Writing Great S

Writing
Great Specifications

USING SPECIFICATION
BY EXAMPLE AND GHERKIN

KAMIL NICIEJA

FOREWORD BY GOJKO ADŽIĆ

MANNING
SHELTER ISLAND

Manning Publications Co.　　　　Development editor:　Marina Michaels
20 Baldwin Road　　Technical development editors:　Alain Couniot
PO Box 761　　　　　　　　　　　　　　　　　and Jonathan Thoms
Shelter Island, NY 11964　　　　　　　Review editor:　Aleksandar Dragosavljević
　　　　　　　　　　　　　　　　　Project editor:　Tiffany Taylor
　　　　　　　　　　　　　　　　　　Copyeditor:　Tiffany Taylor
　　　　　　　　　　　　　　　　　Proofreader:　Katie Tennant
　　　　　　　　Technical proofreader:　Alessandro Campeis
　　　　　　　　　　　　　　　　　　Typesetter:　Dottie Marsico
　　　　　　　　　　　　　　　　Cover designer:　Marija Tudor

ISBN 9781617294105
Printed in the United States of America
1 2 3 4 5 6 7 8 9 10 – EBM – 22 21 20 19 18 17

brief contents

contents

foreword

To many agile teams, *specifications* is a dirty word, and any discussion about written documentation is heresy. Yet long-term product success depends on new members joining teams, scaling up and growing products and organizations, and reconciling the needs and demands of an ever-growing number of user groups and stakeholders. Those tasks are almost impossible without capturing knowledge in some form that allows sharing and doesn't rely on a single person's memory.

This book deals with those parts of the delivery process that typically fall between the cracks of the three Cs of user stories. The *Card, Conversation, and Confirmation* technique for working with user stories plays a pivotal role in directing software delivery today, but many delivery teams struggle to capture the results of conversations and document them in a way that will make confirmation easy. Kamil's suggestions and techniques will help you do that, not just in the short term, but over many years as a software product keeps evolving, and when you need to remember discussions you had months earlier in order to inform future cards and conversations.

Specification by example (SBE) with Gherkin presents a way for teams working in an iterative delivery model to capture knowledge about their intentions and about what their software products do. Most books in this area focus on either tool-specific automation mechanisms or high-level teamwork processes for collecting the right examples, but there's very little literature out there about the style and form of good examples that will guide development. That's why this book is so important.

The omnipresent Given-When-Then style of describing examples is close to natural language, but that familiarity is a double-edged sword. On the one hand, it makes it easy for anyone to get started, which is fantastic because it lowers the bar for teams to start a conversation. But Gherkin (the geek name for that format of specifications) is also aimed at supporting automated validation and long-term documentation, and that requires a lot more formality and structure than natural language does. Without considering that dark side of Given-When-Then examples, many teams get some short-term benefits at the significantly increased cost of long-term maintenance. Kamil tackles this problem with several simple techniques that are easy to remember, and lots of concrete examples that will help you put things into perspective.

The ideas in this book are close to some informal approaches I've seen working with many successful teams. Kamil presents them as structured patterns, such as "Starting with a Then" and "Specifying intentions and outcomes over the UI," so you can remember them easily. The tips and tricks to work with scenario outlines will save you months of rework and hassle, helping you deal with possibly the most important and most difficult topic for anyone new to this way of documenting examples. Several chapters also have homework exercises that you'll be able to use to immediately to try out new knowledge and ideas.

I particularly like how the later part of the book touches on domain modeling and creating a ubiquitous language. Kamil does a nice job taking those concepts from good architectural practices and translating them to the world of collaborative specifications.

—Gojko Adžić
Author, *Specification by Example* (Manning, 2011)

preface

In 1968, there were only 10,000 installed computers in all of Europe. That year, NATO funded a conference that, even though its topic was little known to a wider audience, hosted more than 50 people from 11 different countries. Held in Garmisch, Germany, the conference talked about software engineering and represented the first appearance of programming as an engineering discipline. The event would later become known as the first of two NATO Software Engineering Conferences (the second was held a year later); both played major roles in promoting widespread acceptance of software development.

After the conference, the NATO Science Committee was ordered to compile a report that summarized the discussions.[1] Every time I read this report, I'm amazed by how insightful it was and that parts of it remain relevant. "We tend to go on for years, with tremendous investments, to find that the system, which was not well understood to start with, does not work as anticipated," said J. W. Graham during a panel on feedback through monitoring and simulation. "We work like the Wright brothers built airplanes: build the whole thing, push it off the cliff, let it crash, and start over again." Decades have passed, but not a lot has changed.

Graham's committee gathered to discuss whether there was a better way to do software engineering. They focused on the use of simulation during design, an idea introduced by Brian Randell in a working paper. "The important point [in building better software] is the use of simulation," continued Graham. By *simulation,* he meant what we today call *test automation*—a deterministic environment with predefined inputs and

---

[1] *Software Engineering: Report on a Conference Sponsored by the NATO Science Committee, Garmisch, Germany, 7th to 11th October 1968,* eds. Peter Naur and Brian Randell (Scientific Affairs Division, NATO, 1969), http://mng.bz/jn3d.

predictable outcomes. "Simulation is a way to do trial and error experiments. If the system is simulated at each level of design, errors can be found and the performance checked at an early stage." In other words, the earlier in the process we test, the sooner we can find mistakes. When we consistently test after every change in design, errors tend to disappear. In the end, we get better software.

Throughout the rest of the discussion, other participants followed Graham's train of thought. Alan Perlis chimed in, clarifying the relationship between tests and design: "A software system can best be designed if the testing is interlaced with the designing instead of being used after the design." Test a little, code a little. If this sounds familiar, that's because Perlis's approach reemerged as test-driven development (TDD) in the late 1990s. Modern TDD requires software engineers to write tests before any application code. Ideally, TDD should actively prevent defects by improving code design. Perlis predicted that, too: "A simulation which matches the requirements contains the control which organizes the design of the system. ... The critical point is that the simulation becomes the system." According to his vision, tests *guide* software design and organize it. TDD does the same. A test-driven process relies on repeating a short development cycle called the *red-green-refactor* loop. Initially, new tests fail the simulation because no application code has been written yet (and, in most test-automation engines, failed tests appear in red). But as new code is written, more and more tests start to pass—and they turn green as a result. The loop is repeated until all tests pass. And so, step by step, the simulation becomes the system.

TDD was created and promoted by Kent Beck. Thirty years divided Beck and Perlis, but as personal computers and software engineering engulfed the world, the underlying problems programmers faced remained the same. TDD has a fatal flaw, though. Although, as Perlis said, a simulation that matches the requirements can control and organize the design of a system, the use of simulation doesn't address the problem of collecting the correct requirements in the first place. Thus, a good simulation can perfectly organize the wrong system, rendering itself useless. That's why programmers never design software systems alone—they work with designers, testers, business analysts, product managers, and so on. But TDD is a highly technical process. Would it be possible to harness the benefits of feedback through simulation on a higher level of abstraction, without relying only on low-level code, and in a more collaborative way? Fortunately, in the last decade or so, attempts to answer this question have resulted in a lot of innovation (for example, TDD evolved into behavior-driven development [BDD]).

This book focuses on an innovation called an *executable specification*: a specification that's written in natural language *and*, at the same time, can be run as a program—or, more specifically, as an automated test. The use of natural language instead of code means everyone, whether they can program or not, can discuss the requirements, as well as their tests and implementation. The use of simulation means we can have the simulation control the design of the system and then become the system itself, by interlacing design and testing.

I first became familiar with the topic at Monterail—a web development studio working with enterprise clients and startups from all over the world—where I was responsible for implementing executable specifications. Thanks to executable specifications, Monterail's delivery teams were able to deliver software of higher quality. In a year or so, we wrote more than 500 Gherkin scenarios for highly complex products including procurement software, webinar/webcast software for marketers, and a packet-capture product family that can transform any server into a precision network-monitoring device.

I started my career at Monterail as an engineer and then moved to product management. I wrote executable specifications, I implemented them, and I tested them. Around that time, I read Gojko Adžić's *Specification by Example* (Manning, 2011, www.manning.com/books/specification-by-example), which was pivotal to the way I approach the topic of software quality. In early 2015, I participated in Product Owner Survival Camp in Vienna, where Ellen Gottesdiener, Gojko Adžić, David Evans, and Christian Hassa held their workshops. During a coffee break, a coworker of mine (who also attended) and I mentioned to Gojko that we were thinking about releasing a free ebook with tutorials for writing executable specifications. Gojko's book is great, but it focuses on the process and key practices, leaving implementation aspects aside. Although many books discussed how to write tests, for some reason almost nobody was talking about writing the specification layer—the stuff that humans can read, not just machines. We agreed that it was a topic worth exploring. The joint project didn't work out, but Gojko introduced me to Manning's Mike Stephens; and, some time later, the idea for my own book took off—all thanks to that meeting in Vienna.

There are many different kinds of executable specifications; an attempt to discuss all of them in a single book wouldn't be practical. So, we'll explore two of these approaches—specification by example (SBE) and Gherkin—that are increasingly popular. Together, they offer programmers, designers, and managers an inclusive environment for clear communication, discovering requirements, building a documentation system, and writing acceptance tests. My goal in this book is to help you create such an environment in your organization so that we, as an industry, may continue progressing on the path set in 1968 by the pioneers of our industry.

I wish you good luck in your journey with SBE and Gherkin. But I also want to thank you. I truly believe that delivery teams all over the world wield tremendous power and have great responsibility to the people who use their software—and increasingly, that's millions of users. Every attempt to improve software quality—including yours—should be applauded.

acknowledgments

I thank everyone who contributed to this book, especially the people at Manning: publisher Marjan Bace and everyone on the editorial and production teams, including Alessandro Campeis, Alain Couniot, Bert Bates, Dan Maharry, Marina Michaels, Mike Stephens, Janet Vail, Tiffany Taylor, Katie Tennant, Dottie Marsico, and Jonathan Thoms. Having some confidence in the topic I wanted to write about, I thought I was the one who was here to teach; but, rightfully, it was I who ended up being schooled. I learned so much from you—all while you were working hard to move the process along as swiftly as possible.

Thanks go to the amazing group of technical peer reviewers led by Aleksandar Dragosavljevic: Ivo Alexandre, Costa Alves Angelico, James Anaipakos, Dane Balia, Keith Donaldson, Ruben Gamboa, Aurélien Gounot, Burk Hufnagel, Edgar R. Knapp, Unnikrishnan Kumar, David Madouros, Russell Martin, Markus Matzker, Nasir Naeem, David Osborne, Mike Reidy, and Craig Smith.

My thanks to Gojko Adžić, who wrote the foreword and introduced me to Manning.

I want to thank the great people at Monterail who worked with me from 2013 to 2015 and contributed to many of the ideas you'll read here. They helped me see SBE and Gherkin from every angle: development, testing, and product design.

Many friends helped improve early drafts of the book or got me through blocks and obstacles. For their invaluable comments and continuing support, I thank Bartek Jarmołkiewicz, Magda Mól, Dominik Porada, and Piotrek Zadworny.

I also want to thank my cofounders at Ada:[1] Adam Stankiewicz and Natalia Świrska. The company was born at the same time as the idea for this book. Thank you for your patience and encouragement.

---

[1] Ada is an AI-powered personal assistant that will help you rent your next apartment: http://adarenting.com.

Finally, a big thank-you goes to my family. I wouldn't have done any of the work I'm proud of today without my parents. Mom, you've always believed in me: thank you for being the very first reader of my short stories, back when I was in school. Dad, I often think of the times when we had fun together learning our first programming language, Visual Basic. I was 10 years old then. I'm older now, but it's still fun.

I once read that people write in an attempt to advise their past selves. Since childhood, I've wanted to write a book—although I imagined it would be a novel. At some point, I came to believe it would never happen, but the universe works in funny ways. To anyone who struggles with a goal that feels distant and daunting, I want to quote Nike's Phil Knight: "The cowards never started, and the weak died along the way. That leaves us." Don't give up. Thank you for your work.

about this book

The goal of this book is to help you learn to do the following:

- Capture requirements and acceptance criteria as executable test cases
- Master the Gherkin language as a practical, communicative way of writing software specifications
- Collect valuable examples
- Write easy-to-automate specifications
- Design stable executable specification suites with good test coverage
- Balance the specification style and documentation style in Gherkin scenarios
- Manage specification suites in large projects

Who should read this book

For readers who came here with preexisting knowledge of both specification by example (SBE) and Gherkin: this is an intermediate-level book designed for anyone who's tasked with writing or updating a specification in Gherkin or who's responsible for implementing an SBE process using Gherkin in their organization. If those are issues you deal with on a daily basis, you'll find answers here.

For readers who came here to learn from scratch: many tutorials on the web explain how to set up executable specifications and write testing code. But their authors don't understand that, to anyone but software engineers and testers, automated testing is as vague a concept as any random UX method can be to an average programmer. Those tutorials have good intentions and want to bring everyone to the same table, but whose table is that?

This book is a teaching resource meant for everyone—product and design people, analysts, programmers, and testers. Instead of focusing on technical challenges, it goes into depth about writing the text layer of executable specifications in Gherkin in a clear, understandable, concise manner. Non-engineers can learn how to make essential contributions to design and testing without having to learn programming or write testing code. Engineers and testers, on the other hand, will find SBE and Gherkin helpful for doing more meaningful TDD by striking a stronger chord with nontechnical audiences through executable specifications.

How this book is organized

This book is divided into 11 chapters and an appendix:

- Chapter 1 presents a quick, practical introduction to SBE and Gherkin.
- Chapters 2 and 3 talk about writing scenarios and the theory of the automation layer. Chapter 2 introduces the basics of the Given-When-Then template, and chapter 3 discusses what makes a great scenario.
- Chapters 4 and 5 look at scenario outlines, which are a more advanced way of writing scenarios. Chapter 4 presents the new structure of scenario outlines, and chapter 5 shows why it's important to collect thoughtful examples.
- Chapter 6 is about the life cycle of executable specifications. Before going into more-advanced topics, you need to understand the place of SBE and Gherkin in a real-world software development process.
- Chapter 7 covers living documentation and how to create high-precision scenarios out of unrefined drafts.
- Chapters 8 and 9 are about managing medium-sized specification suites. Chapter 8 talks about grouping unorganized scenarios into whole specifications, and chapter 9 discusses refactoring large specifications into smaller ones.
- Chapters 10 and 11 focus on the largest specification suites. Chapter 10 introduces domain-driven design as a way to prepare medium-sized specification suites for seamless expansion. Chapter 11 is about splitting large specification suites based on their business domains.
- The appendix is a quick tutorial on how to write and run simple, automated tests for feature files with Cucumber and Gherkin. It's intended for readers who are interested in how the automation layer works in practice.

You can read the book from cover to cover or make a quick stop after chapter 2, read the appendix, and then come back to the rest of the book. I highly recommend reading the entire book without skipping chapters—the ordering is intentional and not designed to be rearranged. Some of the chapters include exercises; the answers are provided at the end of the chapter.

Code conventions and downloads

This book contains many examples of source code, both in numbered listings and in-line with normal text. In both cases, source code is formatted in a `fixed-width font like this` to separate it from ordinary text.

In many cases, the original source code has been reformatted; I've added line breaks and reworked indentation to accommodate the available page space in the book. In rare cases, even this wasn't enough, and listings include line-continuation markers (➥). Additionally, comments in the source code have often been removed from the listings when the code is described in the text. Code annotations accompany many of the listings, highlighting important concepts.

The source code for all examples in this book is available from the publisher's website, www.manning.com/books/writing-great-specifications.

About the author

Kamil Nicieja began his career as an engineer and then moved to product management. He's now CEO of Ada (http://adarenting .com), an AI-powered personal assistant that will help you rent your next apartment. He's experienced SBE's benefits first-hand both in development and in business, and he's seen what happens when management and development misunderstand each other or don't develop common domain concepts together from both points of view. In addition to writing this book, he blogs at www.nicieja.co about entrepreneurship, startups, and technology.

Book forum

Purchase of *Writing Great Specifications* includes free access to a private web forum run by Manning Publications where you can make comments about the book, ask technical questions, and receive help from the author and from other users. To access the forum, go to https://forums.manning.com/forums/writing-great-specifications. You can also learn more about Manning's forums and the rules of conduct at https://forums .manning.com/forums/about.

Manning's commitment to our readers is to provide a venue where a meaningful dialogue between individual readers and between readers and the author can take place. It isn't a commitment to any specific amount of participation on the part of the author, whose contribution to the forum remains voluntary (and unpaid). We suggest you try asking the author some challenging questions lest his interest stray! The forum and the archives of previous discussions will be accessible from the publisher's website as long as the book is in print.

about the cover

The figure on the cover of *Writing Great Specifications* is captioned "Habit of a Moorish Priest in 1695." The illustration is taken from Thomas Jefferys' *A Collection of the Dresses of Different Nations, Ancient and Modern* (four volumes), London, published between 1757 and 1772. The title page states that these are hand-colored copperplate engravings, heightened with gum arabic.

Thomas Jefferys (1719–1771) was called "Geographer to King George III." He was an English cartographer who was the leading map supplier of his day. He engraved and printed maps for government and other official bodies and produced a wide range of commercial maps and atlases, especially of North America. His work as a map maker sparked an interest in local dress customs of the lands he surveyed and mapped, which are brilliantly displayed in this collection. Fascination with faraway lands and travel for pleasure were relatively new phenomena in the late eighteenth century, and collections such as this one were popular, introducing both the tourist as well as the armchair traveler to the inhabitants of other countries.

The diversity of the drawings in Jefferys' volumes speaks vividly of the uniqueness and individuality of the world's nations some 200 years ago. Dress codes have changed since then, and the diversity by region and country, so rich at the time, has faded away. It's now often hard to tell the inhabitants of one continent from another. Perhaps, trying to view it optimistically, we've traded a cultural and visual diversity for a more varied personal life—or a more varied and interesting intellectual and technical life.

At a time when it's difficult to tell one computer book from another, Manning celebrates the inventiveness and initiative of the computer business with book covers based on the rich diversity of regional life of two centuries ago, brought back to life by Jefferys' pictures.

Introduction to specification by example and Gherkin

1

How well we communicate is determined not by how well we say things, but how well we are understood.

> —Andy Grove

The money is all on the right [side of the product life cycle], in the area of certainty [where the product is mature]. I work on the left, with uncertainty. I'll never be rich.

> —Chris Matts

Humanizing technology is perhaps *the* greatest challenge of software engineering. The technology industry must strive to show tremendous empathy for other people's problems. We're making tools for everyone out there. In the messy world of organizational politics, broken workflows, human errors, and biases, technology experts must figure out how to successfully deliver great software. It's an important responsibility.

To do our job well, we have to

- Make sure we deliver *the right software*
- Deliver it *the right way*

Delivery teams are naturally competent in delivering software the right way. As an industry, we've developed tools, standards, and methodologies that make our designs beautiful and usable—and our code performant, secure, and easy to maintain. We keep getting better at refining and reinventing our best practices.

"The right software" part, though … what does that even mean? Every time I explain to someone what this book is about, I tell them that, as programmers, we're taught to *write code*—algorithms, design patterns, abstractions. Or, as designers, we're taught to *design*—organize information and create beautiful interfaces. But when we get our entry-level jobs, our employers expect us to "deliver value to our clients." And the client may be, for example, a *bank*. If I'd been working for a bank when I started my career, it would have quickly come up that I know next to nothing about banking—except how to efficiently decrease my account balance. So I would have had to somehow *translate* what was expected of me into code. I would have needed to build a bridge between banking and my technical expertise if I wanted to deliver any value. "This," I say, "is what the book is about: building bridges between technology and business." Over the course of multiple projects I've had the privilege to work on, I've come to believe that these bridges can only be built with empathy—understanding other people's problems—and inclusive communication.

Even though engineers should be good at building bridges, our industry seems to have a problem with delivering *the right software*. In practice, delivering the right software requires securing the right requirements. I'll talk more about requirements in a moment. For now, I'll say the following:

- A 1994 study showed that 31.1% of projects were canceled before they were completed, and 52.7% of projects cost 189% of their original estimates.[1]
- In larger companies, rare successful projects had only 42% of the originally proposed features.[2]
- In 2000, IBM and Bell Labs studies showed that 80% of all product defects are inserted at the requirements-definition stage.[3]

---

[1] The Standish Group, "The CHAOS Report" (1995), http://mng.bz/40M3.
[2] Ibid.
[3] Ivy Hooks and Kristin Farry, *Customer-Centered Products: Creating Successful Products Through Smart Requirements Management* (AMACOM/American Management Association, 2001).

- Requirements errors consume from 28% to more than 40% of a typical project's budget.[4]
- Requirements defects account for the vast majority of the total cost of all defects—often 70% or more.[5]
- In 2008, almost 70% of companies surveyed set themselves up for both failure and significantly higher costs by their use of poor requirements practices.[6]

What are the consequences? Commercial organizations across the European Union lost €142 billion on failed IT projects in 2004 alone, mostly because of poor alignment with business objectives or business strategies becoming obsolete during delivery.[7] So although we're pretty good at maintaining our technical standards of excellence, we apparently still have a lot to learn when it comes to understanding what businesses need from us.

In this chapter and throughout the book, I'll introduce you to a selection of bridge-building methods for translating business objectives into working software that, in my experience, results in great and meaningful products and services. This chapter will begin your in-depth journey of learning to write *executable specifications in Gherkin* according to the key practices of *specification by example*.

Specification by example (SBE) is a collaborative software development approach that facilitates collaboration by illustrating software requirements with concrete examples and automated acceptance tests. Because SBE is a process, you'll need some tools that will help you implement that process. This is why you're going to learn *Gherkin*. Gherkin is a business-readable, domain-specific language that's easy for nontechnical folks to understand. As such, it makes translating requirements into code easier.

In a way, the book is an advanced Gherkin tutorial with some product-design ambitions. I'll talk more about the reasons for choosing Gherkin later in the chapter. But when I was first learning SBE's key patterns, I found that, although locating material on automated acceptance tests and eliciting better requirements is easy, there aren't many resources available on writing great executable specifications. By *great*, I mean well-written and easy to read in terms of sentences and words, not code. That makes my ambition small, because I chose a specific topic for the book. I care about making sure that well-elicited requirements aren't misrepresented by poorly written specifications. At the same time, I realize that writing executable specifications is a cross-disciplinary matter. Whenever I can, I'll talk about making your requirements better and more specific with clever Gherkin techniques. Other times, I'll point you toward specific books that talk about requirements, product design, or marketing, in hopes they will answer your further questions.

---

[4] Ibid.

[5] Dean Leffingwell and Don Widrig, *Managing Software Requirements: A Use Case Approach*, 2nd ed. (Addison-Wesley Professional, 2003).

[6] IAG Consulting, "Business Analysis Benchmark" (2008).

[7] Gojko Adžić, *Impact Mapping* (Provoking Thoughts, 2012).

This chapter offers an overview of what a specification is and how SBE and Gherkin fit into the software development landscape. If you're a non-engineer, you'll learn how to make essential contributions to automated testing without having to learn to write testing code. (Don't worry about technical lingo. I use it rarely and explain it when I do.) Engineers and testers will find SBE and Gherkin helpful in striking a stronger chord with nontechnical audiences through automated specifications. You'll also begin to see SBE as a single process to guide product development through requirements analysis, design, development, testing, and so on.

1.1   *What's a specification?*

Imagine that you and the team you work with have been brought in to work on a new version of a management system for a local public transport company. To get on with work, you need a list of functionalities, user stories, blueprints, sketches—anything that will let you write some code or make a UI mock-up. You need a specification.

> **DEFINITION** *Specification*—An analysis of a system and its design, made to plan and execute the implementation

The word *specification* can mean a written document or an act of specifying. You'll see that I switch freely between both meanings. Whenever it's important to make a clear-cut distinction, I'll use a term like *specification document* or *specification process*. But you can assume that most of the time, I have the broad meaning of the word in mind.

In the case of the example public transport company, to devise a specification, you have to agree on a list of requirements and functionalities the new release must satisfy.

> **DEFINITION** *Requirement*—A capability or condition that must be met or possessed by a solution to satisfy market needs or a contract, a standard, a specification, or other formally imposed documents

For example, you and the business owners may agree that a good requirement would be to apply discounts when students or retirees buy tickets. Other examples could relate to handling season tickets, performing online payments, managing customers, and reports.

Delivery teams can write down their requirements in a functional requirements document, but they may also encapsulate requirements in use cases, which are shorter, or use user stories as tickets for a future in-depth conversation about the requirements. The final method depends on the software development process chosen by the team.

1.2   *Why do teams need specifications?*

Traditionally, specifications have had a bad reputation in the software development community. The reason is half psychological, half practical.

Psychologically, specifications seem to promise the same success as following a cooking recipe. They invite a "Follow the steps, and everything will be all right" mindset. The promise is as reassuring as it is deceiving. In practice, creating a complete specification is extremely difficult, if not impossible.

No software development team functions without specifications, though. Whether you write an official document or have a casual conversation about the requirements during a workshop, you're still specifying.

The one and only reason teams need specifications is *information asymmetry*. Teams need to distribute information evenly among the stakeholders to create the best possible product. If they don't, they'll miss critical requirements and make an incomplete product—or even a broken one.

> **DEFINITION** *Information asymmetry*—A situation in which one party has more or better information than another

To reduce information asymmetry, teams create specifications—recipes defining *what* needs to be done or *how* it needs to be done. Specifications can help fight information asymmetry in two ways:

- A specification can define acceptance criteria that help examine whether a team has delivered a complete system that works.
- A specification can provide a common language that allows technical and nontechnical stakeholders to understand each other when they talk about requirements.

We'll now go into more depth on both of these topics.

1.2.1 Defining acceptance criteria in specifications

Assume that you and the public transport company's management team have agreed that the system you're building should include two subsystems:

- An internal management application for updating bus schedules
- A mobile timetable application with journey-planning functionality

Sounds reasonable, doesn't it? The capabilities for both the employees of the company and its customers are clearly defined. But are they really?

Every time you analyze a requirement, you'll eventually stop talking about general capabilities of the system and start thinking in terms of concrete, discrete quality measures that the application must meet. When discussing our public transport company, I said that a good requirement would be to apply discounts when students or retirees buy tickets. But how can you determine whether that requirement is satisfied without going into more detail? For example, you'd need to declare that students can have a 30% discount and retirees can have a 95% discount. These two declarations would allow you to say that the requirement was in fact satisfied and implemented correctly. Such quality measures are called *acceptance criteria*.

> **DEFINITION** *Acceptance criterion*—A condition or quality measure that a software product must meet to satisfy requirements

Acceptance criteria *illustrate* requirements. You should be able to use a criterion to evaluate the system and get an unambiguous confirmation that the system either passes or fails your test: for example, "A bus road should consist of at least two bus stops." Right, and that's how the system behaves. "Timetables for work weeks should be different than timetables for weekends." Oops, we forgot about that; let's go back to the drawing board. You should be able to get a binary response to every criterion—as in *yes* or *no* questions. Without that binary response, you can't say whether the system is complete and works as it should.

Raw requirements are often too difficult to comprehend without further analysis. Without clear acceptance criteria for each of the requirements, delivery teams can't plan any work ahead and deliver any value in a predictable way. When there's not a good specification, functionality usually suffers from rework or bugs that cause delays and cost a lot. Good acceptance criteria ensure that the implemented solution meets the demands of your stakeholders.

1.2.2 *Building a ubiquitous language into specifications*

Imagine for a moment that after you finish the beta version of the mobile journey planner, the customer support department receives a phone call from an angry customer:

> The customer begins, *"I downloaded the app to help me during my two-day stay in the city. But I can't get where I want!"*

> *"What street are you on? What's wrong?"*

> *"I've got a meeting in Edison. I used your app to get there, but I can't find the building I'm supposed to enter. It's all wrong!"*

> *"Wait—do you mean Edison Street or Edison Business Center? They're two different places."*

The customer wanted to plan the journey without knowing what street the destination building was on, but the application didn't support such a behavior. To add insult to injury, the mobile app chose Edison *Street*, located elsewhere in the city, as the final destination, because it couldn't find Edison *Business Center* in the database.

The result? The user and the application spoke two different languages, and the confused customer got lost. The dictionary of the developers who built the app was restricted to streets; after all, bus stops inherit their names from where they're located. That's how the system works, the team said. What they didn't know was that their customers don't think about the rules of a system—they only want to arrive on time.

To avoid similar mistakes, delivery teams should strive to grasp the language their users speak and align their language with this language. The result of this alignment is often called a *ubiquitous language.*

> **DEFINITION** *Ubiquitous language*—A common language between developers and domain experts

A ubiquitous language is "a language cultivated in the intersection of [technical and business] jargons."[8] The development of journey-planning software requires knowledge in two different domains: journey planning and software. Experts in both areas must communicate understandably.

DEFINITION   *Domain*—What an organization does, and the world it does it in

The journey planners will use the jargon of their field and have limited understanding of the technical dictionary of software development. Developers, on the other hand, will understand and discuss the system in terms such as objects, methods, and design patterns. Having a single common language eliminates the cost of mental translation and reduces the number of misunderstandings—the ratio of noise in the signal—in discussions between technical and nontechnical stakeholders. Translation blunts communication and makes domain learning anemic.

   The journey planners from the example can also be called *domain experts*. Domain experts help you create a ubiquitous language. When either the business side or the technical side discovers a misunderstanding, they can use the opportunity to improve their shared dictionary and avoid the same mistake the next time. This way, they build a shared *domain model*, which will improve in quality over time.

DEFINITION   *Domain expert*—A person who is an authority in a particular area or topic. The term usually refers to a domain other than the software domain.

DEFINITION   *Domain model*—A simplification of the real-world business domain. It's an interpretation of reality that abstracts the aspects relevant only to solving the problem at hand.

The ubiquitous language fuels the domain model. Having a shared dictionary of important business concepts creates a platform for discussing data, behaviors, and relationships within the model in a meaningful way, with a certainty that everybody is on the same page. In the journey-planning example, the team thought that a *destination* was the same as a *street*, but it turned out that users assumed there are other kinds of destinations, such as *buildings* and *points of interest*. Having established a baseline, the team can use the common language to establish clear relationships between the concepts of destinations, streets, buildings, and points of interests.

   A specification can help develop the ubiquitous language. It's a container where all important domain concepts can be stored after they're encountered and analyzed by the team. When that happens, and the process is thorough and successful, the specification becomes a documentation of the domain, the knowledge base of the delivery team. When a specification fails to contribute to the ubiquitous language or doesn't create a truthful domain model, the team may misunderstand requirements, which often leads to expensive rework.

---

[8]   Eric Evans, *Domain-Driven Design* (Addison-Wesley, 2003).

1.3   *Common specification pitfalls*

Much of software engineering is about building systems right, but specifications, requirements, and acceptance criteria are about building the right system. From time to time, every software engineer experiences a painful push-back caused by a sloppy analysis of the requirements. You, too, know what's at stake. This section should help you identify some pitfalls you yourself may have encountered.

I want to discuss these five anti-patterns:

- Over-specification
- Hand-offs
- Under-documentation
- Speci-fiction
- Test-inability

I named each anti-pattern in a distinctive way that will help you remember what it's about. Hopefully, as you go through the sections that follow, the names of the anti-patterns will become clearer to you, and I'll achieve my goal.

1.3.1   *Over-specification*

A popular first instinct meant to defend a project against ambiguity and insufficient planning is to try to design and plan as much as we can up front. I call that *over-specification.*

> **DEFINITION**   *Over-specification*—Doing too much specification up front

It's definitely easier to remove or change a requirement during an analysis phase; the more time we invest in implementing it, the more unmotivated we become when we have to kill it. The up-front approach aims to remove useless implementations, design flaws, and predictable errors as early as possible in exchange for a longer analysis phase. But software development teams must also understand that over-specification can lead to a state of *analysis paralysis.*

> **DEFINITION**   *Analysis paralysis*—A productivity block created in search of the perfect—unattainable—design

In extreme cases, bureaucratic or regulated environments may demand over-specification by requesting specification documents that can run into thousands of pages. (Bear in mind, though, that analysis paralysis isn't limited to written specifications.) But unless you're making software for surgeons, analyzing every single detail in advance often feels unnecessary—even harmful.

1.3.2   *Hand-offs*

Handing off requirements looks like a classic waterfall mistake—an artifact from the past—but I still see agile teams struggling with hand-offs, often due to their organization's internal politics. Any requirement can be handed off.

DEFINITION   *Hand-off*—A situation in which somebody analyzes requirements without the input of the delivery team, signs off on the scope by writing down the analyzed requirements, and later hands off those requirements to the delivery team to complete

Hand-offs result in a fragmented communication flow between business and delivery. In my experience, people who hand off requirements are often business users, managers, analysts, product owners, or designers, depending on the chain of command in a given organization. In a management-oriented company, managers are more likely to create an environment where they can decide on the list of requirements and the scope, trying to maintain control over important decisions. I've seen the same thing happen with design teams in design-oriented organizations. And engineers, too, can hand off requirements if they're within their areas of expertise. (Think of technical, nonfunctional requirements such as performance, security, or low-level integrations.) Nobody's a saint.

Such organizations mistake the communication structure for the organizational structure. A company can be management-oriented, design-oriented, or engineering-oriented and still have a healthy, collaborative, and inclusive process.

Hand-offs cause various problems with delivery. A team that only receives a specification won't understand the context in which the requirements were collected. Their decision-making abilities will be impaired when it comes to split-second decisions. The team won't be able to make on-the-fly decisions because they won't know the thought process that led to making the requirements the way they are. They will only see the final result—the specification. They may also be too afraid to change anything. And in over-specified documents, contradictions and ambiguities can occur easily. When hand-offs like these happen, misunderstandings creep in and cause expensive rework to appear later in the process.

TIP   Don't let documentation replace communication.

1.3.3   Under-documentation

Many delivery teams burnt by over-specification discard it in favor of an implementation-first approach, eradicating any up-front practices. An implementation-first approach optimizes for writing software without dealing with wasteful documentation and specifications. It rejects huge design commitments before customers prove they want the solution—and the only way to prove it is to hack some code together and release it as soon as possible, rejecting any process that doesn't help write production code. For example, Extreme Programming advocates use no extra design documents and let the code speak for itself. Running code doesn't lie, as a document might. The behavior of running code is unambiguous.

Initially, the implementation-first approach feels efficient, especially in young companies—but as the organization grows and the product matures, diseconomies of scale kick in. Not everyone is a coder. Communication and decision-making start causing trouble, and adding new people to the team slows work instead of making it faster. I call such a specification anti-pattern *under-documentation*.

> **DEFINITION**   *Under-documentation*—Discarding documentation and letting code speak for itself in order to speed up development

Underdocumented teams are left with no clear path to track decisions made in the past. Institutional memory suffers; when people who worked on implementation become unavailable, temporarily or permanently, they take their knowledge with them. Building long-term understanding within the company often requires additional facilitation. Many teams hurting from under-documentation realize its downsides too late when fixing the problem gets painful.

> **TIP**   Don't let *agile* be an excuse to ignore documentation.

1.3.4   *Speci-fiction*

Documentation and specification artifacts grow obsolete easily. As your product evolves over time, requirements often evolve, flat-out change, or turn out to be poorly defined and have to be refined. Documentation and specifications, like all internally complex documents, are often too difficult to update on a regular basis without introducing some inconsistencies. Outdated and unwanted, they become *speci-fiction*. (Yes, I invented the word. No, I'm not a poet.)

> **DEFINITION**   *Speci-fiction*—A specification that poses as a single source of truth but that can't be one because nobody cares to update it

If you've ever struggled with outdated documentation, you're already familiar with the phenomenon of speci-fiction. Sometimes documents are left outdated because of multiple last-minute changes. In this case, the *fiction* in speci-fiction is that a new reader would be led to falsely believe that the specification or documentation describes the entire system *as it is*, when the working system is, in fact, different, because the requirements were changed during the release frenzy. Speci-fiction is only an illusion of correctness—an illusion that occurs when no single, reliable source of truth exists.

1.3.5   *Test-inability*

The INVEST mnemonic for agile software projects is a common reminder of the characteristics of a good-quality product backlog item such as a user story (see table 1.1). Much of INVEST is beyond the scope of this discussion; I won't expand on the topic directly, but I already talked about such characteristics as *valuable* and *small* when I discussed the difference between the right delivery and the right software at the beginning of this chapter and when I talked about over-specification and long specification documents.

Table 1.1   The INVEST mnemonic

Letter	Meaning	Description
I	Independent	The story should be self-contained.
N	Negotiable	The story should leave space for discussion about its scope.
V	Valuable	The story must deliver value to the stakeholders.
E	Estimable	The delivery team should always be able to estimate the size of the story.
S	Small	The smaller the story, the easier it is to analyze and estimate correctly.
T	Testable	The story should support test development.

I'd like to focus on the testability part, which many teams overlook. I've met many programmers and testers who, when working on a user story, weren't sure where to start, what to test and what not to test, how much to test in one go, what to call their tests, and how to understand why a test fails.

According to INVEST, testability should be baked into a good user story, because testability lays the foundation for quality. How can you be sure that you delivered any business value if you don't know how to test its implementation? Or how can you know that you'll continue to deliver value in the future, regardless of any system changes or errors? What I call *test-inability* is a team's failure to answer questions like these—a failure that originates in a bad specification process.

> **DEFINITION**   *Test-inability*—Lacking clear measures of value that can support development

1.4   *Meet specification by example and Gherkin*

Delivery teams choose the implementation-first approach despite its shortcomings because it gives them the freedom, agility, and productivity they love. On the other hand, the up-front approach has the upper hand in consistently producing somewhat reliable documentation. Is there any method that combines the best of both worlds? Fortunately, yes. Of the many tools and methodologies introduced by the community to reshape traditional specification methods, I find two particularly interesting and explore them in the book: SBE and Gherkin.

Specification by example, a set of practices that sprang from the agile acceptance-testing tree, is a collaborative approach to defining software requirements based on illustrating executable specifications with concrete examples. It aims to reduce the level of abstraction as early in the process as possible, getting everyone on the same page and reducing future rework.

Gherkin, a business-readable domain-specific language, provides a framework for business analysis and acceptance testing. Gherkin helps you understand requirements from the perspective of your customers. By forcing you to think about what a user's workflow will look like, Gherkin facilitates creating precise acceptance criteria. The

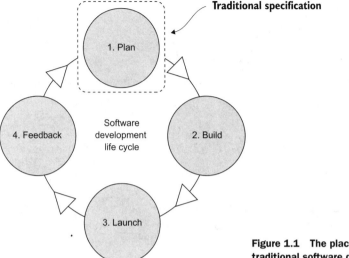

Figure 1.1 The place of specifications in the traditional software development process

book uses a Cucumber version of Gherkin's syntax. If you don't yet know what that means, don't worry—I'll explain everything in chapter 2.

SBE and Gherkin reimagine the traditional software development process. Every software development process follows similar phases as functionality progresses from conception to release (see figure 1.1). In most agile software development methodologies, the phases are as follows:

- Planning implementation
- Building the product
- Launching the product
- Getting feedback

Many teams also fall into a trap of treating specifying as a one-time *activity* that occurs during the planning phase, instead of as a *process* that keeps occurring as requirements evolve and change, which they often do throughout development. Teams that don't treat specification as a long-term process often behave like *automata*—machines designed to automatically follow a predetermined sequence of operations. In such a case, the sequence is defined during the planning phase and must be followed as long as no problems occur. But when a problem *does* occur, it's often already too late.

With SBE and Gherkin, as shown in figure 1.2, we follow a different paradigm. This paradigm requires us to use practices that must be performed throughout the entirety of a project—from analysis to maintenance. You'll see why when I talk more about *designing acceptance tests* (a testing activity) and *building living documentation* (a maintenance activity). Instead of creating a static document with requirements, I'll talk about a system of dynamic specification documents that *constantly evolves* along with the product.

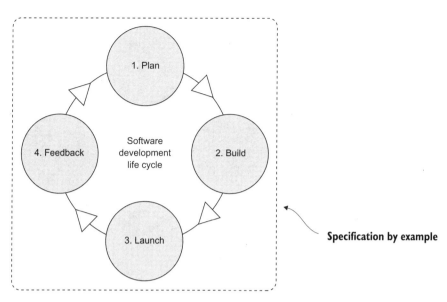

Figure 1.2   SBE reimagines the software development process by prolonging the specification process so that it takes place throughout the entire project.

If you're curious about what a specification written in Gherkin looks like, look at this example:

```
Feature: Setting starting points and destinations

   Scenario: Starting point should be set to current location

     Given a commuter that enabled location tracking
      When the commuter wants to plan a journey
      Then the starting point should be set to current location

   Scenario: Commuters should be able to choose bus stops and locations

     Given a bus stop at Edison Street
       And a Edison Business Center building at Main Street
      When the commuter chooses a destination
      Then the commuter should be able to choose Edison Street
       But the commuter should be also able to choose Edison Business Center
```

In order to help you write specifications like this, the upcoming chapters will apply SBE's key process patterns to Gherkin. You'll be able to offer programmers, designers, and managers an inclusive environment for clear communication, discovering requirements, and building a documentation system.

1.4.1   Key process patterns

Teams that apply SBE successfully introduce seven process patterns into their work-flow.[9] In an SBE process that uses Gherkin—which, as you'll see later, is only one of

---

[9]   Gojko Adžić, *Specification by Example* (Manning, 2011).

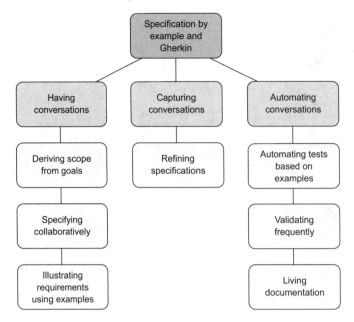

Figure 1.3   A high-level look at SBE's process patterns

several ways of applying SBE—these seven patterns can be split into three distinct groups revolving about the central concept of *conversations* (see figure 1.3).

Patterns focused on *having conversations* aim to increase the knowledge flow between the delivery team and the business as well as within the delivery team, without sacrificing agility. Patterns that deal with *automating conversations* ensure that the specifications stay up to date throughout the project's life cycle, allowing nontechnical stakeholders to check whether the use cases they care about work well within the system.

Capturing conversations links analysis and automation. Having conversations can't be a separate development activity, just as you can't write automated tests for the sake of writing tests. That's where the real magic begins, and where you'll meet Gherkin— it will let you write down your conversations in a form that's easy to automate.

1.5   *Having conversations that identify business needs*

The main premise of SBE and Gherkin is that frequent conversations between domain experts and the delivery team lay a foundation for the entire development process (see figure 1.4). Here are some examples of conversations:

- The public transport company's management wants to build new modules into their timetables system, and you discuss their business needs together.
- An angry customer explains that your mobile app shouldn't interpret Edison Business Center as Edison Street because they're not the same thing.

- Two engineers discuss whether the system should treat a bus route as a collection of 2D points on a map or a straight line between the start point and the destination point.
- A commuter files a bug report about the bus-scheduling functionality.
- You read customer feedback on social media and discover what new functionalities users want.

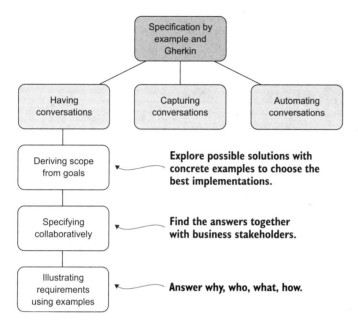

Figure 1.4 Having conversations should provide delivery teams with all the answers necessary to understand a project's goals, and who customers are and what solutions they need.

From these examples, we can reason that a *conversation* means a discussion between the business and the technology. Business domains and technology domains interact because they have to—if you want to create *any* software, let alone working software or, sometimes, even successful software, the team must understand the business context and have required technical excellence. The sections that follow analyze the topics that such interactions can follow.

1.5.1 *Deriving scope from goals*

Conversations typically revolve around four questions:

1. Why are we building this?
2. Who are we building this for?
3. What exactly are we going to build?
4. How will we build it?

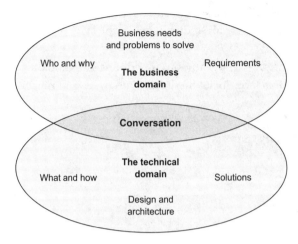

Figure 1.5 **The business and technology domains must meet over the course of a conversation if you want to understand the business goals and set the optimal project scope.**

Some answers come from the business domain and others from the technology domain (see figure 1.5). Usually, the business domain provides the *who* and the *why*, and the technology domain provides good *what* and *how* answers.

In general, answering questions at the top of the list will give you enough input to ask and answer the questions at the bottom. Such a practice—getting from business objectives to programmable solutions—is what SBE's practitioners call *deriving scope from goals*. Over the last five years, deriving scope from goals emerged as probably *the* most important practice in the modern landscape of software development.

Every major conference now features someone talking about the value of delivery people understanding business goals and designing software according to their company's objectives. Techniques such as impact mapping, feature injection, and user-story mapping have spread widely, changing the business analysis landscape. I, too, will talk about these techniques throughout the book.

The questions I listed help delivery teams understand why a solution is needed and who needs it. Answering them means discussing the company's goals and establishing success metrics. The goals and metrics, in turn, allow you to determine the scope of future work the team must deliver and build a framework that will let the team say whether they're making progress in terms of reaching their goals.

1.5.2 *Illustrating requirements with examples*

SBE and Gherkin require delivery teams to support their conversations with practical examples. *Illustrating requirements with examples* helps reduce the level of abstraction and leads to clearer acceptance criteria—especially if the examples are concrete instead of vague.

Humans prefer stories illustrated with examples. Say you were a lawyer who wanted to explain to your friend how splitting royalties works. If you said, "The writers should split the salary based on their contribution," your friend might not have a good idea of what you meant. Each of you might understand the concept of "contribution" differently. But let's change that to "Here's an example: John, Gilly, and Robbie wrote a 250-page book together. John and Gilly wrote 100 pages each, so they should get 40% of the salary, because they each wrote 40% of the book—and Robbie, who wrote only 50 pages, should get 20% of the salary, just as 50 is 20% of 250." This time, your friend would probably grasp the full idea in a split second.

Clear storytelling invites good examples, because examples help us build better mental models of the new concepts we encounter. They're anchors. Links. Cognitive shortcuts. Most important, they reduce the likelihood of misunderstanding the purpose of a story. Requirements illustrated with good examples inherit all these benefits. They're simpler to digest and easier to keep in your head.

Let's look at a conversation without any concrete examples and a conversation full of examples to see if that's true. Here's the first conversation:

> *"Okay, so how should the application work?"*

> *"I suppose that when commuters download our mobile app, they should be able to provide a starting point and a destination point, and see a timetable with all the bus lines and departure times they might find helpful in getting to the destination. It's very simple, really."*

> *"Seems that way."*

Such a conversation raises more questions than it answers. What are the starting points and destination points? Are they streets? Bus stops? Buildings and other places? And what exactly may a commuter "find helpful in getting to the destination?" There's no way we can know for sure.

What would happen, though, if we asked for concrete examples during the discussion?

> *"OK, so how should the application work?"*

> *"Let's not jump to conclusions. Imagine for a moment that you're going to the city, say, on a business trip. How and when do you get there?"*

> *"Well, I guess I might arrive a day earlier to be sure nothing goes wrong."*

> *"So we're going to need a functionality to filter the timetables by date."*

> *"Yes, we are. But let's consider what happens if the you're a bit more happy-go-lucky and arrive in the city an hour before the meeting. You don't have enough time to check where you are. Or maybe you don't know the exact street you must arrive at."*

> *"Wow, we might need to implement a GPS geolocation functionality so we could help users know their current location."*

> *"Yeah, and there should be an option to search for locations such as parks, buildings, and restaurants instead of only bus stop names."*

> *"Seems that way."*

Conversations with examples look similar to short stories about a system's behaviors. Good stories are vivid and build a platform for fertile discussion between the people who read them. Bad stories confuse readers and leave people clueless. The same is true for good and bad specifications.

1.5.3 *Specifying collaboratively*

As you'll see in the sections to come, SBE and Gherkin redefine the distinction between analysis, design, and implementation by building a bridge between requirements and code. The practitioners should see the act of specifying as a process of continuous discovery through reducing their uncertainty about the requirements. Specifying is not a single activity or a phase to go through. In an agile process, requirements evolve as a project progresses because rarely does the knowledge exist up front to specify an application adequately.

Every time you have a conversation about your product, every time you ask a question about a requirement, every time you encounter a bug, every time you hear customer feedback—you're discovering whether your assumptions about the product are true or false. You're learning.

Sometimes, though, organized effort may be required to produce a reliable, repeatable specification process in a complex environment with multiple stakeholders. In such cases, SBE encourages specifying collaboratively by inviting the stakeholders to specification workshops or holding smaller, more regular meetings within the delivery team.

The participants should use the specification workshops to capture and refine good, concrete examples that emerged when the delivery team tried to derive scope from the business goals. They should then match the examples with requirements and acceptance criteria, letting the examples guide their analysis efforts.

Depending on the size of the team and the complexity of the product, specification workshops can range from multiday sessions featuring every important stakeholder to short, regular meetings between product owners, senior engineers, and designers. These workshops put a strong emphasis on knowledge sharing. Including diverse participants guarantees exploring multiple perspectives and covering different angles. Knowledge should flow freely within the team. Analysts, designers, developers, and testers should strive to understand what they're about to build, asking as many questions as they deem relevant. To achieve a common perspective on how customers will use the software, participants should learn the ubiquitous language of the business owners and the customers. Long story short, they should build a short-term understanding of the requirements that will guide their efforts in planning and during implementation.

> **WARNING** The topic of organizing and facilitating specification workshops, although important, is beyond the scope of the book, which focuses on writing skills. I only talk about workshops briefly in section 7.4. Chapter 7 is also where I mention a few resources and techniques for organizing workshops. For now, I advise you to read Gojko Adžić's original *Specification by Example*, chapter 6 talks about collaborative specification.

1.6 *Long-term benefits of automating conversations*

After the delivery team collects examples, team members create specifications out of conversations recorded in Gherkin. They automate the conversations and examples with software tests, validating the tests frequently to make sure the specifications stay up to date (see figure 1.6).

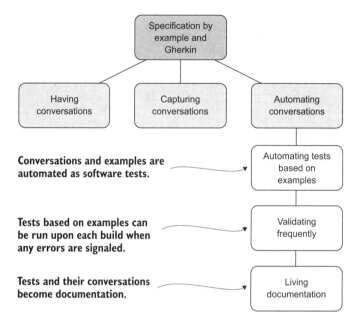

Figure 1.6 Automation turns conversations into executable test cases that, if validated frequently, become long-term system documentation.

I'll now talk about the elements of the automation process and why automating specifications gives delivery teams an enormous advantage. Don't be surprised that I haven't yet discussed recording conversations in Gherkin, even though the translation process is a prerequisite for automation. I want you to understand the benefits and challenges of team specification and automation first, so that you'll be free to draw your own conclusions when we explore Gherkin.

1.6.1 *Automating tests based on examples*

SBE requires delivery teams to use conversations to collect meaningful examples that help the team understand the requirements. From examples, tests are created. Good examples make tests better and more business-driven by covering real-world use cases provided by business stakeholders and customers. In the end, tests verify whether the delivery team implemented requirements correctly. You can see the schematics of this process in figure 1.7.

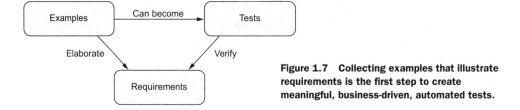

Figure 1.7   Collecting examples that illustrate requirements is the first step to create meaningful, business-driven, automated tests.

Automating ties conversations and examples to system behaviors. Tests return binary responses about every conversation you capture. A conversation either passes your test, meaning the behavior was implemented correctly, or it fails the test, meaning the system is incomplete or broken.

If an example passes the test, you know that the acceptance criterion illustrated by the example is still relevant. If the test is failed, you're notified that the changed code base no longer satisfies the acceptance criteria. If that's the case, the examples should change to reflect that—and sometimes the code has to change, too. (The code could be right and the example now outdated, or the example could be right and the code wrong. In each case, you fix a different thing.)

Why is that? Imagine that the example public transport company introduces new express buses. These vehicles skip most of the bus stops on their way, in order to get to the destination point more quickly. Your team now needs to add express buses to the mobile app. It's a simple change in terms of code: somebody must add a new attribute to the database that determines whether a bus line is an express line or a regular one. Easy peasy. You make the change quickly and then take a lunch break.

That's when all hell breaks loose. (Almost.)

The team forgot that the timetables module isn't the only one affected. The mobile app also features a live map that shows how the buses closest to the user move around. A commuter can check which buses are which in the legend on the map. The legend is generated automatically, but adding the new type of express bus broke the programming logic behind it. As a result, the legend has disappeared. For the few days before you notice the problems, commuters not only aren't able to distinguish express buses from regular buses—they aren't able to find *any* buses on the map.

If you had any documentation in place, the change made it inaccurate and outdated. Nobody updated the document, because your team wanted to have lunch. That's what usually happens: people forget, production hotfixes creep in, the Four Horsemen of the Apocalypse drop by. And when the dust settles, your carefully prepared documentation no longer reflects the current state of the system. In this case, it doesn't tell the reader that there are two types of buses, and it doesn't explain the difference between them. Step by step, with every hotfix and every negligent change, the documentation becomes irrelevant.

1.6.2   *Validating frequently*

None of these problems would arise if your conversations and examples were automated. When conversations are run as tests, you can regularly track which ones behave correctly and which ones don't. If you test frequently and your specification is exhaustive, you'll get instant feedback after you make a change to the code base.

You can validate during the development process or before a release—what matters is that you must do it often. The more often you test, the sooner you can spot possible errors.

Captured conversations should be validated against both the existing system and new code as it's being written. If you validate conversations frequently, you can have as much trust in the specification as you have in the code. This way, you create a more accessible way to review implemented requirements for all stakeholders.

Because SBE and Gherkin see development as a process of constant discovery through reducing uncertainty about requirements, the model of the system is, by definition, not fully defined from the beginning—it's only defined *well enough*. It evolves continuously based on feedback from stakeholders, and new examples and domain concepts enter the specification as new elements are added to the code. To make sure these new examples fit into the system, delivery teams need a process of *continuous integration*.

> **DEFINITION**   *Continuous integration*—A software development practice where members of a team integrate their work frequently. Each team member should integrate as often as possible, leading to multiple integrations per day. Each integration is verified by an automated build to detect integration errors quickly.

If the team uses a testing tool (like Cucumber, a Gherkin-compatible test runner), the tests can be run on each software build. If any errors are signaled, they can be caught early and fixed, letting the "integrate, build, test" process start again—this time, successfully.

1.6.3   *Living documentation*

As much as we'd like it to be otherwise, only working production code holds the truth about the system. Most specifications become outdated before the project is delivered. Because every product is a machine made out of thousands of moving parts, the dating problem becomes a curse of all software projects.

Outdated documentation may *seem* like a reliable source of knowledge about the system, but it only misleads its readers. An automated, frequently tested specification—as well as the examples included in it—is resistant to such problems. The direct connection between scenarios and code often reduces the damage by cultivating a system of *living documentation*.

> **DEFINITION**   *Living documentation*—Documentation that changes along with the system it documents, thanks to the link between the text and the code as well as frequent validation.

When tests keep specifications in check, they let specifications with examples evolve into a documentation system. Using executable specifications as living documentation means taking advantage of automation to facilitate learning within the team and their decision-making abilities. When Gherkin scenarios are free of unnecessary technical bloat, well written, accurate, and full of business-oriented examples and domain vocabulary, they can serve as a *single source of truth* that everyone uses to learn about the functionalities in question.

Thanks to frequent validation, you know that your tests, examples, and conversations are up to date; and when you trust your tests, you can use them as documentation for the entire system. You can track every test back to its origin—the conversation you had with your stakeholders about the requirement. When in doubt, you or anyone else on your team can always check the captured conversation. Frequent validation also guarantees that the documentation must change every time the underlying code changes, because the documentation is connected to the code through tests.

A living documentation system should benefit everyone. Specifying collaboratively, illustrating requirements with examples, and refining specifications for readability—all these measures should involve everyone who matters in the requirement-analysis process, or a few dedicated people can make the requirements as easy to understand as possible for everyone else. Everyone involved should be able to read the results, too. Tools such as Relish, Cucumber Pro, and CukeHub can even integrate with a code repository of your choice and publish the scenarios in a private cloud where you can collaborate and share executable specifications and test results with other team members, as easily as you can share a document in Google Docs.

1.7   *Capturing conversations as executable specifications*

Okay, so automating conversations offers a lot of benefits. But *how* do we automate them? At the beginning of section 1.6, I promised that we'd come back to the topic of recording conversations in a language that will help you optimize them for automation. This section discusses the refinement process that makes free-flowing conversations easy to automate (see figure 1.8).

Specification workshops allow for having conversations. Programmers and testers are responsible for automation. How does the translation process happen? Should programmers store conversations as comments in their testing code? That would be ridiculous—but the records have to be written somewhere, don't they? A free-flowing conversation is, by definition, an unreliable medium that only stimulates short-term memory. We need long-term storage.

As introduced earlier, Gherkin is *the* tool for capturing conversations about requirements in a formalized way, clarified by extracting essential information and removing noise. Gherkin facilitates knowledge sharing among all stakeholders,

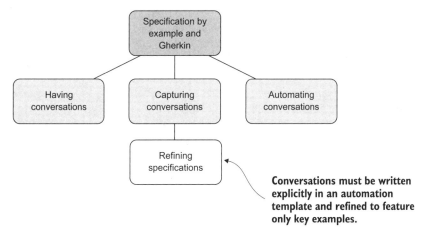

Figure 1.8   The capture process aims to preserve verbal product-design chats and translate them to lightweight, long-term, formalized stories that, in time, can be used to put together system documentation.

regardless of their technical skill. It does so by conveying tests and requirements in a ready-for-automation template that's expressed in plain English and that uses the ubiquitous language of a product.

Gherkin focuses on capturing conversations as *scenarios*. Scenarios preserve essential information and remove noise by extracting concrete actions from conversations.

DEFINITION   *Scenario*—A concrete example that illustrates a business rule

Following is an example of a scenario. Remember the conversation about how the mobile app for journey planning should work?

> *"Let's imagine that you're going to the city on a business trip. When do you get there? ... If you're a bit happy-go-lucky and arrive in the city an hour before the meeting, you don't have enough time to check where you are."*

> *"Wow, we might need to implement a GPS geolocation functionality, so we could help users know their current location."*

Here's the same conversation expressed in Gherkin:

```
Given a commuter that enabled mobile location tracking
 When the commuter wants to plan a journey
 Then the starting point should be set to current location
```

This sequence is called the *Given-When-Then* template. I'll talk about it in detail in chapter 2, where you'll learn the basics of using the template.

Thanks to its focus on user actions, Gherkin is a great language for conveying *behavioral requirements.* Just as having conversations improves a delivery team's short-term understanding, capturing conversations ensures that they don't let that knowledge slip through their fingers in the future. Scenarios achieve that and remind us that we don't need 100-page functional requirements documents to capture what's valuable. We don't even have to write all the scenarios up front. We can capture a few scenarios at a time, as we discuss each new requirement. A few months in, we'll have a huge library of relevant scenarios. We only need to be consistent.

> **DEFINITION** *Behavioral requirement*—A requirement formed as a story about how users behave when they interact with the system. Whereas normally requirements can be formed as abstract statements, behavioral requirements always talk about examples of using the system.

The contents of the template should use nontechnical language that relies heavily on real-world business concepts. Notice how the example mentions *commuter*, *journey*, and the *starting point*—concepts borrowed from the business vocabulary of the public transport company—but doesn't say anything about low-level development procedures or the application's user interface. Scenarios captured using the Given-When-Then template should stay at a business-readable, code-free level at all times, improving the domain model and building its ubiquitous language.

> **WARNING**   If you see anything about a connection to the database in a Gherkin scenario, or read about buttons or any other UI element, somebody made a huge mistake.

Because programmers and testers can automate anything put in the Given-When-Then template, scenarios written in Gherkin become *executable specifications*. This book will teach you to write executable specifications in Gherkin and use the Given-When-Then template. You'll also learn the rest of the Gherkin syntax required to capture design conversations in a form that easily translates to executable specifications.

> **DEFINITION** *Executable specification*—A specification that can be run as an automated test

The syntax serves as a link between speech, text, and automated code. It lets you progress naturally from one to another. Gherkin also provides techniques to organize scenarios into full documents, link similar behaviors, and simplify capture and automation, all while keeping things at a business-readable level derived from the ubiquitous language.

Most executable specifications contain many scenarios, and every scenario needs multiple examples. In its rough form, an example is like a quick note or a doodle. It makes sense when you look at it a day after you made it, but try examining it six months later—not so meaningful anymore, right? That's why successful teams don't use raw examples; they *refine* them. A team extracts the essence of key examples and turns it into clear, unambiguous, organized specification documents, as shown in figure 1.9.

As new requirements appear, acceptance criteria generate new examples, and every example generates a new scenario. To refine executable specifications, teams merge similar examples, reject examples that introduce noise, and choose the most

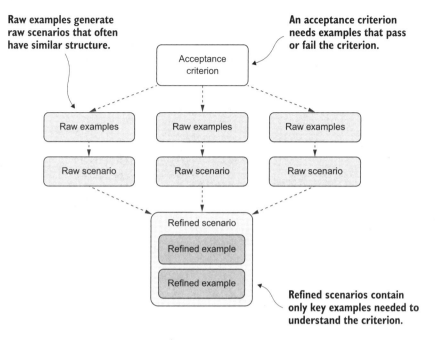

Raw examples generate raw scenarios that often have similar structure.

An acceptance criterion needs examples that pass or fail the criterion.

Acceptance criterion

Raw examples   Raw examples   Raw examples

Raw scenario   Raw scenario   Raw scenario

Refined scenario
  Refined example
  Refined example

Refined scenarios contain only key examples needed to understand the criterion.

Figure 1.9   The process of refining raw examples extracted from collected acceptance criteria into refined scenarios with key examples

meaningful or descriptive examples. The result is an executable specification in its final form, ready to become the foundation for the living documentation system.

1.8   *Making software that matters*

You've now begun the journey of mastering executable specifications written in Gherkin according to SBE's key practices. As you learn more about SBE and Gherkin, we'll focus on practicing techniques that help you avoid common specifying pitfalls. When software engineers and designers don't put enough thought into their specifications, the cost is measured in weeks of work and hundreds of thousands of dollars wasted.

The benefits of SBE and Gherkin go far beyond reducing rework. You'll get better insight into your business domain and reduce friction caused by inevitable translation costs that come up when a business requirement becomes working software. People made these tools and processes because they wanted to guarantee that the software they help build will make sense to customers. They wanted to make software that matters.

SBE, BDD, or ATDD?

When I started my journey with executable specifications, like many other practitioners I was confused by the naming issues around the topic of agile acceptance testing. When I found out that many people call SBE *behavior-driven development* (BDD) or *acceptance test-driven development* (ATDD), I didn't understand the difference.

(continued)

My confusion was deepened by the fact that I became interested in SBE after reading Gojko's book, but the first project where I was able to practice writing executable specifications used Gherkin. In his book, Gojko wrote that he didn't "want to use any of the *Driven Development* names, especially not Behavior-Driven Development." But Gherkin was invented by Dan North and Chris Matts, and Dan North is the main face of BDD. I was perplexed.

I wanted to avoid naming controversies, because they aren't key to what you're going to learn. I honestly admit that I borrowed freely from both fields, trying to create a mix that will maximize benefits and minimize mental load. Dan North calls BDD a *methodology*; but, quoting Gojko, what I wrote here doesn't form a fully fledged software development methodology. My only goal is to teach you to write great Gherkin specifications *using* SBE practices. So whenever I talk about a practice or an idea derived from SBE, I'll tell you that up front. Everything else will appear under the umbrella term of *Gherkin* and *good Gherkin practices*; if you want to read more about it, you can assume it comes from the field of BDD.

Because this is a book about practical application of executable specifications with examples, it mainly deals with capturing conversations in Gherkin and refining examples. It's a long-ignored topic due to Gherkin's seemingly easy syntax and elusively low entry barrier. Many software engineers and designers think they need a quick tutorial and then can start writing. It's only a simple Given-When-Then sequence, right?

Yes and no. Everything depends on the project you're dealing with. At first, having executable specifications will yield better alignment without much training—but complex products with complicated business domains can go astray quickly. Hundreds of requirements will produce hundreds of Gherkin files you have to manage. And every file will contain multiple scenarios, and every scenario will attach additional example. That sounds like Gherkin and SBE don't fit huge projects well; but, truth be told, huge projects will stretch every process and tool. As you'll see, executable specifications with examples shine the brightest in complex environments—but that's why I'm writing a book, and not a blog post.

You don't have to be able to write testing code to read the book. I'll cover automating conversations only as long as it introduces good patterns that will make life easier for your engineers. Having said that, we should always value business-oriented specs over specs that are easy to automate. Similarly, I won't talk about anything related to having product-design conversations during specification workshops, unless it directly impacts you when writing specifications in Gherkin. There are other resources that teach these skills well enough.

I do expect you, however, to understand the basics of the automated testing *process* and why it matters. Practical knowledge about the QA process will be helpful in some of the later chapters. If you have a technical background or are experienced in working with developers and QA engineers in any agile methodology, you'll be fine. I also expect you to understand what it takes to release a product, from its conception through the public announcement to long-term maintenance. Some of the things we'll discuss will cover not only initial requirements but also possible changes in scope that a product can face at a later stage of its life cycle.

What will you learn? The next chapter explores Gherkin and SBE in practice. You'll begin by capturing requirements and acceptance criteria as executable test cases. As you progress through the book, you'll tackle more-advanced topics. You'll learn to write good scenarios. You'll see how to choose good examples. You'll design business-oriented error checks. When the time comes, you'll move on from thinking about suites of specifications, and you'll learn to organize scenarios into groups of coherent specification documents that readers can navigate easily. I'll also talk about how the ubiquitous language shapes examples and scenarios, and how to evolve specifications into a living documentation system over time.

Right now, though—right now, welcome to specification by example and Gherkin.

1.9 Summary

- A specification is a description of the system design required to implement the system.
- Acceptance criteria let you review whether you've built a complete system.
- A ubiquitous language is a common language among developers, business stakeholders, and end users. It makes every stakeholder sure they're talking about the same things.
- Specification by example is a business-analysis process aiming for "just enough," just-in-time software design. Lightweight examples provide enough initial context to start development and are later refined into more-sophisticated forms.
- Gherkin is a business-readable language for writing specification documents. Gherkin's practitioners capture conversations about requirements in the form of behaviors—also called scenarios—which are examples of how the system is expected to behave.
- An executable specification is a conversation captured using the Given-When-Then template with a corresponding acceptance test. The acceptance test makes sure the delivery team has implemented the underlying requirement correctly.
- Every executable specification's life cycle starts with a specification that later becomes an automated test. Automating the specification ensures that it stays up to date, because the captured conversation is directly tied to testing code. This way, tests become documentation.
- Gherkin and SBE arm you with software development techniques that facilitate knowledge sharing, reduce short-term waste without sacrificing long-term documentation, and help the delivery team deliver software faster and without rework thanks to meaningful, concrete examples of system behaviors that ensure everyone's on the same page.

Part 1

Writing executable specifications with examples

P art 1 of this book consists of six chapters that discuss the ins and outs of writing executable specifications in Gherkin. Chapters 2 and 3 will teach you about Gherkin—the language in which you'll write scenarios. Chapters 4 and 5 discuss the art of writing a special kind of scenario called a scenario outline, as well as choosing good examples. Chapters 6 and 7 talk about what happens when a specification is "finished," explain its life cycle, and go into depth about creating a living documentation system.

The specification layer and the automation layer

If you haven't worked with Gherkin and specification by example (SBE) before, chapter 1 may have shown you your first Gherkin scenario (listing 1.1). We haven't yet written a full Gherkin specification document together, though, and we'll need more practical examples to do that.

Chapter 1 also talked about how conversations captured in Gherkin become automated tests and how automation keeps executable specifications up to date. But we didn't discuss any details. What does *automation* mean in the context of SBE? How can you automate conversations? Are there any tools you can use? These are all legitimate questions.

In this chapter, you'll learn to write a simple executable specification from scratch. Throughout the chapter, you'll work on an example of a calendar application that schedules meetings for its users. (Think Google Calendar.) You'll write a simple scenario about what it takes to create new meetings. By doing so, we'll also explore the basics of the relationship between the two layers of every executable specification, in order to understand the technical limitations behind the Given-When-Then template.

Reading Gherkin listings

A quick note on how to read the Gherkin listings placed here and there throughout the book. Because the goal is to get as close to writing the perfect Gherkin scenario as possible, some of the listings are rated on a scale from *[BAD]* to *[BEST]*. (Not all scenarios are comparable, so not all are rated.)

Listings marked [BAD] are anti-patterns, should be avoided, and are mentioned only to warn you about their bad effects. The [OK] listings are neither good nor bad; they're mediocre. The [GOOD] and [BETTER] listings are at the quality level you should strive for after reading this chapter. And the [BEST] listings contain non-obvious solutions that become possible only after you've applied the advanced tips and tricks from this chapter. The best scenarios don't happen every time, but when they do, it's extremely satisfying.

2.1   *The layers of executable specifications*

Every executable specification has two layers: a *specification layer* and an *automation layer* (see figure 2.1). Without the specification layer, an executable specification wouldn't be a specification. Without the automation layer, it wouldn't be executable. This section provides a brief overview of both.

This book deals mainly with the specification layer and the writing aspect of executable specifications—the art of writing Gherkin. But to do that well, you need to know the basics of the automation layer, too. That's because automation requires the specification layer to be written in a certain way that allows computers to read it.

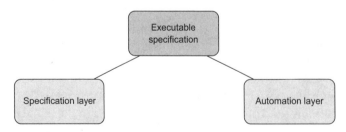

Figure 2.1   Every executable specification in Gherkin has two layers that complement each other and create automated tests written in natural language.

2.1.1 *The specification layer*

Simply put, the specification layer of an executable specification is the document you read when you want to know what you're going to build. Gherkin specifications are usually short, and even a small project will have multiple documents—all of these documents together form a large specification layer for the entire project.

> **DEFINITION** *Specification layer*—Contains text documents written in Gherkin that humans can read

It's important to understand these three elements of the specification layer (see figure 2.2):

- Acceptance criteria
- Scenarios
- The ubiquitous language

I'll talk about acceptance criteria, scenarios, and the ubiquitous language in detail later in the chapter, but here's a brief summary. Chapter 1 said that specifications talk about requirements and acceptance criteria that the delivery team needs to understand if they want to implement new features correctly. Gherkin organizes the acceptance criteria by conveying them as scenarios written using the Given-When-Then template. The scenarios become elaborate expressions of the *ubiquitous language,* which is a common language among developers, business stakeholders, and end users. As you saw in chapter 1, the scenarios are a way to store conversations about requirements in a written form: they're a reflection of how the delivery team talks with the business about important domain concepts. You'll see a similar situation play out later in this chapter.

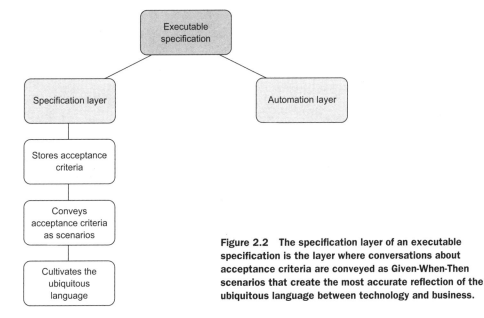

Figure 2.2 **The specification layer of an executable specification is the layer where conversations about acceptance criteria are conveyed as Given-When-Then scenarios that create the most accurate reflection of the ubiquitous language between technology and business.**

Here's an example of some simple Gherkin text:

```
Feature: Teams

    Scenario: Enforcing access rules

    For more information on availability, please look at the
    invite confirmation scenarios later in the specification.
    In short, an unavailable person who already confirmed RSVP
    can be invited to another event at the same time, but will
    be able to attend only one of them.

    Given Mike, Kate, and John were assigned to the same team
      And Ada was assigned to another team
     When Kate and Mike schedule a 1 hour long meeting at 4 p.m.
     Then John should see that Kate and Mike will be unavailable
      But Ada shouldn't be able to see Kate and Mike's meeting
```

As explained in chapter 1, the sequence within each scenario is called the *Given-When-Then template*. The template and some other repeatable structures visible in the example are what enable automation of every Gherkin document.

The specification layer is created by writing *feature files*.

> **DEFINITION** *Feature file*—A file with a .feature extension written in Gherkin that groups related scenarios within a document that provides a specification for a single functionality

As a matter of principle, both technical and nontechnical stakeholders can have access to the specification layer of the specification suite. They should be at least able to read and understand it if they have to. But as I mentioned, the specification layer also has to be formatted in a way that allows for automation, so some constraints, predefined grammar, and strict syntax are always present. This chapter will show you the basics of Gherkin's automation syntax later on.

> **DEFINITION** *Specification suite*—A collection of all executable specifications and the testing code for a single project. This collection is usually put in the real codebase where it can be automated and executed.

2.1.2 *The automation layer*

The programmers and testers on your team will use scenarios to write the testing code. The testing code is the *executable* part of your executable specifications. Every part of the specification suite related to executing automated tests is contained within an *automation layer*.

> **DEFINITION** *Automation layer*—The automation layer executes a simulation of the implemented application to see if the code behaves as defined in the specification.

To make a long story short, every time you want to write a Gherkin specification like the one shown earlier, you have to add a new .feature file to the specification layer of

Specification suite

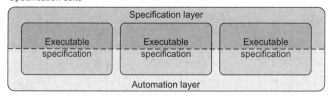

Figure 2.3   A specification suite, as well as every executable specification in the specification suite, can be split into two layers— the specification layer and the automation layer—which work together to create a functional testing process.

your *specification suite,* write the scenarios there, and then add the testing code to the suite (see figure 2.3).

A specification suite is a kind of test suite. In software development, a *test suite* is a collection of test cases that are intended to be used to test a software program to show that it implements a specific set of behaviors. Because the tests for executable specifications share some qualities with traditional tests but are different in other aspects, the name should be both familiar and new—thus, a specification suite.

It's important to understand these three aspects of the automation layer (see figure 2.4):

- The automation layer is a *simulation* of a working application that behaves as the Given-When-Then scenarios tell it to.
- The simulation performs *acceptance tests* that check whether the system under test behaves in an acceptable way.
- The automation layer is designed to be a *feedback loop* that makes accepted specifications pass the testing process and rejects specifications that weren't accepted, marking them as broken.

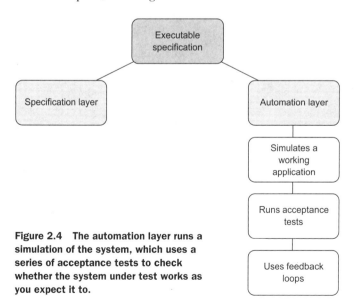

Figure 2.4   The automation layer runs a simulation of the system, which uses a series of acceptance tests to check whether the system under test works as you expect it to.

I'll talk about feedback loops more in chapter 6 when we get to the topic of an executable specification's life cycle.

As an example of how the automation layer works, suppose you want to test whether a calculator app works well. To do so, you need some samples of addends and the results you expect the calculations to return. The automation layer will then be able to execute the testing code responsible for performing calculations and see whether the result returned by the code matches the expected result defined in the specification (see table 2.1).

Table 2.1   An example of the automation layer's behavior

Input given	Automation layer	Expected output
1 + 0	The testing code runs …	1
1 + 1	The testing code runs …	2
1 + 2	The testing code runs …	3
1 + (-1)	The testing code runs …	0

Running the automation layer with Cucumber

The Given-When-Then template's syntax enables automation. That's why tools like JBehave and Cucumber use Gherkin, which is a more elaborate evolution of the template. But Gherkin isn't the only available option. Different tools for automated acceptance testing impose their preferred syntax differently. Some tools, like FitNesse, use a wiki-like system as the main way of organizing the specification layer.

JBehave, Cucumber, and FitNesse are all *test execution engines*.

> **DEFINITION**   *Test execution engine*—A type of software that's written to automatically test other software. Throughout the book, I use terms such as *test execution engine*, *test runner*, *testing framework*, and *automation framework* interchangeably.

This book teaches a Cucumber-flavored version of Gherkin.

> **DEFINITION**   *Cucumber*—A testing framework that can match Gherkin feature files with testing code. It lets programmers run the code that automates the scenarios.

Cucumber emerged from the Ruby community, but it also supports or has an equivalent for .NET, C++, JS, Lua, PHP, Python, and JVM. It can run Gherkin files written in more than 60 spoken languages—among them Chinese, French, Arabic, and Pirate English.[a]

---

[a] https://github.com/cucumber/cucumber/wiki/Spoken-languages.

The division of labor is simple (see the following figure). Gherkin handles everything related to capturing conversations about the business logic, from rewriting acceptance criteria as scenarios to modeling the business domain using the ubiquitous language. Cucumber, on the other hand, allows the delivery team to test the system using the same examples that were captured during the analysis and design phases.

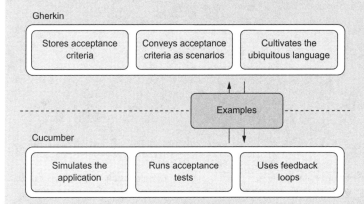

Examples act as a link between Gherkin and Cucumber. The system is tested using the same examples that were collected when the delivery team first analyzed the requirements.

Why did I choose Cucumber and Gherkin for the book? According to the popularity of its open source repository, Cucumber is rising as the most popular testing framework supporting executable specifications, decisively beating both JBehave (10 times as popular) and FitNesse (twice as popular). But I discuss a lot of techniques throughout the book that can come in handy for people who use other test runners, too. (Unfortunately, there are some differences between Cucumber's Gherkin and JBehave's Gherkin in terms of syntax and indentation; due to the scope of the book, you'll have to research the differences between Cucumber and JBehave on the your own.)

You're probably wondering, "Will this book teach me to automate executable specifications with Cucumber?" Spoiler alert: it won't. If you want to read more about automating Gherkin tests with Cucumber, read the appendix. It's a quick tutorial about how to write and run simple automated tests for your feature files. I have to warn you, though: the appendix covers only the basics.

A huge variety of learning resources is already available that teach how to deal with the automation layer, so instead this book focuses on mastering the Gherkin layer—a topic that's underrated by many developers and testers. Also, because you can use Gherkin with many programming languages such as Ruby, Java, and Python, I wanted to stay as language agnostic as possible. If you're curious about how to write and execute automated tests, you can easily find a lot of articles on the web. This chapter includes a brief introduction to the topic of automation, explaining only as much as is needed to understand the depths of the specification layer.

2.2   *Writing your first Gherkin scenario*

At the beginning of this chapter, I mentioned that you'll work with an example of a calendar application for teams, similar to Google Calendar (see figure 2.5). Every calendar application must allow teams to schedule meetings—to keep things simple, that's the one and only thing you're going to specify today.

Figure 2.5   You could imagine your application is a simpler clone of Google Calendar, Microsoft Outlook, or any other popular scheduling software you and your friends use.

2.2.1   *Feature*

It's time to write some Gherkin. This section presents a step-by-step tour of writing your first scenario. To begin, create an empty text file in any text editor of your choice.

Every Gherkin .feature file starts in a similar manner. You've already seen it twice in previous examples of executable specifications:

```
Feature: Scheduling
```

Feature is Gherkin's word for indicating that a new specification has begun—what follows is the name of the feature being documented. Conventionally, every feature file consists of a single Feature in order to encourage writing many small files rather than a few large specifications.

> **WARNING**   Don't get too used to the Feature keyword. In chapter 8, you'll replace it with more-advanced keywords such as Ability and Business Need that allow for better categorization of requirements.

Below the Feature line, you can add a description of the feature. It's expected to describe the business value of this feature or to provide additional information that makes the feature easier to understand. In this book, I call this a *specification brief*.

> **DEFINITION**   *Specification brief*—Specification line containing important pieces of information such as an answer to the question of why a specification was written in the first place, who the most important stakeholder is, and why they need it.

For the time being, let's keep the feature file simple. Given the example's scope, you'll specify only one or two scenarios. You should inform the reader where other scenarios can be found.

Listing 2.1 Feature line followed by a specification brief

```
Feature: Scheduling

    Because scheduling is a huge functionality, this
    specification file describes only the most important
    high-level scenario.
    You can find more detailed scenarios in the rest
    of the files inside the "meetings" folder in the
    specification suite.
```

Specification brief

From the point of view of Gherkin's syntax, the first line is the most important, because the Feature: part can never be changed. (Okay, there are two exceptions, but I'll talk about them at the end of the book.) The spaces in front of what follows are important, too, because the spaces tell Cucumber what the file's structure is. There are no strict rules or limitations regarding vertical spacing between the first line and the specification brief. Personally, I like to add a blank line because I think it makes the document clearer. But if you don't agree, you don't have to do that.

> **Exercise 1**
>
> Write the rest of the specification brief that explains who will use the scheduling features and why they need them, based on what you know about the application. You can draw some inspiration from the description of the app at the beginning of this section.

2.2.2 Scenario

In chapter 1, I said that Gherkin captures behavioral requirements. Behavioral requirements are formed as stories about how users behave when they interact with the system. In Gherkin, these stories are called *scenarios*. In this section, you'll start writing your first scenario.

Listing 2.2 Your first scenario

```
Feature: Scheduling

    Because scheduling is a huge functionality, this
    specification file describes only the most important
    high-level scenario.
    You can find more detailed scenarios in the rest
    of the files inside the "meetings" folder in the
    specification suite.

    Scenario: Creating a meeting        <----  Name of the scenario
```

In this example, the Scenario line lets both the reader and the automation framework know that a new scenario begins below it. If a scenario needs additional elaboration, you can place any amount of free-flowing text between the Scenario line and the first Given. It's similar to the specification brief, and that's why it's called a scenario brief. There are multiple ways to use the free-flowing space, as we'll discuss throughout the book: for example, to provide definitions for domain-specific concepts, which you'll see in action in chapter 7 during the discussion of living documentation.

Every scenario should do the following:

- Define context (the Givens)
- Describe an event that occurs within the system (the Whens)
- Ensure that expected outcomes take place (the Thens)

The sequence is called the *Given-When-Then template.*

The Givens explain what needs to happen so you can watch the rest of the scenario take place. The Whens neatly organize the template around a single behavior of the system, so a reader doesn't have to wonder what the purpose of the scenario is. The Thens clarify the consequences of taking that action.

The Given-When-Then template is a simple yet powerful tool. It often works as a harmonious system. A slight change anywhere may influence a new change elsewhere. Givens, Whens, and Thens influence each other, but sometimes they force entire scenarios to change—and when scenarios change, sometimes entire specifications must change as well. I talk more about this in chapter 3, which covers all the details of the template.

2.2.3   *Given*

Ah, the Givens. Givens answer a single question: what are the prerequisites that allow the scenario to happen?

For example, when a scenario's main action is, as in this case, creating a meeting, there must be some users who will be able to perform the action—so a user account must have been created first.

Listing 2.3   [OK] Your first Given

```
Feature: Scheduling

  Because scheduling is a huge functionality, this
  specification file describes only the most important
  high-level scenario.
  You can find more detailed scenarios in the rest
  of the files inside the "meetings" folder in the
  specification suite.

  Scenario: Creating a meeting

    Given a user            ◁──── Given that's been added to the scenario
```

TIP You can see that there are two more spaces before the `Given`. Scenarios require additional indentation because it helps Cucumber understand which `Given`s, `When`s, and `Then`s belong to which scenarios.

`Given a user`—that sounds vague, doesn't it? All apps have users. And pretty much anyone can be a user. First, this naming doesn't explain anything. Second, you're working hard to make your application unique; the specification should reflect that, too.

Listing 2.4 [BETTER] Your first `Given`, reworked

```
Feature: Scheduling

  Because scheduling is a huge functionality, this
  specification file describes only the most important
  high-level scenario.
  You can find more detailed scenarios in the rest
  of the files inside the "meetings" folder in the
  specification suite.

  Scenario: Creating a meeting

    Given a team member              ⟵------- A more specific Given
```

Better! Now, you can at least see that the scheduling feature is about collaboration. A *team member* sounds a bit abstract, though—and software should be made for real people.

Listing 2.5 [BEST] Your first `Given`, reworked a second time

```
Feature: Scheduling

  Because scheduling is a huge functionality, this
  specification file describes only the most important
  high-level scenario.
  You can find more detailed scenarios in the rest
  of the files inside the "meetings" folder in the
  specification suite.

  Scenario: Creating a meeting

    Given Mike, a member of our team      ⟵----- A Given with a real person
```

Users play key roles in scenarios, and it's a good practice to use unique, real names for several reasons. I talk about them in the next chapter, when I introduce the topic of outside-in development. Right now, I'll give you a simple example. Let's say that two users appear in a single scenario. Calling them *team member 1* and *team member 2* would sound awkward, wouldn't it? That's why you'll specify Mike—because Mike doesn't sound awkward, and when things aren't awkward, more people read and understand them. Hello, Mike. Do you like Gherkin? (I bet he does. It's the sole reason you brought him into existence).

2.2.4   *When*

Givens create the context in which the rest of the scenario takes place. Let's keep the momentum going and specify what the main action of the scenario should be. And, because Whens describe key actions the user performs, this is the perfect job for a new When. Let's add one to the scenario.

Listing 2.6   Your first When

```
Feature: Scheduling

  Because scheduling is a huge functionality, this
  specification file describes only the most important
  high-level scenario.
  You can find more detailed scenarios in the rest
  of the files inside the "meetings" folder in the
  specification suite.

  Scenario: Creating a meeting

    Given Mike, a member of our team
    When Mike chooses 2 p.m. as a start time for his meeting
```

Main action of the scenario

Prerequisite needed for the main action to happen

As you can see, you're aiming for an example as concrete as possible: in addition to the user introduced in the previous step, you've added specific hours. Also notice that the second step is aligned to the right so the word When ends at the same place Given does. This is a community convention that you'll see in many feature files, but it isn't obligatory. You could also write

```
Given Mike, a member of our team
When Mike chooses 2 p.m. as a start time for his meeting
```

without aligning the When to the right under Given. We'll continue to use this convention throughout the book, though.

Note that the scenario has already introduced some simple terms into your product's ubiquitous language: a meeting, a team member, a start time. If programmers or designers read the scenario, they'll adopt this dictionary without having to invent their own terms. Left to their own devices, technical experts often invent artificial names because they don't know any better, and introducing artificial terms almost always widens the communication gap between business and delivery, instead of bridging it.

Every scenario should preferably have only one When, because that makes scenarios clearer and easier to read. I'll talk more about such design rules in chapter 3, where you'll learn about specifying user tasks and choosing the right abstraction level for your scenarios.

2.2.5   *Then*

An action without an outcome is wasted. The part of the Given-When-Then template that asserts the outcome is the Then—so why don't you add it to the scenario?

Listing 2.7 Your first Then

```
Feature: Scheduling

  Because scheduling is a huge functionality, this
  specification file describes only the most important
  high-level scenario.
  You can find more detailed scenarios in the rest
  of the files inside the "meetings" folder in the
  specification suite.

  Scenario: Creating a meeting
    Given Mike, a member of our team
    When Mike chooses 2 p.m. as a start time for his meeting
    Then he should be able to save his meeting
```

Predicate

Main action

Consequence of the action

Thens describe consequences. In this case, choosing a valid start time for a meeting results in successfully creating the meeting. A Then is usually a concrete representation of the rule your criteria try to enforce. The representation is usually a *change* in the system. For example, it may be something new that was created—like Mike created his first meeting—but it may also be something that was removed or rephrased.

The main difference between the scenario in listing 2.7 and the acceptance criteria you usually see is that the scenario seems much more personal. That's because

- Acceptance criteria are the abstract rules of the system; scenarios tell stories about people who use the system according to these rules.
- Human beings discuss and remember stories much better than they do abstract rules.

Adding a Then means that, in eight simple steps, you've arrived at a full Gherkin specification starting from an empty text file. You now have a simple test that specifies what needs to happen if you want to create an event.

Exercise 2

Write a simple scenario for canceling a meeting. Remember to specify proper consequences, so people won't show up to canceled meetings!

2.3 Understanding the structure of steps and scenarios

Now's the perfect time for a quick theoretical break. Let's slow down to process all the information discussed regarding the specification layer, from the standpoint of the automation layer. Givens, Whens, and Thens are also known as *steps*.

DEFINITION *Step*—The smallest unit of any Gherkin specification. It's usually a single line of text.

All steps work on two levels:

- A step describes the business logic of the application in natural language.
- Each step is closely related to its underlying testing code, which checks whether the business logic described is implemented properly.

From the technical point of view, every step consists of a restricted *keyword* and the step's *content* written in natural language that follows the keyword:

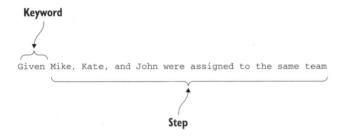

DEFINITION   *Keyword*—A special word used to optimize the specification layer for automation. Keywords are imposed and enforced by the test execution engine. They must appear in every executable specification written in Gherkin.

Every keyword has a specific function to serve:

- `Given`s execute testing code needed to run a scenario: for example, creating accounts or prepopulating the database with example data.
- `When`s execute the main action of a scenario that's expected to change the state of the application by adding new data to the database, editing existing data, or integrating with an external service like email.
- `Then`s measure consequences of a scenario's main action to check whether the state of the application changed as you expected it to.

There are also other keywords such as `But` and `And`—they're replacements that help you avoid using the same word multiple times in a row. They make scenarios flow more naturally.

Here's a full list of the keywords supported by Gherkin. Some of them you already know; others you'll meet later in this chapter and in the chapters yet to come:

- `Feature`
- `Background`
- `Scenario`
- `Given`
- `When`
- `Then`
- `And`
- `But`

- Scenario Outline
- Examples

Scenarios and features use keywords to maintain their structure, too.

You probably remember the `Feature` keyword. In chapter 8, you'll learn that `Feature` can be replaced with more-specific keywords such as `Ability` and `Business Need`. They can help you differentiate between your requirements and organize them in a clearer way—but for now, `Features` are all you need. Similarly, the `Scenario` keyword lets both the reader and the automation framework know that a new scenario has begun.

> **Exercise 3**
> Find all the keywords in the Gherkin file that you've written so far in this chapter, separate the keywords from the steps, and write the results in a table. Try to memorize the keywords; they're the most basic ones, but they're also the most popular.
>
> **Understanding indentation in Gherkin's syntax**
> You may have noticed that, like Python and YAML, Gherkin is a line-oriented language that uses indentation to define structure. You can use spaces or tabs, but it's usually considered a good practice to use spaces, because they maintain the structure more easily on everyone's computers.
>
> Line-oriented languages require you to keep every command within a single line. You can't write a two-line `Given`, for example. The only exceptions to the single-line rule are free-flowing descriptions such as the specification brief and scenario briefs. Free-flowing descriptions aren't part of the Given-When-Then template, and they don't make any difference when it comes to automation. That's why you can format them however you want.

Now is the perfect time for the quick theoretical break to end. You can be proud of yourself. A few pages in, you already know most of Gherkin's syntax. Be alert, though: we're not done yet.

2.4 Testing different outcomes

Let's review the scenario again. It's a good practice to do so once in a while, for two reasons. First, Gherkin is prose—sometimes a bit awkward, but still prose. And prose striving for readability and clearness needs constant reviewing—especially if it's written by technical people. (Ask my editors.) Second, every scenario is also a test, and delivery teams should continuously work on improving their tests in case they missed anything when they wrote them in the first place.

Listing 2.8 Expected output of the scenario

```
Feature: Scheduling

  Because scheduling is a huge functionality, this
```

```
specification file describes only the most important
high-level scenario.
You can find more detailed scenarios in the rest
of the files inside the "meetings" folder in the
specification suite.

Scenario: Creating a meeting

  Given Mike, a member of our team
    When Mike chooses 2 p.m. as a start time for his meeting
    Then he should be able to save his meeting
```

Have you noticed anything weird?

This scenario looks perfect—*too* perfect, some might say. Mike accomplished a total success without breaking a sweat. How often does that happen in reality? As a person whose job is to make software for a living, you know the answer all too well. It *never* happens. When real people interact with software, not only does a total success rarely occur, but sometimes it's flat-out impossible—and the results look more like carnage.

Developers, designers, testers, and analysts can never assume that customers will use their products in a linear manner. They must always prepare to specify multiple paths a user can choose.

To see why, let's get back to the example. We've taken SBE's commitment to concrete examples seriously: you can't get more concrete than the 2 p.m. start time in the When. Have you asked yourself, though, whether there's any possibility that the start time may fail? For example, what would happen if Mike chose 2 p.m. as the start time, but it was already 3 p.m.? Wouldn't that break the scenario?

Listing 2.9   Two similar scenarios with different outcomes

```
Feature: Scheduling

  Because scheduling is a huge functionality, this
  specification file describes only the most important
  high-level scenario.
  You can find more detailed scenarios in the rest
  of the files inside the "meetings" folder in the
  specification suite.

  Scenario: Creating a new meeting successfully

    Given Mike, a member of our team
      And that it isn't 2 p.m. yet          <--- Prerequisite that guarantees a positive outcome
      When Mike chooses 2 p.m. as a start time for his meeting
  Positive  Then he should be able to save his meeting
  outcome

  Scenario: Failing at creating a new meeting

    Given Mike, a member of our team
      And that it's already 3 p.m.          <--- Prerequisite that guarantees a negative outcome
      When Mike chooses 2 p.m. as a start time for his meeting
      Then he shouldn't be able to save his meeting   <--- Negative outcome
```

By writing two different *outcomes* for the same action, you've written your first comprehensive test in Gherkin. You can either pass or fail a test. In order to make sure your specification suite has acceptable scenario coverage, you must specify both what happens when a user takes a successful approach, as well as an unlucky approach.

Testers usually call scenarios with positive outcomes *happy paths*. Beginning with the happy-path scenario is a good way to establish a key example as a foundation from which to think about other possibilities. Fortunately, testing heuristics suggest a multitude of other paths, including angry paths, scary paths, embarrassing paths, forgetful paths, and so on. We'll talk more about all the possibilities in chapters 4 and 5, which are about choosing good examples for your executable specifications.

> **Exercise 4**
>
> What are other circumstances that may result in failures when Mike creates a meeting? Write a third scenario that adds more detail to the specification. You can use a scheduling conflict in Mike's calendar as a reason for failure, or you can invent your own example.

2.5 How the automation and specification layers interact

The two scenarios in listing 2.8 are your first real tests written in Gherkin. But didn't I say in chapter 1 that SBE's practitioners *automate* their tests? How does that happen? I talked a bit about Cucumber, the test execution engine, earlier in this chapter, but I haven't said anything concrete. How are you going to write good tests in Gherkin without learning to write real testing code in Cucumber? Is that even possible? Let's decouple these worrisome questions and take them one by one.

2.5.1 Step definitions

Cucumber executes the testing code within something called a *step definition*.

> **DEFINITION** *Step definition*—An implementation of the testing code for a single step. Step definitions are containers for the testing code that must be executed in order to run the steps in the automation layer.

For example, let's consider possible step definitions for testing a notification email that's sent after Mike creates his event. You can find some practical examples of step definitions in table 2.2.

Table 2.2 What needs to happen under the hood to test whether an email was sent?

Keyword	Testing code in the step definition
Given	Establish connection to the database, populate it with some testing data, or configure the application to a desirable state
When	Simulate sending an email based on the data fetched from the database
Then	Check if the email was sent by integrating with the mailing service's internal queue

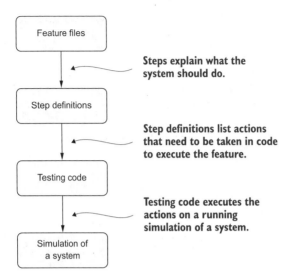

Steps explain what the system should do.

Step definitions list actions that need to be taken in code to execute the feature.

Testing code executes the actions on a running simulation of a system.

Figure 2.6   Gherkin features test a simulation of the working system with testing code executed through step definitions.

In theory, the relationship between features, steps, and step definitions is pretty simple. Figure 2.6 illustrates the high-level flow.

Every feature contains multiple scenarios that contain multiple steps. These steps have corresponding step definitions that are responsible for running the automation code that affects a simulation of a system, as well as checking whether the code yields expected results.

2.5.2   *Matching steps with step definitions*

A middle-sized Gherkin project can contain between 200 and 600 scenarios. If you assume that every scenario has at least 3 steps, each of which is one of each kind, that's between 600 and 1,800 steps in a single specification suite. And remember that, unlike keywords, a step's content isn't predefined; you can write whatever you like as long as it fits within a single sentence and makes sense, given the rest of your scenario. All in all, that's a lot of content and a lot of step definitions to execute. How does that happen?

In general, Gherkin files must be parsed by a testing framework that matches steps and their step definitions (see figure 2.7). That's precisely what Cucumber does.

From a technical point of view, every step's content is matched with a step definition within the automation layer—like in a search-and-replace operation in any text editor you've ever used. Here's the general rule for matching step definitions:

```
Step's content <- Testing code
```

You can read this expression as the general rule, "the left-hand side can be replaced with the right-hand side." When anything that matches the left side—a step—is found, it's replaced with whatever the right side—testing code—contains. Table 2.3 lists some simple, practical examples with dummy testing code written in Ruby. If you want a more advanced explanation, check out appendix A.

Step

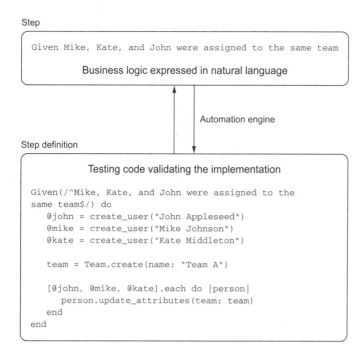

Figure 2.7   The testing code contained in step definitions is matched to examples and scenarios through regular expressions executed by the automation engine. Steps and their step definitions are inseparably connected. Steps describe the business logic in natural language; step definitions allow the automation engine to run the testing code needed to check whether the step's business logic is implemented correctly.

Table 2.3   Specific steps matched with their step definitions

Step's content	Step definition's code	Purpose
`Mike, a member of our team`	`@mike = User.create(name: "Mike")`	Create Mike's account.
`that it isn't 2 p.m. yet`	`Time.freeze("1 p.m.")`	Freeze the time of the system's simulation to make sure the event is valid.
`Mike chooses 2 p.m. as a start time for his meeting`	`@meeting = Meeting.create(start_time: "2 p.m.", user: @mike)`	Attempt to save Mike's meeting in the database.
`he should be able to save his meeting`	`expect(@meeting.saved?).to eq true`	Ensure that the system saved Mike's meeting properly.
`he shouldn't be able to save his meeting`	`expect(@meeting.saved?).to eq false`	Ensure that the system didn't save the incorrect meeting.

You'll notice, first, that Cucumber rejects keywords when matching a step. Cucumber behaves like that because in some advanced cases, you may want to write interchangeable steps; for example, you may want a When from one scenario to become a Given in another scenario. I'll talk more about why you might want to do so in chapter 3. Second, Cucumber matches the rest of the step with the testing code in a step definition with the step's name.

Only together can Gherkin and Cucumber work as an end-to-end tool. The specification layer elaborates requirements and acceptance criteria in natural language using important real-world examples. The examples, expressed in steps, become links that connect acceptance criteria with automated tests—the automation layer—through regular expressions (see figure 2.8). The tests make sure the system behaves as the requirements should require it to.

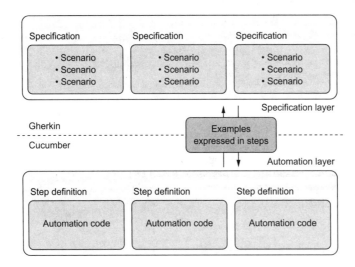

Figure 2.8 Examples, expressed in steps, act as a link between Gherkin and Cucumber. Steps, scenarios, and feature files constitute the specification layer. Step definitions and the testing code are the fundamentals of the automation layer. Together, the specification layer and the automation layer create an executable specification suite.

You could write scenarios without using Cucumber, but they wouldn't be executable. And if they weren't executable, they wouldn't become acceptance tests. Without acceptance tests, you couldn't easily know when to update the scenarios when the system breaks or changes. And why would you keep outdated scenarios? You'd probably discard them just as you discard the sticky notes with user stories after you finish the story.

That's why the system works only if every acceptance criterion becomes a scenario, scenarios become tests, and tests control the design of the system by validating the system frequently with the testing code. These three steps make a cohesive whole: a specification process that covers your development efforts from start to end.

Testing and checking

A question that's often asked when the topic of automated tests comes up is, "Why don't we get rid of all of our testers and automate all of our testing?" But you never hear anyone say, "Why don't we get rid of all of our developers and automate all the development?" Trying to answer why is an interesting thought exercise.

Developers do the smart thing and call their automated work *compiling*. Testers, too, could differentiate between testing that requires thought and can't be automated and the checking that's done with automation. When you design scenarios and think about the possible inputs and expected outputs, you're doing exploratory *testing* that could never be done without a conscious mind. Once you design the scenarios, you can automate most of them with testing code—and that's the *checking* part. Some tests are more complicated than simple, easy-to-replicate checks, and that's why they can never be fully automated.

2.6 *Finishing the Gherkin crash course*

And—you're finished. After reading this chapter, you're ready to write Gherkin specifications for any project.

Let's review what you've done:

- You analyzed your acceptance criteria using concrete examples of how you expect users to use the product in their natural environment.
- You captured these examples as Given-When-Then scenarios to prepare them for future automation.

You ended up with a specification that's different from traditional requirements documents:

- It's much smaller, because Gherkin requires you to break down the scope of your work into singular features. Small specifications fit well into iterative processes that focus on getting small chunks of work done quickly and repeatably.
- It's concrete and doesn't leave much to a reader's imagination. By making the solution easier to comprehend, concrete examples allow engineers to produce working code more quickly.
- It's ready to be tied up with implementation code through automated tests in order to maintain consistency with the system at all times. The document will stay up to date, because when anything changes, the link between code and scenarios will be broken. If the specification is validated frequently, the delivery team will be able to spot broken scenarios quickly.
- It's not wasteful. The specification acts as a link between the analysis, design, implementation, and testing phases. The system doesn't require a separate testing phase that would enable testers to determine whether requirements are satisfied—if they trust the specification, they can focus on exploratory testing and more-difficult edge cases. No other development artifacts are introduced.

What this chapter didn't cover is Gherkin's full syntax. Don't worry; you can find a full specification of the Gherkin language in Cucumber's repository on GitHub. But in my opinion, you can feel free to skip it. Throughout the book, you'll see that the key to writing good Gherkin lies somewhere other than getting to know the intricacies of its syntax—and you'll learn the handiest tricks on the fly.

The real difficulty in using Gherkin is its flexibility. In addition to the keywords, you can type almost anything you want in any order you can imagine. Such flexibility can lead you astray if you're not careful. In the next chapter, you'll see how to protect yourself.

2.7   *Answers to exercises*

EXERCISE 1   Write the rest of the specification brief that explains who will use the scheduling features and why they need them, based on what you know about the application.

```
Like it or not, meetings are the lifeblood of every organization.

Our calendar app is meant for busy teams who work in collaborative
environments, have to manage multiple meetings a day with different
clients, and want to be as mobile as they can. They need smart reminders,
help with different time zones, and a professional meeting management
solution.

This feature, then, being the simplest meeting management form we could
come up with without compromising on powerful capabilities, is the core
part of our product.

Please be careful and make sure everything is tested properly.
Everything else in this application could break and people would still
forgive us; if this feature breaks, we'll all be doomed.
```

EXERCISE 2   Write a simple scenario for canceling a meeting.

```
Given a meeting by John and Anna at 4 p.m.
  And that it is 3 p.m. now
When Anna cancels the meeting
Then the event should be removed from the calendar
  And John should be notified about the canceled event
```

EXERCISE 3   Find all the keywords in the Gherkin file that you've written so far in this chapter, separate the keywords from the steps, and write the results in a table.

- Feature
- Scenario
- Given
- When
- Then
- And
- But

EXERCISE 4 What are other circumstances that may result in failures when Mike creates a meeting? Write a third scenario that adds more detail to the specification.

```
Given Mike, a member of our team
  And another event in Mike's calendar at 2 p.m.
 When Mike chooses 2 p.m. as a start time for his new meeting
 Then he should not be able to save his meeting
```

2.8   *Summary*

- A full Gherkin specification is called a *feature*. A single feature is typically contained in its own file that ends with a .feature extension. A feature typically specifies the behavior of a single functionality.
- The specification layer contains specification files with the .feature extension, written in plain English and filled with domain-specific terms and concepts.
- The automation layer and the specification layer heavily influence each other. You can't have a good specification layer without understanding the basics of the automation layer.
- Given a set of expected inputs and outputs, the automation layer executes a simulation of the application to see whether the working code behaves as expected.
- Cucumber is a testing framework that matches Gherkin steps with step definitions and lets you run testing code.
- Givens, Whens, and Thens are called *steps*.
- Steps begin with keywords that help Cucumber parse the feature file.
- Step definitions are containers for all the testing code that must be executed to run a step.

Mastering the Given-When-Then template

3

This chapter covers

- Writing scenarios for the real world
- Using realistic data in scenarios
- Understanding advanced rules for using Given-When-Then
- Getting unstuck when writing scenarios
- Generating ideas for new scenarios

In chapter 2, we explored the two layers of executable specifications: the specification layer and the automation layer. We focused on the specification layer and writing it. But if you ever tried to write a blog post, you know that *just* writing and *great* writing aren't the same thing. Likewise, writing scenarios and writing great scenarios can be quite different.

This chapter will teach you to write great scenarios. Chapter 2 taught you the basics of the Given-When-Then template, and this chapter is an advanced course. Expressive scenarios incorporate a vivid vocabulary of domain language that helps readers understand requirements more easily. But Gherkin's syntax is so easy that sometimes it seems repetitive—and therefore boring. Boring scenarios are easier to skim. You *must* learn to write expressive scenarios if you are to establish a connection with your readers.

My goal for this chapter was to write it like a practical cheat sheet. You'll be able to use it like your personal Gherkin Manual of Style—similar to the way the *Chicago Manual of Style* is a style guide for American English (it's been published since 1906 by the University of Chicago Press). Its 16 editions have prescribed writing styles widely used in publishing. Like English, Gherkin is a language—so an advanced manual will help you in the future.

Chapter 1 said that each Gherkin scenario is like a short story about a product. More parallels can be drawn between Gherkin and literature. An expert can rate each literary work in three areas: style, composition, and story. *Style* is all about the beauty of the language. *Composition* is about clarity and coherence of thought. *Story* is what happens to the heroes. Great Gherkin, too, can be rated using the same methodology—so the chapter you're reading right now is split into the following three sections:

- The style section (3.1) talks about the highest-level guidelines you should focus on when trying to write beautiful Gherkin scenarios. I'll explain why your scenarios should focus on stakeholders and be written in an outcome-oriented way.
- The composition section (3.2) expands on the structure of the Given-When-Then template and how you can write new scenarios more easily.
- The story section (3.3) explains what to do when you don't know what to write, by teaching methods to generate new ideas and get unstuck.

This chapter is organized around a collection of tips from these categories. Whenever I start a new tip, I'll begin by mentioning the category it belongs to. Most of the tips will be introduced in the order of this list, so you can expect style tips to appear in the style section, and so on. Sometimes, though, I'll mention techniques from other sections if they seem relevant but aren't important enough to warrant separate subsections—for example, I might include a story tip in the composition section. So don't be surprised.

3.1 Choosing the right style for your Gherkin scenarios

Exercises in Style is a classic book by the French author Raymond Queneau. The plot is simple: a man gets into an argument with another passenger on a bus. But this anecdote is told 99 more times, each in a radically different style: as a sonnet, an opera, in slang, and with many more permutations. Each style used in *Exercises* highlights different elements of the same story—and so, readers perceive each retelling differently, noticing different nuances every time.

Like Queneau, you can write your scenarios in different styles. This section will teach you what works best with Gherkin. We'll try to dissect what makes a scenario expressive. I'll talk about what you should focus on when writing new scenarios—what to emphasize and what to hide. I'll also discuss why trying to create software models that stick to the real world as closely as possible ultimately results in building better software.

3.1.1   *Doing outside-in development with Gherkin*

Starting with this section, you'll be working on an example application we'll name Queneau after the French author. Queneau is a text editor with features that let writers easily imitate different styles, exactly like its namesake.

WRITING USER-ORIENTED SCENARIOS

One of Queneau's competitive advantages is that the app can teach you to imitate the style of popular authors, such as Raymond Queneau himself and, let's say, Vladimir Nabokov. It does so by instructing you to revise your text like the chosen author would. In Nabokov's case, Queneau would instruct you to shorten your sentences, remove any adverbs, avoid passive voice, and so on. Thanks to what you learned in chapter 2, I can easily demonstrate such functionality using a Gherkin scenario.

> **Listing 3.1   [OK] An example scenario**

```
Scenario: Detect sentences that are too long

  Given text with a sentence that is too long:
    """
    As he crossed toward the pharmacy at the corner he involuntarily turned
    his head because of a burst of light that had ricocheted from his
    temple, and saw, with that quick smile with which we greet a rainbow or
    a rose, a blindingly white parallelogram of sky being unloaded from the
    van—a dresser with mirror across which, as across a cinema screen,
    passed a flawlessly clear reflection of boughs sliding and swaying not
    arboreally, but with a human vacillation, produced by the nature of
    those who were carrying this sky, these boughs, this gliding façade.
    """
  When the content is analyzed
  Then the sentence that is too long should be detected
```

The scenario looks fine—but if you scratch the surface, doesn't it seem lifeless? After all, writers will use your text editor to bring hundreds of beautiful and despicable characters to life. This scenario looks out of touch compared with what your end users will do with the product. By talking about system operations like analyzing and detection, which are highly technical, the scenario is clearly written in a style your users wouldn't want to read. And because more people read books written by authors like Nabokov than books written by technical people, you should do something about it if you want nontechnical stakeholders to read your scenarios, too.

Using multiline doc strings

If you need to write a step that won't fit on a single line, you can use *doc strings*. A doc string follows a step and begins and ends with three double quotation marks. Here's an example:

```
Given a text:
    """
    There is no rule on how to write.
    Sometimes it comes easily and perfectly;
    sometimes it's like drilling rock
    and then blasting it out with charges.
    """
```

Doc string

Doc strings allow you to write long error messages or email contents in your scenarios. Sometimes longer texts have a lot of business value. For example, in heavily regulated environments where mistakes are expensive, you might want to test your error messages with executable specifications.

To see what I mean, let's look at a revised version of the scenario from listing 3.1.

Listing 3.2 [GOOD] User-oriented scenario

```
Scenario: Detect sentences that are too long

  When Vladimir writes a sentence that is too long:
      """
      As he crossed toward the pharmacy at the corner he involuntarily turned
      his head because of a burst of light that had ricocheted from his
      temple, and saw, with that quick smile with which we greet a rainbow or
      a rose, a blindingly white parallelogram of sky being unloaded from the
      van—a dresser with mirror across which, as across a cinema screen,
      passed a flawlessly clear reflection of boughs sliding and swaying not
      arboreally, but with a human vacillation, produced by the nature of
      those who were carrying this sky, these boughs, this gliding façade.
      """
  Then he should be notified that the sentence could be shortened
```

Without changing much of the content, focusing on the person in front of the screen shifts attention to answering an important question: can you do something to improve Vladimir's life? Is it the most efficient way to help him? Can he achieve his goal easily? Having answered these questions, you might, for example, notice that if Queneau highlighted the sentence that could be shortened immediately after Vladimir wrote it, the app would distract him instead of helping him focus. Should you introduce two different modes, one for writing and one for editing? Editing mode would suggest possible changes. Vladimir would be able to switch between modes at will, depending on what he wanted to do at the moment.

Listing 3.3   [BEST] Discovering user benefits with Gherkin

```
Scenario: Detect sentences that are too long

  The EDIT MODE highlights all the suggestions made by
  our text editor directly in the text.

  The WRITE MODE hides the suggestions, so the author
  can focus on writing without any distractions.

  When Vladimir writes a sentence that is too long:
    """
    As he crossed toward the pharmacy at the corner he involuntarily turned
    his head because of a burst of light that had ricocheted from his
    temple, and saw, with that quick smile with which we greet a rainbow or
    a rose, a blindingly white parallelogram of sky being unloaded from the
    van—a dresser with mirror across which, as across a cinema screen,
    passed a flawlessly clear reflection of boughs sliding and swaying not
    arboreally, but with a human vacillation, produced by the nature of
    those who were carrying this sky, these boughs, this gliding façade.
    """
  Then he should be notified that it could be shortened in the Edit Mode
  But he shouldn't be notified about that in the Write Mode
```

> **TIP**   Hashing out Gherkin scenarios is a great way to brainstorm and discover new features. Writing a Given-When-Then scenario is even cheaper than drawing a sketch or making a mock-up. I find collaborating over Gherkin scenarios particularly valuable in asynchronous, remote work environments.

DEFINING ACTORS IN SCENARIOS

In chapter 2, when you were polishing your first `Given` in listing 2.7, I asked you to call the user in the scenario *Mike*. I told you that the reason to do so was that when two users appear in a single scenario, calling them *team member 1* and *team member 2* sounds awkward.

Real names and user-oriented scenarios facilitate empathy, and this is important. In one project, I called the user in most of my scenarios *Simona*. Every time I wrote a scenario, I imagined that she was anxious to get her work done as quickly as she could, because she had a sick child at home. I wondered whether there was anything more I could do to make her work easier. In user-centered design and marketing, what I did with Simona's scenarios is called creating a *persona*. Personas are fictional characters created to represent the different user types that might use a product in a similar way. So every time I mentioned Simona, I meant every person similar to her—a certain demographic, a customer segment. But these are abstract terms. A good persona is much more real.

Should you write steps with step definitions that have no testing code?

When I was learning how to use Cucumber and Gherkin, I was told that writing steps with step definitions that don't execute any testing code was a bad practice. Here's a quick example:

```
Given Vladimir's desire not to be distracted
 When he turns on the Write Mode
 Then only the paragraph he's working on should be fully visible
  And the other paragraphs should be dimmed out
```

How on earth could you write testing code to check whether a user *feels distracted*?

At first glance, the step feels redundant. Including it seems like unnecessary work for whoever will implement the acceptance tests. A developer would certainly tell you that doing so increases the complexity of the test suite for no reason.

I think the answer becomes clearer if you keep in mind that scenarios emerge *before* you start thinking about tests and testing code. With specification by example (SBE) and Gherkin, you follow an end-to-end paradigm of building a dynamic specification system that *constantly evolves* along with the product. And when you embrace the mindset of organizing your development process around collecting examples and refining scenarios, then you can see a fluid progression between development phases.

Imagine that you're sitting in a specification workshop, trying to analyze the Write Mode feature. It would be extremely natural to write that Vladimir doesn't want to be distracted, because that's why you invented the feature in the first place. You could even rename the Write Mode to something like Focus Mode and make it a big element of your marketing value proposition for Queneau.

This is why I think that instead of not writing steps with empty step definitions, you should make a habit of not writing steps that don't bring any *value*. These are two different things.

Had you looked at this situation only from the perspective of the system, you would have seen only system attributes—data coming in and going out of your application, the inputs and outputs. In some cases, this isn't a bad approach—and yes, there can be other cases. From a technical point of view, every scenario must be written from the perspective of an *actor*.

DEFINITION *Actor*—Anything that influences an action or a process taking place in the system under design

There are three types of actors:

- Stakeholders
- Organizations
- Systems

A *stakeholder* is someone with a vested interest in the behavior of the use case, even if they never interact directly with the system. Stakeholders come in all sorts of flavors. They're the people who use the software you create, but they can also be economic buyers, decision makers, business partners, or insiders.

But organizations and systems can be actors, too. For example, an external service provided by a business partnership may shape your product and deserve a mention in your scenarios.

OUTSIDE-IN DEVELOPMENT AND USER-ORIENTED SCENARIOS

You can write Gherkin scenarios for all three types of actors, but I strongly advocate taking the perspective of a specific group of stakeholders: the *end users*. End users are the people who interact with your product. They experience how your software works in the real world. In general, you should use the tools you choose in a way that can yield the most benefits. But the software development community has come to a broad consensus that the user-centered perspective works best. That's why, as an industry, we've reoriented most of our tools, such as user stories, to focus on people. I've already mentioned how UX designers and marketers use personas to empathize with abstract customer segments. Gherkin, too, fits this trend well.

> **TIP** [STORY] To elicit better requirements, understand *who* needs a suggested solution and *why* they need it. If you need help to better understand your stakeholders, try creating a user journey map. A *user journey map* is a visual or graphic interpretation of the overall story, from an individual's perspective, of their relationship with an organization, a service, a product, or a brand, over time and across channels. Unfortunately, creating user journey maps goes beyond the scope of the book.

In the world of software, focusing on stakeholders is also called *outside-in development*. At times, outside-in development is like literature, too. Storytellers have to keep in mind what's interesting to their audience, not what's fun to do as a writer. Those objectives can be very different. Even systems-heavy solutions can be analyzed from this perspective. Systems are designed by people; they're used by people; they're managed by people. The outside-in approach forces you to think about the people who define software requirements and try to understand *why* they want what they want. In general, try to write your scenarios for end users when you can—but when you can't, don't lose sight of the people behind systems and machines.

> **DEFINITION** *Outside-in development*—A software development methodology that aims to create successful software through understanding the goals and motivations of stakeholders

This section isn't meant to exhaust the topic of outside-in development. That's a separate art of finding, analyzing, and managing stakeholders on different levels, both inside your organization and outside of it. As I just outlined, it's more complex than focusing on end users. For example, some stakeholders may be hidden from your

> ## Outside-in terminology and behavior-driven development
>
> Outside-in terminology belongs to the Gherkin domain but not to the SBE domain, which means you may not hear it much when talking with people who use non-Gherkin executable specifications like FitNesse. Behavior-driven development (BDD)—which is mostly associated with Gherkin through the figure of Dan North, who had a hand in creating both BDD and Gherkin—is often defined as "a second-generation, *outside-in*, pull-based, multiple-stakeholder, multiple-scale, high-automation, agile methodology."
>
> Bonanza of keywords aside, I took the liberty of integrating outside-in methods into this chapter and also chapter 5. But I believe that mentioning the terminology mix-up explicitly here is a fair thing to do.

view. This usually happens when a new, weird requirement emerges, and you have no idea where it came from—because it doesn't sound like a request people you usually talk to would make. (Hint: It may have been enforced by a silent stakeholder.) Machine-to-machine solutions are another example. I can't cover them all in this chapter. But I wanted to achieve two things: to give you a guideline—a rule of thumb that will maximize results and minimize effort; and to give you a platform from which to investigate outside-in development on your own.

3.1.2 *Gathering realistic data*

I started writing short stories when I was in middle school. I couldn't write very well, so I at least wanted the stories to be cool. I wrote about stuff I thought was exciting. It was also stuff I knew nothing about. The results always turned out to be boring because my stories lacked detail and depth. It took me a few years to realize that people liked my writing more when there was something *true* and *realistic* at the core of a story rather than when it was shouting "cool" all over the place but felt fake. Good Gherkin writers should also hate fake stories—fake examples, fake actors, and fake domain concepts—because fake data often results in making misinformed decisions. Let me explain why.

Table 3.1 contains three examples of rules that Queneau implements to help writers edit their text files more easily. All three examples were devised to illustrate system rules somebody took for granted. But the correct approach for illustrating requirements with examples is to find examples that constitute a *source* of each rule. As a strong fundamental, grounded in the real world, the source provides validation of whether a rule makes sense. The examples in the table don't—they're more like fragile crutches.

If you put the table in a Gherkin scenario, it wouldn't break the test-execution engine. The examples were designed *not* to break it.

Fake scenarios with fictional examples poison your decision making. Outside-in development relies on analyzing people, processes, and rules *outside* of your system to incorporate them *in* your application. The role of data in Gherkin is to inform

Table 3.1   [BAD] Fictional examples of acceptance criteria in Queneau

Rule	Example
Avoid long sentences	This is a sentence that is too long and, while it's certainly pretty, it might therefore be too complicated for a reader to comprehend at a glance—so you should consider shortening it or breaking it into smaller pieces.
Replace difficult words with simpler alternatives	This extraordinary sentence contains a difficult world—*extraordinary*—that you could replace with a simpler word such as *special*.
Avoid adverbs	Adverbs should be limited, *preferably* removed.

decisions and ensure continuity of research and discovery in the software development process. Examples and scenarios should empower future readers to understand the context they were written in, so that anyone who decides to push the feature forward can build on top of what the original writers intended.

Look at the examples again. If you were to make a change to this scenario six months after its conception, would you—a person who hasn't worked on this project before—be able to understand *why* such sentences were chosen? No. They would seem arbitrary.

Ultimately, what we're after is authenticity—both in software and in writing. Authentic stories strive to tell you something impactful and true. Similarly, authentic, impactful software understands you and your needs.

3.1.3   *Favor specifying intentions and outcomes over the user interface*

The two previous chapters talked about how the Given-When-Then template works well with behavioral requirements. *Behaviors* are actions performed by actors and meant to make a change in a system. Understanding how high-level these actions should be is a difficult topic that many Gherkin writers struggle with. I'll talk about it multiple times throughout the chapter. This section will give you an introduction to help you understand the general rule for how abstract or concrete behaviors should be.

I have to begin by saying that Cucumber and Gherkin are typically associated with end-to-end system testing. This heritage is the reason a lot of people write Gherkin scenarios that talk about what's tested in the automation layer: the user interface.

> **DEFINITION**   *End-to-end tests*—Tests that check whether the flow of an application is behaving as expected from start to finish, by running a simulation of the entire system in a browser and emulating real users clicking through the UI

To understand what I mean, look at the following scenario. It specifies a simple exporting feature built into Queneau.

Listing 3.4 [BAD] Interface-oriented scenario

```
Scenario: Exporting documents

  Given "Export" button from the "File" menu was clicked
  When Vladimir types "Lolita" into the "Name" text field
   And he chooses "PDF" from the file type select field
   And he chooses a "1955" destination folder from a select field
  Then a file "Lolita.pdf" should appear in folder "1955"
```

Now, imagine that you change the location of the Export button in the example, putting it in the Edit menu instead of File. It's a minuscule change, but you'd have to rewrite both the step and the step definition in question.

If the specification has to change every time the UI changes—when a button disappears, for example—then building trust is more difficult, because humans instinctively value stability over chaos. Writing about buttons, forms, links, and input fields is a limiting approach to harnessing the benefits of a business-readable DSL like Gherkin in bridging the communication gap between technology and business.

Some of the confusion comes from the fact that Gherkin scenarios are about behaviors, and thinking about behaviors can automatically prime you to imagine a UI to interact with. But throughout the book, I favor a different approach: writing Gherkin specifications that describe the business logic of a system, as well as the intentions of actors and the outcomes they can or can't achieve. So instead of talking about buttons or links, you talk about business goals, customers, requirements, and acceptance criteria—because *that's* what the business cares about.

> **TIP** [STYLE] Don't write scenarios about the UI. Write about business outcomes. Nobody cares about the UI; they care if they can get their job done.

Favoring specifying intentions and outcomes over the UI is a practical tip for writing more-bulletproof scenarios. But from a theoretical point of view, the discussion is about preferring one style of writing over another: interface-oriented style, which is also called *imperative style*, or outcome-oriented style, also known as *declarative style.*

Imperative style is simple, is intuitive, and reflects what manual testers do. That's why almost everybody who is new to Gherkin naturally starts with this style. In contrast, declarative style describes *what* the user does, but not *how* they do it—the *how* part is pushed into step definitions and handled by the automation layer. The real difference between the imperative approach and the declarative approach comes down to different levels of abstraction. Imperative writing is less abstract and more concrete, whereas declarative writing is more abstract. Liz Keogh, a BDD mentor, argued once that "there's no such thing as declarative and imperative"[1] and "every declarative is a chunking-up of something else, and every imperative is a chunking-down, and you can chunk up and down to different levels of abstraction." *Chunking up* and *chunking down* are terms from the domain of natural language processing, and they mean becoming more abstract or more specific, respectively.

---

[1] Liz Keogh, "There's No Such Thing as Declarative and Imperative," June 17, 2013, http://mng.bz/QO51.

> **Exercise 1**
> Rewrite listing 3.4 in declarative style.

But choosing the right level of abstraction isn't only a stylistic choice. It's also about composition. For example, the more abstract you decide to be, the shorter your scenarios will be and the fewer steps they will contain. And that can be good or bad. Shorter scenarios can be easier to read, discuss, and remember—but they can also be too short to allow readers to grasp difficult domain concepts and their consequences in full. So the choice of abstraction level shouldn't be automatic. I'll talk more about how to make a good decision in the next section (which talks in general about compositions) and, particularly, in section 3.2.4. I'll also revisit the topic in chapter 8, where I'll talk about splicing scenarios into specifications while maintaining a reasonable level of abstraction.

3.2   *Composing Gherkin scenarios*

In literature, *composition* involves structuring a story to the best of your ability in order to achieve a specific storytelling effect. This section discusses the rules of composing Given-When-Then templates designed to facilitate outside-in development:

- *Low-level composition*—How to phrase Gherkin steps
- *High-level composition*—How to balance `Givens`, `Whens`, and `Thens` in your scenarios

These rules should help you write easily readable Gherkin scenarios more quickly.

3.2.1   *Starting with a Then*

Every writer knows that there's something terrifying about a blank page. Even if you know what you want to write about, transforming thoughts into words is difficult. The same applies to Gherkin scenarios. It may seem counterintuitive, but the easiest way to start writing a Gherkin scenario is to begin with the end in mind—the `Then`—just as most good writers never start writing without figuring out the ending. This should get you unstuck quickly. It also brings other benefits, such as better collaboration with business users to elicit better requirements.

> **TIP**   Starting with examples of outputs can help engage business users in the discussion even before any scenarios are written and will give them a clear picture of what they can get out of the system. Outputs are often easier to discuss than inputs because, usually, outputs already "exist" in the real world. For example, when you're trying to automate a manual process with software, the expected outputs of the process are easy to retrieve from existing results. Now you only need to figure out the automation process.

> **TIP**   To help achieve better outcomes, examine a behavior that already exists, and try to improve it.

What are the other benefits? The truth is, no one is ever in the market to buy a "product." Think about it. Nobody wants to buy a drill for the sake of buying a drill. Sometimes, though, people need a hole in a wall. In marketing, mistaking the source of demand is called *marketing myopia.*[2]

> **DEFINITION** *Marketing myopia*—The mistake of paying more attention to the specific products a company offers than to the benefits and experiences produced by these products.

Customers want to buy a specific *outcome* your product will produce. And Thens *are* the outcomes. That's why you should start with both getting the right Thens and getting the Thens right, by which I mean your users should want the outcomes you're specifying, and the outcomes should be described clearly to the delivery team. Everything else should build on top of that.

> **TIP** [STYLE] To facilitate outside-in development, use the following template to phrase most of your Thens: *<an actor> should be able to <achieve a result.>.*

Starting with Thens fits into a larger narrative than writing good Gherkin or even making software. *Principles of Marketing*, for example, is a must-read resource for all marketing students. You won't find a line of code in it—not even a mention of an application or a server. The Jobs-to-be-Done framework[3] also developed a concept of customers *hiring* products to yield specific outcomes, rather than buying new stuff. Doing outside-in development can fit into new business practices like these as they spread among companies.

3.2.2 *Using only one When per scenario*

In prose, each form of fiction can only contain a story specific to its length. Short stories focus on a single hero or theme. Novels feature casts of multiple characters and gently intertwine their subplots.

If you try to apply the structure of a novel to a short story without recomposing it, you'll fail. Many book adaptations fail as movies for the same reason. They try to fit too many themes and characters into a movie that's two hours long, confusing viewers with rushed plots and undeveloped characters.

Ideally, a scenario should be three sentences long and feature one Given, one When, and one Then. Just as short stories focus on only one theme, each scenario should be composed to talk about only one acceptance criterion.

Let's say that, in Queneau, there's a readability score feature that lets writers know when they violate too many suggestions, making the text hard to read. Here's a scenario describing that.

---

[2] Philip T. Kotler and Gary Armstrong, *Principles of Marketing* (Prentice Hall, 2013).
[3] First described in the 2005 *Harvard Business Review* article "Marketing Malpractice: The Cause and the Cure," by Clayton M. Christensen, Scott Cook, and Taddy Hall.

```
Listing 3.5   [BAD] Scenario with two Whens
```

```
Scenario: Improving readability score

  Given Vladimir's low readability score
  When he goes into the Edit Mode
   And he simplifies the text
  Then his readability score should improve
```

Tell me: does the readability score improve *only* when you use Edit Mode?

When you use two `When`s for one outcome, you can never be sure which `When` caused the outcome to happen. In listing 3.5, intuition suggests that *both* `When`s are necessary for the readability score to improve. But are they? Why would the score improve only if you used Edit Mode? Does that mean if you made the same changes in Write Mode, the readability score wouldn't go up? That's ridiculous. To avoid such confusion, think of `When`s as *user tasks* performed by actors, and try to specify only one user task per scenario.

DEFINITION   *User task*—A high-level instruction that describes a single business activity

To determine whether a `When` you wrote is a user task, ask whether the actor could perform the task without turning on a computer. "Revising content" is a user task because you can revise manually, too. "Choosing destination folder for a text file" isn't a user task, because it's too low level—it deals with the tech domain instead of the business domain.

When you write a scenario with two user tasks, you make the scenario more difficult to analyze. Coupling always means some interaction between multiple rules, and

The Screenplay Pattern

Task-oriented thinking comes from an acceptance-testing practice called the *Screenplay Pattern*, brought to life by Antony Marcano and later refined by Andy Palmer. I stumbled on the Screenplay Pattern thanks to Jan Molak and John Ferguson Smart, who expanded on the subject in a series of articles.[a]

The Screenplay Pattern is a user-centered approach to writing high-quality automated acceptance tests based on good software-engineering principles. From a high-level point of view, the pattern organizes tests around actors who perform user tasks in order to accomplish their business goals. The approach is similar to the one I take in the book.

Developers and engineers will find the pattern helpful in avoiding redundancy and organizing test code according to patterns such as the Single Responsibility Principle and the Open-Closed Principle. Non-engineers can also use the Screenplay Pattern to organize Gherkin scenarios more easily.

---

[a] Jan Molak, "From Acceptance Tests to User Guides," March 31, 2016, http://mng.bz/VU1u.

interaction means new inputs and outputs to take care of. Given Gherkin scenarios' optimal length, it would be like trying to fit a novel into three sentences. But when you aim to use only one task per scenario, you can clearly see what's being tested in the scenario.

> **TIP** [STYLE] User tasks take place in the present and should be phrased in active voice to differentiate them from contexts and outcomes.

But sometimes a scenario with multiple Whens is an acceptable choice. Each high-level user task is comprised of multiple lower-level activities called *user actions*. For example, when you want to print a document, you have to choose a format *and* pages to print *and* a quality of printing to achieve the final objective. (There are many other options to choose from, but I'm simplifying for the sake of the example.)

Listing 3.6   [GOOD] Scenario with multiple user actions

```
Scenario: Printing documents

  Given a 50 pages long draft
    When Vladimir wants to print in the letterhead format
    And he chooses to print all the pages
    And he chooses to print in low quality
    Then the printer should print 50 low quality A4 pages
```

None of these steps is a standalone user task; you must complete all three to get a meaningful result. If you only use multiple Whens to convey user actions, there also isn't any confusion about whether the steps are all required for the scenario to take place in the real world.

> **TIP** [COMPOSITION] To distinguish small user actions and big user tasks, remember that user tasks should allow actors to proceed to Thens. If a When needs additional clarification, it's a user action.

Exercise 2

Rewrite the user actions from listing 3.7 as a user task.

When you set out to write a new scenario, should you write about user tasks or user actions? That depends. I'll come back to this in section 3.2.4, which discusses choosing the right level of abstraction for your scenarios.

3.2.3   *Specifying prerequisites with Givens*

In sci-fi and fantasy, imaginary worlds often *enable* writers to tell the stories they want to share. Let me give you an example. The events of *The Lord of the Rings* wouldn't happen if not for the One Ring, a magical item that's central to the plot. The ring is an element of the fictional universe that author J. R. R. Tolkien created; but because its appearance sets the action in motion, it's also a *prerequisite* necessary for the rest of the story to happen.

Givens have a role in scenarios that's similar to world-building in storytelling. A Given creates a *snapshot* of the represented world and its history *before* the action of the scenario can take place. The snapshot stays static until the actors change it with their actions.

> **TIP** [STYLE] Don't phrase Givens as actions. Use passive voice in past tense, or phrase each Given as a list of things that need to happen before the actors can move the action forward.

But how can you create a snapshot in text? Use lists, because you can often rearrange lists easily, or use passive voice in past tense—but always remember to reserve actions for Whens. Actions are usually scenario specific and thus can't be moved freely; lists, on the other hand, are universal, because you can rearrange items more easily. And it's often important to phrase Givens flexibly, because although different scenarios need different snapshots, you'll often want to reuse elements you've already created for other scenarios. To illustrate, here's an example of an action within a Given.

> **Listing 3.7   [BAD] An active Given**

```
Given Vladimir writes a sentence in his draft:
    """
    It was love at first sight, at last sight,
    at ever and ever sight.
    """
```

I might suspect that this step was copied from another scenario where it was used as a When to specify some action. The problem is that without looking at the testing code, you'll know little about this step's implementation. The implementation can, for example, depend on other Givens that were useful when the step was a When but will only make your new scenario less clear if you have to include them.

Here's how you could rewrite the problematic step to be standalone and flexible.

> **Listing 3.8   [GOOD] A passive Given**

```
Given text:
    """
    It was love at first sight, at last sight,
    at ever and ever sight.
    """
```

Now you have a step that is clearly distinct and can later be automated in a way that's easy and safe to reuse in other scenarios.

Think of Givens as building blocks. These blocks are used to build a coherent world where your scenarios can take place. Passive blocks tend to fit with each other more easily. You can just list necessary prerequisites, instead of trying to awkwardly stitch together a few active sentences from other scenarios.

Exercise 3

Rewrite the following step into a passive `Given`: `Given Vladimir wants to write a new book.`

REUSING GIVENS WITH BACKGROUNDS

Sometimes you'll need the same prerequisites for all the scenarios in a single feature file. Gherkin makes that easier with *backgrounds*.

To better understand what a Gherkin background is, imagine you're writing a book that features multiple narrators. Each of the narrators tells their part of the story in a separate chapter. All the chapters are happening simultaneously. To let the reader better understand the plot, you decide to add a prologue written in third-person narrative mode that explains the basic context for all the other chapters. For example, the book may be a historic action novel that pictures a chaotic aftermath of a medieval city's burning. The prologue describes events that led to the burning. The chapters deal with the aftermath from the perspective of subsequent narrators. If Gherkin's scenario can be compared to the book's chapters, then a background is exactly like the prologue.

DEFINITION *Background*—A list of steps that run before each one of the scenarios in the same feature file

You can use a background to extract steps that are necessary to understand all other scenarios in a specification, without repeating them in every scenario. Let's say you choose to implement a search-and-replace function in Queneau. A simple implementation will need four new scenarios: one for search, one for search and replace, one for a success scenario, and one for a failure scenario.

Listing 3.9 Scenarios with redundant `Givens`

```
Feature: Search and replace

  Scenario: Successful search

    Given a text:
      """
      It was love at first sight, at last sight,
      at ever and ever sight.
      """
    When Vladimir searches for "was"
    Then he should be pointed to the word "was" in the text

  Scenario: Unsuccessful search

    Given a text:
      """
      It was love at first sight, at last sight,
      at ever and ever sight.
```

The same Givens in all scenarios

```
    """
    When Vladimir searches for "best"
    Then he should see that there is no such word in the text

Scenario: Successful search and replace

  Given a text:
    """
    It was love at first sight, at last sight,
    at ever and ever sight.
    """
    When Vladimir wants to replace "was" with "is"
    Then the text should be:
    """.
    It is love at first sight, at last sight,
    at ever and ever sight.
    """

Scenario: Unsuccessful search and replace

  Given a text:
    """
    It is love at first sight, at last sight,
    at ever and ever sight.
    """
    When Vladimir wants to replace "best" with "greatest"
    Then the text stay as it was:
    """
    It was love at first sight, at last sight,
    at ever and ever sight.
    """
```

The same Givens in all scenarios

Here's the same specification, simplified thanks to a background.

Listing 3.10 Givens refactored into `Background`

```
Feature: Search and replace

  Background:
    Given a text:
      """
      It was love at first sight, at last sight,
      at ever and ever sight.
      """

Scenario: Successful search

  When Vladimir searches for "was"
  Then he should be pointed to the word "was" in the text

Scenario: Unsuccessful search

  When Vladimir searches for "best"
  Then he should see that there is no such word in the text

Scenario: Successful search and replace

  When Vladimir wants to replace "was" with "is"
  Then the text should be:
```

The Background keyword

Redundant Givens from all four scenarios put in the background

```
        """
        It is love at first sight, at last sight,
        at ever and ever sight.
        """

    Scenario: Unsuccessful search and replace

      When Vladimir wants to replace "best" with "greatest"
      Then the text stay as it was:
        """
        It was love at first sight, at last sight,
        at ever and ever sight.
        """
```

As you can see, backgrounds are put after the specification brief but before the scenarios. When you run the test-execution engine, it will execute both of the Givens before running each scenario.

> **Should you use backgrounds?**
>
> Sometimes a background is a useful tool. We managed to go from 49 lines of text in listing 3.9 to 37 in listing 3.10, a decrease of almost 25%. And the more scenarios you have, the greater the decrease will be.
>
> Having said that, I don't advise using backgrounds too often. Many Gherkin practitioners think backgrounds are prone to being misused and that they make the specification layer too technical. Everyone should be able to read a Gherkin scenario and understand it even without knowing Gherkin's syntax—backgrounds make this harder. If you feel like you have to use backgrounds frequently, you should think about using broader-concept steps or split your specification into several smaller feature files.

3.2.4 *Choosing the right abstraction level*

In section 3.2.2, I said that you may want to write about high-level behaviors called user tasks that consist of other, low-level behaviors: user actions. Due to the amount of time I'm spending talking about ambiguity and clarity, you may think that being explicit and listing every possible action in your scenarios is the default way to go. But being verbose isn't always a good idea.

THE DISADVANTAGES OF BEING OVERLY SPECIFIC

Look at the following scenario, which talks about versioning drafts. The person who wrote it chose to make changes in the newer revision using low-level user actions.

Listing 3.11 Scenario that should be more abstract

```
Scenario: Revising drafts

  Given a draft of "Lolita"
  When Vladimir writes:
```

```
"""
Chapter 29
"""
And he marks the paragraph as a H1
And he writes:
"""
It was love at first sight, at last sight,
at ever and ever sight.
"""
Then the new draft should replace the previous draft
```

The scenario is technically okay, but it's too verbose given its purpose. Writing two new paragraphs with specific examples isn't required to check whether new drafts replace older drafts. It makes the scenario more difficult to read. But what if you simplified it?

Listing 3.12   Scenario at the correct abstraction level

```
Scenario: Revising drafts

  Given a draft of "Lolita"
   When Vladimir makes a new revision
   Then the new draft should replace the previous draft
```

Much better!

Unfortunately, no single rule exists for choosing the right level of abstraction. But don't worry about that right now. Even though you're trying to write the best scenarios you can, I wouldn't expect that to happen every time—and that's fine! Finish the first draft and see what other people think. Ask your teammates, or find a third-party reader. Iterative improvement is much better than nonexistent perfection. The following subsection offers some tips that should help you choose the optimal level of abstraction.

HOW MANY STEPS SHOULD YOU AIM FOR IN A SCENARIO?

Remember how I talked about starting new scenarios by writing their Thens? The level of abstraction of a particular scenario should depend on Thens, too, making them as obvious as possible. When you begin with the end in mind, you can work back to a correct abstraction level, thinking about the minimal set of user tasks and prerequisites needed to achieve the outcome you want.

> **TIP**   [STYLE] As a rule of thumb, keep your scenarios at an abstraction level that allows you to aim for as few Givens, Whens, and Thens as possible without sacrificing readability.

In general, you should explain the details necessary to understand the purpose of a scenario. If there's a user flow that *must* be part of a scenario, because the scenario can't take place without it, but it isn't crucial to understanding the scenario's essence, then you should only mention it briefly and consider wrapping it in a broader concept. This is what I did in listing 3.12 when I removed several specific steps, such as making a paragraph into a header, and wrapped them in the broader concept "making a new revision."

On the other hand, you should always have readers in mind. Will they understand what you intended if you simplify a scenario too much? For example, in the next scenario, do you know what Vladimir did to make the readability score go up?

Listing 3.13 Scenario that should be less abstract

```
Scenario: Improving readability score

  Given Vladimir's low readability score
  When he simplifies the text
  Then his readability score should improve
```

I have no idea. *Simplifying* can mean a thousand things.

Exercise 4

Rewrite listing 3.13 to reduce its level of abstraction. For the purpose of the exercise, you can assume that there's only one way to improve the readability score: by making long sentences shorter.

My personal rule of thumb, which can help you to choose the right abstraction level, says that you should be detailed when you introduce a new domain concept or a new user flow to the specification suite, explaining as much as you deem necessary. Corridor testing is useful to determine whether you're specific enough.

> **DEFINITION** *Corridor testing*—Informal, ad hoc solicitation to gain quick user feedback or data. Named after the classic example of spotting someone across a corridor and asking for their opinion.

Remember that a concept important to one scenario may not be as important to others. It's okay if you explain a particular user flow in detail in one scenario and only mention it briefly in other specifications. You can be briefer and act as though the reader is someone who already knows the concept you're writing about whenever you mention anything that already exists somewhere else in the specification suite.

In prose, getting the right abstraction level is easy, because the reader is usually reading chapters in a linear manner. For example, if I taught you what an executable specification is in chapter 1, I can expect that you already know what it is when you read chapter 3. A specification suite doesn't work this way. A reader with any level of knowledge about the system can jump into any specification file at any moment. But don't worry about that right now. Chapter 7, which discusses living documentation, talks about creating universal glossaries of concepts that will help you regulate the level of abstraction of particular steps throughout the specification suite. And chapters 8 and 9 present some techniques for organizing scenarios and specifications in a manner that's easy to follow even though the reading process isn't linear.

3.3   *Telling Gherkin stories with impact*

Gherkin scenarios tell stories about behaviors performed by actors. Whereas the previous sections taught you why the outside-in style matters and how to structure stories, they didn't address the most important issue many writers face: what to write about. How do you write meaningful scenarios that make your software better? Where should you start? How can you make sure all inputs and outputs are covered properly and your tests are good? This section offers some methods for writing scenarios that have real impact.

3.3.1   *Writing warm-up narratives*

A good way to get started when you're stuck with a new requirement is to write a short, free-flowing narrative about the requirement in action. You can do this after you gather some initial examples and acceptance criteria but before you write any scenarios in Gherkin. Here's an example.

> **Listing 3.14   Warm-up narrative**

```
"If your story is ready for rewrite, cut it to the bone.
Get rid of every ounce of excess fat. This is going to hurt;
revising a story down to the bare essentials is always
a little like murdering children, but it must be done."
—Stephen King

Writing is hard. Many authors struggle to get anything done.
There's something terrifying about a blank page, but there's
something terrifying about an unrevised page, too. What can
you do to make a writer's life easier?
```

Sketch out a few moments of a day in the life of one of the actors. In this narrative, invent a person you can empathize with, and capture, briefly, the mental state of that person, their goals, or the conditions that drive them to act as they do.

When writing, don't think about implementation yet. Ignore any technical limitations of your current system, and don't focus on the new features you'll have to develop to support the behavior. You don't have to worry about edge cases, either. The point of this exercise is to write *anything*. You can always rewrite the narrative into the Given-When-Then template later.

> **Exercise 5**
>
> Write a warm-up narrative for Vladimir and the Focus Mode feature. Focus Mode, mentioned in section 3.1.1, is a distraction-free writing mode designed to help the writer stay in the flow. Does the narrative cause you to imagine new solutions that would help Vladimir write something more easily?

If you think the narrative captures the business situation well enough, you can also put it into the specification brief. As long as you keep a beginner's mind and write nothing about your system in the narrative, it shouldn't be redundant to the scenarios in the specification. Instead, it should capture a broader business perspective and the *need* for the requirement that arose long before your team wrote any code.

3.3.2 *Vetting acceptance criteria with examples*

A great way to generate new scenarios is to take advantage of the fact that acceptance criteria and examples vet each other. By *vetting*, I mean that finding an acceptance criterion you haven't yet considered can lead to adding new examples to your scenarios (see figure 3.1). But examples that are unexpected, weren't considered seriously at first, or were discovered later in the process can also generate new acceptance criteria (see figure 3.2).

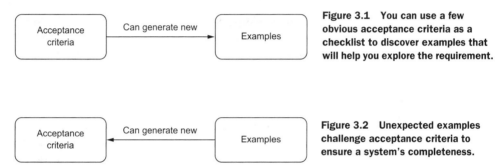

Figure 3.1 You can use a few obvious acceptance criteria as a checklist to discover examples that will help you explore the requirement.

Figure 3.2 Unexpected examples challenge acceptance criteria to ensure a system's completeness.

Examples illustrate acceptance criteria. So when you take on a new example, you also agree to apply a new rule to your design or modify an existing one.

You can start your analysis with either looking for examples or gathering an initial list of acceptance criteria. There isn't a strict rule for that, because you'll probably go back and forth multiple times during development.

Where you start from depends on the conversation you want to have. Exploring examples first works best when you don't have a good grasp of the system's rules yet or when you want to challenge the stereotypical assumptions of your interlocutors. Collecting acceptance criteria first works better when you or your stakeholders have a good initial understanding of what you're about to build—for example, when you're automating a well-described process that's an industry standard.

3.3.3 *Exploring contexts by questioning Givens*

It's easy to get stuck again after you finish writing a scenario. I can't tell you how many times I've said "So—that's it!" after writing a scenario, only to discover much later that my complacency led me to overlook a subtle edge case that I then had to take care of. I was surprised the first time it happened. But after a similar situation occurred a few weeks later, I knew I had to be more careful. The problem was, even when I was cautious, the sense of closure I felt after writing each scenario made it difficult to look at it again with fresh eyes.

One of the methods I encountered when I wanted to solve this problem is called *context questioning*.[4] To use this pattern, ask yourself, "Is there a context that, for the same event, produces a different outcome?"

Let me give you an example. Here's a scenario you've already seen in this chapter:

```
Scenario: Revising drafts

  Given a draft of "Lolita"
    When Vladimir makes a new revision
    Then the new draft should replace the previous draft
```

Are there any other `Given`s that produce different `Then`s for the same event? Are there any kinds of drafts that, when Vladimir makes a new revision, *shouldn't* replace the previous edit?

What if Queneau stores the drafts in the cloud? You could, for example, encounter a synchronization conflict in the same draft between two devices, such as a mobile phone and a laptop. When a sync issue arises, you probably shouldn't discard any of the drafts—neither the one you store in the cloud nor the one that's being saved.

3.3.4   *Exploring outcomes by questioning Thens*

Context questioning is a great technique to get you unstuck and help you write scenarios that are more complete, but it isn't the only one. In the same book, Liz Keogh talks about *outcome questioning*. To question outcomes, ask yourself, "Is there another outcome that also matters?"

Let's stay in the same area as the previous example: saving files in the cloud. Suppose Queneau offers a free 50 MB cloud plan for everyone. When a user runs out of space, they should upgrade to continue using the cloud feature:

```
Scenario: Upgrading cloud plans

  Given a 50 MB limit on Vladimir's cloud drive
    And 50 MB of text documents on Vladimir's cloud drive
   When Vladimir tries to save a new revision in the cloud
   Then he should be upgraded to a plan with more space
```

Haven't you forgotten something? I once heard that making a profit is a nice thing to do in the software business—so maybe you should also make sure you charge Vladimir's credit card. Here's the scenario after outcome questioning:

```
Scenario: Upgrading cloud plans

  Given a 50 MB limit on Vladimir's cloud drive
    And 50 MB of text documents on Vladimir's cloud drive
   When Vladimir tries to save a new revision in the cloud
```

---

[4]   I first read about context questioning in a book called *Behaviour Driven Development* by Liz Keogh (Leanpub, 2015).

```
Then he should be upgraded to a plan with more space
And his credit card should be charged $5
```

But there are two separate outcomes here. Should they be in the same scenario, or in different ones? A good rule of thumb is to ask whether they can happen separately. If they can't, they should be in the same scenario. But if they can, you need to ask whether the outcomes are related to the same business domain. If they aren't, they're probably two separate requirements and should be separated so the specification suite will be organized more clearly and have good searchability. I'll talk more about this in chapters 8 and 9, which explore the topic of organizing scenarios and specification suites.

Exercise 6
Are concepts such as *cloud features* and *buying extra space* in the same domain as *charging the user's credit card*?

I'll talk about the concept of the specification suite as a map of requirements more in chapters 8–11. For now, we'll use the rule of thumb I discussed previously.

3.4 *Answers to exercises*

EXERCISE 1 Rewrite listing 3.4 in the declarative style:

```
Given a draft to export
 When Vladimir saves "Lolita" as a PDF
 Then a formatted PDF should appear where Vladimir saved it
```

EXERCISE 2 Rewrite the user actions from listing 3.7 as a user task:

```
Given a 50 pages long draft
 When Vladimir wants to print the entire draft as low-quality A4
 Then the printer should print 50 low quality A4 pages
```

EXERCISE 3 Rewrite the following step into a passive Given: Given Vladimir wants to write a new book:

```
Given a new book idea by Vladimir
```

EXERCISE 4 Rewrite listing 3.13 to reduce its level of abstraction. For the purpose of the exercise, you can assume that there's only one way to improve the readability score: by making long sentences shorter:

```
Given text with a low readability score:
  """
  As he crossed toward the pharmacy at the corner he involuntarily turned his
  head because of a burst of light that had ricocheted from his temple, and
  saw, with that quick smile with which we greet a rainbow or a rose, a
  blindingly white parallelogram of sky being unloaded from the van—a dresser
```

```
with mirror across which, as across a cinema screen, passed a flawlessly
clear reflection of boughs sliding and swaying not arboreally, but with a
human vacillation, produced by the nature of those who were carrying this
sky, these boughs, this gliding façade.
"""
```
When Vladimir breaks his long sentence into multiple ones:
```
"""
As he crossed toward the pharmacy at the corner
he involuntarily turned his head.
--
A burst of light ricocheted from his temple.
--
He saw, with that quick smile with which we greet
a rainbow or a rose, a blindingly white
parallelogram of sky being unloaded from the van.
--
It was like a dresser with mirror across which,
as across a cinema screen, passed a flawlessly clear
reflection of boughs sliding and swaying.
--
It did so not arboreally, but with a human
vacillation, produced by the nature of those who
were carrying this sky, these boughs,
this gliding façade.
"""
```
Then his readability score should improve

EXERCISE 5   Write a warm-up narrative for Vladimir and the Focus Mode feature:

```
"Every writer is at heart a
procrastinator, because writing is an exhausting difficult
process—especially writing prose. Vladimir knows that, too, even though
he may not want to admit it so easily.
```
```
"When the deadline comes, he won't have a choice anymore and he'll be
forced to focus and get rid of any distractions under pressure. Here's
where we and our Focus Mode can help.
```
```
"So what, possibly, can distract a writer sitting in front of his PC?
Other programs—Facebook, Twitter, and so on—so we'll make the
editor full screen.
```
```
"But what about the sentences he already wrote? He'll want to edit them
even though it would be better to move on for now and do it later—so we
can, for example, dim all the sentences apart from the one that's
currently being written.
```
```
"Vladimir certainly listens to music, because everybody listens to music.
But is the music Vladimir listens to the right music to increase his focus?
We could provide a short ambient playlist built into our Focus Mode that
would guarantee to boost his productivity based on new psychology
research."
```

EXERCISE 6   Are concepts such as *cloud features* and *buying extra space* in the same domain as *charging the user's credit card*?

There are at least two domains in play here:

- The *payments domain* should only deal with processing payments, managing credit cards, and dealing with refunds.
- The *cloud domain* doesn't necessarily have to be connected to the payments domain.

For example, you could easily imagine a change in Queneau's business model that would make all the cloud features available for free. In that case, you'd need to keep all the cloud scenarios but remove from them all mentions of paid and free plans. To avoid that, you should specify cloud functionality and paid plan limits separately.

3.5   *Summary*

- Outside-in development is a methodology that aims to build a clear understanding of the goals and motivations of stakeholders.
- Start writing your next scenario with a `Then` to put emphasis on outcomes that are important for stakeholders.
- To keep scenarios short, sweet, and simple, aim to use only one `When` per scenario.
- `When`s should describe business rules and business-driven behaviors, instead of system implementations or the UI.
- To separate context from actions and consequences, write `Given`s using passive voice and past tense.
- A warm-up narrative briefly sketches out a few moments in a day in the life of one of the actors.
- Vetting examples means exploring the boundaries of acceptance criteria by adding or removing examples and checking whether the criteria are still valid.
- Context questioning means looking for other possible `Given`s and `Then`s for the same `When`s.
- Outcome questioning means looking for other possible `Then`s for the same `Given`s and `Then`s.

The basics of
scenario outlines

4

Chapters 2 and 3 explored the art of writing scenarios. You learned several techniques that make creating new scenarios easy and fun. And that's fantastic! After all, the gentle learning curve is what makes Gherkin so beginner-friendly. But this simplicity is also what makes creating a stable specification suite difficult from a long-term perspective. Gherkin is almost too easy to write, so it's also easy to pick up bad habits.

While writing this chapter, I looked at several of my first feature files: some were longer than 500 lines, even though most of the scenarios were similar. As I read the full specification, I understood why. The feature was a reporting system for conversion metrics. The scenarios looked as if I wrote a main scenario and then copied it multiple times to play with different metrics, changing only the numbers and trying to make sure the calculations would be implemented exactly as they should be. I had good intentions, but I wasted a lot of space—and the readability wasn't perfect, either. Looking back, I saw that my desire to be precise backfired. Going through one feature file took almost an hour, as I tried to re-create my thinking. When I finished, I felt sorry for my former teammates.

Surely there must be a better approach than copying and pasting scenarios! Today, I can laugh at my former self, because I know one: *scenario outlines*.

> **DEFINITION** *Scenario outline*—A template that similar scenarios can share so you don't have to repeat the same Given-When-Then template throughout your feature file

Scenario outlines look similar to normal scenarios, but there are some differences that I'll talk about throughout the chapter.

The process of getting from raw scenarios to reusable scenario outlines is usually iterative, as you'll see later. When I talked about key process patterns of SBE in chapter 1, I called the process *refining examples*. That means taking raw examples and doing the following:

- Merging similar examples
- Removing irrelevant examples
- Focusing on key examples
- Making sure key examples are easy to understand

Outlines can help you do all that efficiently.

Using scenario outlines is a difficult skill to get right. That's why we'll explore the topic in two connected chapters. This chapter covers the basics: you'll go through a tutorial to learn the syntax, and you'll learn how to apply that syntax to a real-world project. You'll also see that outlines can change—grow or shrink—over time, and why that happens. After you understand how outlines work, we'll examine the advantages and disadvantages they bring to the table. Then, chapter 5 will talk about advanced techniques for using scenario outlines—techniques that elevate the upsides to their full potential, simultaneously reducing the downsides.

4.1 *Example shopping application*

A single example runs through the course of chapters 4 and 5: an e-commerce shopping application similar to Amazon—*the everything store*. Like Amazon, this company hopes to become *the* go-to retailer of books, movies, music, and games, along with electronics, toys, apparel, sports, tools, groceries, and garden items.

The company's plans for the future are ambitious. Right now, though, the store sells only books in digital formats, such as PDFs and audiobooks. It's still an early-stage start-up; building a digital shop was the easiest way to release the minimal viable product and start growing revenue.

Now, management feels that it's high time for the company to move from digital-only to selling physical items, too. They choose to begin selling physical-format publications, such as hardcovers, paperbacks, and audio CDs, for two reasons. First, the company is already a book-selling start-up, so there will be no rebranding expenses. Second, and more important, shipping publications in physical formats will require building a working shipping infrastructure. The company can use such an infrastructure in the future to add new products such as toys and tools.

4.2   *Using scenario outlines*

This section reviews an existing feature file for one of the core functionalities of the store: shipping orders. Because shipping digital products isn't the same as selling physical ones, you'll need to add some new scenarios to specify new shipping capabilities for the system.

Along the way, you'll notice that the scenarios become too similar, which makes for boring reading, and that the feature file grows in size, which doesn't seem efficient. You'll then rewrite the feature file by merging multiple scenarios into a single scenario outline.

4.2.1   *Spotting redundancies in Gherkin scenarios*

Management has given you a green light to implement shipping physical orders. Even though this is a huge change, you won't start from scratch. Fortunately, your system already has basic functionalities, such as an order-status page, that you can expand on. In addition, you can connect with external shipping APIs and let other companies handle behind-the-scenes shipment management. The only thing you have to do right now is specify how customers will order shipping for the new formats you're going to offer, and implement the scenarios.

Before you do that, though, let's look at the two existing scenarios. They were written a few months ago to handle the most basic use cases.

Listing 4.1   Two simple initial scenarios

```
Feature: Shipping

  Scenario: Shipping PDFs

    Given a PDF book in Simona's cart
      When she pays for it
      Then the book should be sent to a mobile device

  Scenario: Shipping audiobooks

    Given an audiobook in Simona's cart
      When she pays for it
      Then the book should be sent over email
```

With digital books, the case is simple. They're sent either by email or directly to a mobile device such as a Kindle reader. Going physical will force you to let customers provide their shipping addresses and make sure the books they buy are shipped by integrating with external APIs from a shipping company—a task that will probably be handled in the automation layer.

Have you noticed that the two scenarios in listing 4.1 look almost the same? They share the same basic structure due to an *example-counterexample* relationship. Because there are only two ways to ship a digital order—device integration and email download link—each scenario is a counterexample to the other. Whoever wrote this feature file clearly wanted to let you know that the system ships PDFs differently than audiobooks.

To illustrate contrast, examples and counterexamples usually share the same basic structure, differing only in details. In the example's two scenarios, the Whens are identical. They make Simona pay for her order:

```
When she pays for it
```

The repeating When creates the underlying structure of the scenarios. The differences lie in the Givens and Thens, but even they are similar.

In Gherkin, repetition isn't uncommon. Although the syntax looks like a natural language, the scenarios often aren't pretty. They're written and read by technical teams or busy nontechnical stakeholders who often value brevity over beauty. Some redundancies are to be expected—especially in shorter specifications. Even though this isn't a problem in a two-scenario feature file, you'll see that there are cases where repetition becomes too awkward to dismiss in writing and too difficult to maintain in the specification suite long-term.

Let's see what happens when you add the new physical formats and shipping features. Here are the three types of books the company has decided to add:

- Hardcovers
- Paperbacks
- Audio CDs

Unlike the digital formats, these are sent to the user's shipping address by an external shipping company; see table 4.1.

Table 4.1 All book formats

Format	Shipped ...
PDF	To a mobile device
Audiobook	With an email download link
Hardcover	To a shipping address
Paperback	To a shipping address
Audio CD	To a shipping address

The new scenarios should be easy enough to write. After all, you're going to use the same template that you established when you analyzed the initial examples.

Listing 4.2   Scenarios with new shipping options added

```
Feature: Shipping

  Scenario: Shipping PDFs

    Given a PDF book in Simona's cart
    When she pays for it
    Then the book should be sent to a mobile device

  Scenario: Shipping audiobooks

    Given an audiobook in Simona's cart
    When she pays for it
    Then the book should be sent over email

  Scenario: Shipping hardcovers                    ◁───────┐

    Given a hardcover book in Simona's cart
    When she pays for it
    Then the book should be shipped physically
                                                            Three new
  Scenario: Shipping paperbacks                    ◁──────  scenarios

    Given a paperback book in Simona's cart
    When she pays for it
    Then the book should be shipped physically

  Scenario: Shipping Audio CDs                     ◁───────┘

    Given an Audio CD book in Simona's cart
    When she pays for it
    Then the book should be shipped physically
```

Now it's even worse, isn't it? You've ended up with five scenarios that are almost exactly the same. It's an inelegant, inefficient solution. It also isn't perfect from a readability standpoint. I can imagine people reading only the first scenario and then skimming through the remaining examples—which is warranted in this case, but a bad habit in general. What if some of the scenarios hide an important detail despite looking similar to the others? A skimming reader could easily miss that. How can you make sure that won't happen?

4.2.2   *Refactoring redundant scenarios with scenario outlines*

Ideally, you want to have two types of scenarios:

- Scenarios that visually group similar examples together and use the same underlying template for all examples. The visual grouping notifies the reader that it's safe to skim the examples.
- Scenarios that are important enough to stand on their own, letting readers know they should focus when reading them.

The first type of scenarios are, in fact, *scenario outlines*. To understand how scenario outlines work, you'll have to forget the rule about using concrete examples—only for a little while, and only to see whether adding a bit of abstraction will help remove redundancy from your scenarios. You'll also look for a way to visually distinguish similar steps and build a shared template for such scenarios.

In the online store, you've added the new book formats and ended up with five different `Givens` splattered throughout your feature file:

- `Given a PDF book in Simona's cart`
- `Given an audiobook in Simona's cart`
- `Given a hardcover book in Simona's cart`
- `Given a paperback book in Simona's cart`
- `Given an Audio CD book in Simona's cart`

Because they all share the same sentence structure, they can easily be abstracted away into a simple template similar to this:

```
Given a <format> book in Simona's cart
```

We already noted that each of the five scenarios in the specification uses the same `When` to perform the main action, so let's add that step to the template:

```
Given a <format> book in Simona's cart
 When she pays for it
```

The only thing left is taking care of the Thens. Just as there are several kinds of `Givens`, there are also several different kinds of `Thens`:

- `Then the book should be sent to a mobile device`
- `Then the book should be sent over email`
- `Then the book should be shipped physically`

The list is shorter this time, but remember that the three scenarios for hardcovers, paperbacks, and audio CDs use the same `Then` because these formats are shipped using the same method. Despite that, the three `Thens` can be abstracted away into a similar template:

```
Then the book should be <shipped>
```

The result is a scenario template similar to the following.

Listing 4.3 Full scenario template

```
Given a <format> book in Simona's cart
 When she pays for it
 Then the book should be <shipped>
```

Look back for a moment at table 4.1. Notice the `<format>` and `<shipped>` attributes from the scenario template and the header row. You could use the table to put each of the formats in the scenario template, along with an accompanying shipping method.

And if you could make the `<shipped>` attribute dependent on the `<format>` attribute in the automation layer, you could change the outcome of the scenario based on your template every time you executed the specification suite—without changing the rest of the steps!

The good news is, you can do that. The template in listing 4.3 is valid Gherkin. Gherkin lets you group similar scenarios that share the same structure in a *scenario outline*: an automatable template for removing redundancy in similar scenarios. Outlines use visual signs such as attributes and tables to group related examples so you don't have to worry about missing anything important.

4.3   The structure of a scenario outline

Here's what a full scenario outline looks like.

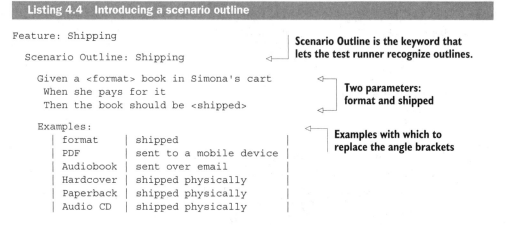

Listing 4.4   Introducing a scenario outline

The result is similar to the process you analyzed back in figure 1.9 (repeated here in figure 4.1), when I talked about the process of collecting and refining examples. Thanks to scenario outlines, you can take *raw examples* from *raw scenarios* and put them into refined scenario groups. Grouping raw examples is possible because every outline is built from three elements: the `Scenario Outline` keyword, parameters, and the `Examples` table. The following sections analyze this structure, starting with the end: the `Examples` table.

4.3.1   The Examples table

The `Examples` table contains all the examples. The syntax is straightforward. Tables can be created easily: use a vertical stroke (|) as the first character of the line, and also separate table cells with it. The first row is the header row containing the `Scenario Outline` parameters. After the header, each example has its own row.

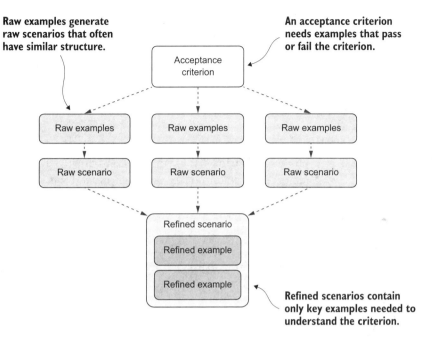

Raw examples generate raw scenarios that often have similar structure.

An acceptance criterion needs examples that pass or fail the criterion.

Refined scenarios contain only key examples needed to understand the criterion.

Figure 4.1 Every acceptance criterion generates new examples; every example generates a new scenario. Teams should refine their specifications to merge similar examples, reject those that introduce noise, and choose the most meaningful or descriptive ones.

4.3.2 *Parameters*

The Scenario Outline parameters go in angle brackets (<>), like <format> and <shipped>. They allow the test runner to paste the examples from the table into the outline you've written.

If you have the following steps

```
Given a <format> book in Simona's cart
 When she pays for it
 Then the book should be <shipped>
```

and the following table, which is a simplified version of the full table

```
Examples:
  | format   | shipped               |
  | PDF      | sent to a mobile device |
  | Audiobook | sent over email      |
```

then Scenario Outline will produce and run two scenarios:

- <format> is replaced with PDF and <shipped> is replaced with sent to a mobile device
- <format> is replaced with Audiobook and <shipped> is replaced with sent over email.

Thus, scenario 1 will run as

```
Given a PDF book in Simona's cart
 When she pays for it
 Then the book should be sent to a mobile device
```

and scenario 2 will run as

```
Given an audiobook in Simona's cart
 When she pays for it
 Then the book should be sent over email
```

Each step from the generated scenarios will have an accompanying step definition in the automation layer that lets each example run as an automated test.

Outlines rely on patterns to match attributes with the examples from the table. When a test runner sees a Gherkin scenario with multiple examples, it runs the scenario template as many times as there are examples, replacing abstract attributes with the concrete values dictated. Each time, it replaces a pattern called <pattern_name> with a corresponding example. Every pattern's name must be written without any spaces and within angle brackets.

> **TIP** If you're curious about how to automate scenario outlines, check out section A.6 in the appendix, which talks about executing scenarios with multiple examples.

With scenario outlines, you can test for multiple cases that share similarities but yield different outcomes. The simplest examples are two contrasting cases for the same acceptance criterion: a *success scenario* and a *failure scenario*. The success scenario defines what conditions are needed for the user to succeed, given the user's intentions. Failure scenarios, on the other hand, define every other behavior that will fall short.

As you can see, merging similar scenarios means writing separate scenarios first and looking for similarities later. It's a simple technique used by beginners. People generally use it in order to not break the *Don't Repeat Yourself* (DRY) principle of software development. This principle, aimed at reducing repetition of information of all kinds, states that you shouldn't write similar code twice.

4.3.3   *The Scenario Outline keyword*

The Scenario Outline keyword at the beginning of listing 4.4—the Scenario Outline: Shipping part—notifies the test runner that it should execute the outline as many times as there are examples in the table. If you need additional information about keywords, the automation layer, and executing scenarios, refer back to sections 2.1, 2.3, and 2.5.

4.4 Advantages of scenario outlines

Now that you understand how to use scenario outlines, let's talk about why you'd want to. In addition to the DRY principle mentioned in the previous section, outlines offer two other advantages for your executable specifications:

- Outlines take much less space.
- Outlines group concrete examples according to high-level business rules.

4.4.1 Shorter feature files

The first and foremost reason to use scenario outlines is brevity. In the example, when you refactored the five scenarios into a single outline, you saved 16 lines—a 52% decrease in length. That's a lot of space, even though shipping functionality is a simple case to specify in terms of business complexity and you didn't have many scenarios to begin with.

4.4.2 Feature files organized by high-level business rules

Scenario outlines also increase your scenarios' level of abstraction without sacrificing the focus on concrete, real-world examples. In the last few years, I've seen and written many feature files that were longer and much more difficult than the one in the example. And although saving space is a nice side benefit, the real problem with longer specifications is that they become more difficult to grasp at a glance because you can't be sure how particular scenarios relate to each other. Here's an example to show you what I mean.

Imagine that you have 10 or more scenarios in a single feature file. Some of the scenarios talk about distinct business rules; others cover different cases of a single complex rule; and, last but not least, some test important edge cases pointed out by testers. If you want to search for a particular scenario, it's much harder to find it in a messy specification suite like that. You'll naturally want to group such scenarios into several easy-to-find cohorts—and scenario outlines let you do that. When you use outlines, you can be sure that every scenario covers only a single business rule and that different applications of that rule are listed in the Examples table. In that regard, Gherkin is similar to legal reasoning. In Gherkin, scenarios are easier to digest when there are only a few rules to obey; but, like in law, the more rules you have, the messier and more complicated an entire codex becomes.

For example, many countries in medieval Europe had laws specifying different penalties for stealing or killing various kinds of livestock. To enforce the rules, the sheriff had to remember that stealing a chicken should cost X and that stealing a cow should cost Y, arbitrary amounts. It would have been much easier to make a general rule that, for example, tied indemnities to the average price of similar livestock in the capital's marketplace. If countries had done that, they could have illustrated the rule with concrete examples based on market prices measured the previous summer, to be sure the sheriff and the citizens were on the same page.

The same principles apply to executable specifications. Remember when you added new book formats to the scenario outline? At first, you had only two specific scenarios without a general rule in place. Each scenario specified how one of the two book formats was shipped. But as you added new examples, the specification got messier, and the abundance of concrete examples didn't look elegant. So from those two scenarios, you derived a general rule for shipping and rewrote it as a scenario outline. In a way, you went through a process similar to how legal reasoning evolved throughout the last millennium—but you did so over the course of a single chapter, instead of 1,000 years. Point for you.

Although scenario outlines won't solve all the problems you'll encounter when managing large specification suites, they can work well on the level of a single feature file. And we'll visit management at the level of the entire suite in chapters 8 and 9.

4.5   *Growing and maintaining scenario outlines*

In the world of continuous deployment and short release cycles, no feature is ever set in stone. Such flexibility lets delivery teams that use iterative software development processes build smaller features that take less time to develop and that can be expanded in the future. As features expand, so do scenario outlines. Although scenario outlines *do* make feature files shorter, they, too, can grow to a size at which managing an outline becomes a problem.

To illustrate how that happens, let's return to the example. Assume that development was smooth and the feature was safely deployed to production. That's great! But it doesn't mean your work is done. Shortly after deployment, you start working on new iterations of your shipping feature. You'll begin by expanding the PDF example:

```
Examples:
    | format    | shipped              |
    | PDF       | sent to a mobile device |
    | Audiobook | sent over email      |
    | Hardcover | shipped physically   |
    | Paperback | shipped physically   |
    | Audio CD  | shipped physically   |
```

Example you'll iteratively expand

When it comes to mobile devices, there are at least three major mobile platforms to consider: Apple's, Google's, and Amazon's. When you first implemented the feature for mobile integration, you decided that books in the PDF format should be shipped directly to a customer's mobile device. You decided to use an external integration provider. The provider maintained a single API endpoint for integrating with all three platforms at once, which was convenient at the time. Unfortunately, your design team decided recently that a shallow integration like that isn't enough in terms of user experience. Each of the three platforms you support has a standalone e-book reader: iBooks, Google Play Books, and Kindle. You'd like to develop a deeper integration with each of these ecosystems, to control the overall user experience without forcing users to install additional apps beyond what they already have.

As you can see, the example that was fine in the past lacks necessary detail in this area. To fix that, the team has agreed that you need to split the single example into three examples—one for each of the new deep mobile integrations. Based on that, you'll then rewrite the application code. And later, you'll have to write new testing code for each example in the automation layer, too.

Let's get ready to work! Here's what a reworked scenario outline could look like.

Listing 4.5   Reworked scenario outline

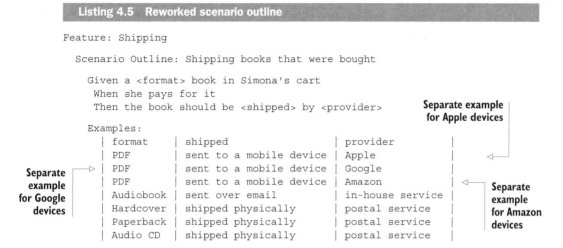

```
Feature: Shipping

   Scenario Outline: Shipping books that were bought

      Given a <format> book in Simona's cart
      When she pays for it
      Then the book should be <shipped> by <provider>

      Examples:
         | format    | shipped              | provider         |
         | PDF       | sent to a mobile device | Apple         |
         | PDF       | sent to a mobile device | Google        |
         | PDF       | sent to a mobile device | Amazon        |
         | Audiobook | sent over email      | in-house service |
         | Hardcover | shipped physically   | postal service   |
         | Paperback | shipped physically   | postal service   |
         | Audio CD  | shipped physically   | postal service   |
```

The automation layer can now have a different technical test for each provider in the step definitions. In terms of numbers, you've removed one example and added three more. The table grew larger. Ten examples aren't difficult to maintain, but you know that selling books is just the first step for your e-commerce company.

At the beginning of this chapter, I mentioned that the company wanted to be *the* online retailer of books, movies, music, games, electronics, toys, apparel, sports, tools, groceries, and garden items—even though it initially only sold books. Soon, the company decided to begin its expansion by adding products such e-readers, tablets, and headphones, chosen to fit into the store's reading landscape. Such products are too precious to be casually shipped by a postal service; they need to be shipped by courier delivery.

As soon as everyone agreed on the details, your team updated the specification to include new examples.

Listing 4.6   [OK] Scenario outline with a growing list of examples

```
Feature: Shipping

   Scenario Outline: Shipping

      Given an <item> in Simona's cart
      When she pays for it
      Then the book should be <shipped> by <provider>
```

With the three new examples, you now have 10 examples overall—which is quite a few. And you're *still* not finished. In the future, there will probably be even more examples as the store grows and new shipment methods appear. Organizing the examples in a more efficient way would probably be a wise thing to do before you end up with a messy specification.

Gherkin lets you organize examples into multiple tables. You can split examples into two or more tables and name each table accordingly to explain what the examples do and why they're there. So if you have a generic table of four numbers that looks similar to this

```
Examples:
    | Number |
    | 1      |
    | 2      |
    | 3      |
    | 4      |
```

you can split it into two tables:

The result is valid Gherkin code that any Gherkin-compatible test runner can easily understand.

That seems like the perfect solution to the problem in the example, so let's use it to tidy up the scenario outline.

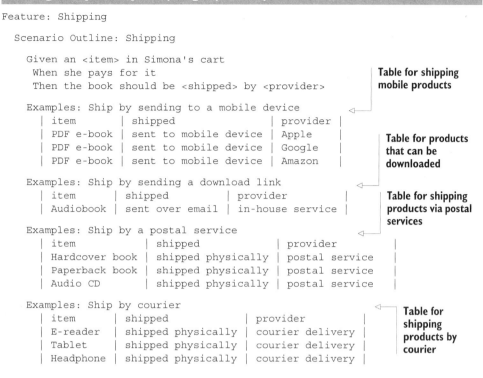

```
Listing 4.7   [BETTER] Examples grouped in separate tables

Feature: Shipping

  Scenario Outline: Shipping

    Given an <item> in Simona's cart
    When she pays for it
    Then the book should be <shipped> by <provider>

    Examples: Ship by sending to a mobile device
      | item       | shipped              | provider |
      | PDF e-book | sent to mobile device | Apple    |
      | PDF e-book | sent to mobile device | Google   |
      | PDF e-book | sent to mobile device | Amazon   |

    Examples: Ship by sending a download link
      | item      | shipped         | provider         |
      | Audiobook | sent over email | in-house service |

    Examples: Ship by a postal service
      | item           | shipped            | provider       |
      | Hardcover book | shipped physically | postal service |
      | Paperback book | shipped physically | postal service |
      | Audio CD       | shipped physically | postal service |

    Examples: Ship by courier
      | item      | shipped            | provider         |
      | E-reader  | shipped physically | courier delivery |
      | Tablet    | shipped physically | courier delivery |
      | Headphone | shipped physically | courier delivery |
```

Table for shipping mobile products

Table for products that can be downloaded

Table for shipping products via postal services

Table for shipping products by courier

This listing organizes examples by shipping method. Each shipping method has its own list of examples. No table is longer than three examples—such a neat categorization!

But let's check whether using multiple tables with examples will bring you more flexibility in the long term. At the moment, you sell and ship these items:

- Digital books on three platforms: Apple, Google, and Amazon
- Physical books
- Audiobooks
- Audio CD books
- E-readers
- Tablets
- Headphones

That's already a lot, but fast-forward a few more months to when the company decides to expand its services once again. This time, management not only wants to sell books and electronics, but also decides to grow the company's entertainment market by adding downloadable movies to the catalogue. And like e-books, movies should integrate out of the box with the three major platforms: Apple's, Google's, and Amazon's.

That should guarantee a few new examples, shouldn't it? But in keeping with the flexibility of scenario outlines with multiple tables, adding the additional rows shouldn't be much of a problem.

Listing 4.8 Tables that can grow while maintaining readability

```
Feature: Shipping

  Scenario Outline: Shipping

    Given an <item> in Simona's cart
    When she pays for it
    Then the book should be <shipped> by <provider>

    Examples: Ship to Apple devices
      | item       | shipped              | provider |
      | PDF e-book | sent to mobile device | Apple    |
      | Movie      | sent to iTunes        | Apple    |

    Examples: Ship to Google devices
      | item       | shipped              | provider |
      | PDF e-book | sent to mobile device | Google   |
      | Movie      | sent to Google Play   | Google   |

    Examples: Ship to Amazon devices
      | item       | shipped              | provider |
      | PDF e-book | sent to mobile device | Amazon   |
      | Movie      | sent to Fire TV       | Amazon   |

    Examples: Ship by sending a download link
      | item      | shipped                   | provider        |
      | Audiobook | send download link to email | in-house service |

    Examples: Ship by a postal service
      | item           | shipped           | provider       |
      | Hardcover book | shipped physically | postal service |
      | Paperback book | shipped physically | postal service |
      | Audio CD       | shipped physically | postal service |

    Examples: Ship by courier
      | item      | shipped           | provider         |
      | E-reader  | shipped physically | courier delivery |
      | Tablet    | shipped physically | courier delivery |
      | Headphone | shipped physically | courier delivery |
```

Movies shipped to Google's service

Movies shipped to Apple's service

Movies shipped to Amazon's service

Adding three new examples was a piece of cake. And even though you now have 13 distinct items in the tables, the feature file still looks extremely organized. Such is the power of good scenario outlines.

As the list of examples has expanded, the structure of the outline has also changed. You've added new parameters, and you've split examples into clear, separated tables. The main takeaway of this section is to remember what many Gherkin writers forget: that scenarios can—and should—be refactored as code. In software engineering, *code refactoring* is the process of restructuring existing computer code—changing the factoring—without changing its external behavior. Gherkin can be refactored, too.

4.6 *Disadvantages of scenario outlines*

I've already said a lot about the upsides of using scenario outlines. You've seen how they can group similar scenarios with reusable attributes and tables according to the DRY principle. Section 4.4 expanded on the topic of how scenario outlines help organize feature files by distinct business rules, resulting in greater readability and searchability. And in the previous section, you saw how a single scenario outline can hold multiple examples without losing its focus. These are all good things. But now let's consider the other side of the story. It's time to talk about the downsides—because there are some.

In truth, the Gherkin community tends to frown on using scenario outlines, because outlines written by inexperienced Gherkin practitioners often look more like code than business-level features. It's true: the attributes, brackets, and tables can sometimes appear scary to people who are new to Gherkin. Unfortunately, that can make outlines less accessible to business stakeholders.

So should you use scenario outlines or not? The answer isn't straightforward. Good, easy-to-read scenario outlines with business-level examples can play a part in getting buy-in from other stakeholders for using SBE. But bad examples can also make accepting SBE much harder for anyone who isn't already convinced about using the methodology.

For example, I worked according to SBE principles on two different projects. In both projects, our team had to use two contrasting approaches. For one project, we got a product owner to work on the scenarios with the delivery team over Git. The product owner was obviously a tech-savvy person who didn't mind seeing scenario outlines, even though they looked a bit technical with all the brackets and tables. For the second project, we never got anyone on the business side to discuss the tests. They found it difficult to talk using Givens, Whens, and Thens and grew discouraged quickly. So we hid *all* of our process and only asked for examples to get them talking about *their* process. We didn't even show them the scenarios, let alone the scenario outlines. We only discussed tables with examples stored in spreadsheets—and nobody said we were too technical. I'll teach you that method in chapter 5.

So yes, scenario outlines can be easily misused—but they can also be effective. My goal is to teach you how to use them well, because, as you've seen, the advantages are huge. This is also why, to make sure you get it right, I decided to explore the topic in two chapters. The first chapter is behind us—on the second step of the journey, we'll talk about advanced techniques for using scenario outlines.

4.7 *Summary*

- Scenario outlines are templates for similar scenarios that can help remove redundancy in your executable specifications according to the DRY principle.
- The Examples table contains the examples and groups them by similarity.
- Each scenario outline can have multiple tables with examples.

- The parameters in scenario outlines allow test runners to paste the examples from the table into the outline.
- Scenario outlines work best when they group examples by business rules that the examples adhere to.
- A scenario outline can grow over time as new examples appear.
- The downside of using scenario outlines is that they can appear too technical and become code-like if you're not careful.

5

Choosing examples for scenario outlines

This chapter covers

- Writing advanced scenario outlines
- Using the outside-in method
- Going beyond the simplest examples
- Testing diverse outcomes
- Fixing bad examples

Did you know that female drivers are 47% more likely than male drivers to be seriously injured in a car crash? When safety regulations were originally imposed on automakers in the 1960s, the government wanted to require the use of two crash test dummies of two slightly different sizes. Doing so would mean that only 5% of men were larger than and 5% of women were smaller than the dummies. But automakers pushed back, and, eventually, the requirement was reduced to only one crash test dummy the size of an average male, making tests more standardized.

Then, in 2011, for the first time female crash test dummies were required in safety testing. The results forced some automakers to slash their safety ratings by more than half, from a top five-star rating to just two stars. According to the test data, when a car slams into a barrier at 35 mph, a female dummy in the front passenger seat registers a 20% to 40% risk of being killed or seriously injured. The average using the male dummy is just 15%.

Even though software is ubiquitous today, software engineering is still a young industry. As such, it has had to borrow useful metaphors, mindsets, and practices from other, more mature fields. For example, civil engineering was a major influence. That's why some of us call ourselves engineers or software architects; it's also why we talk about *building* software.

Automated testing has also had to borrow metaphors. That's why, not coincidentally, the simplest examples are often called *dummies*—just like the fake mannequins in car safety testing. In software engineering, *dummy data* is generic information that doesn't contain any real data but can be used as a placeholder. John Doe, for example, is a dummy name commonly used by testers. Dummies are used whenever a tester or developer needs to make tests pass—they devise a set of dummy values meant to go successfully through the validation systems used in the test, without caring about whether these values will appear in the real world.

But as in the case of female crash test dummies, even the most basic placeholders can influence the results of a test in a dramatic and horrific way. I don't want to argue that *all* kinds of tests should use the most realistic data possible—it wouldn't make much sense for some low-level unit tests, for example—but I strongly believe that *some* tests should. In section 3.1.2, which talked about advanced techniques for writing new scenarios, I made a case for using real-world data when working with SBE. Now, in the middle of this two-chapter journey through the world of scenario outlines, I feel compelled to reiterate.

Coming out of chapter 4, you know how to use scenario outlines to contain multiple examples in reusable templates that are easy to manage and grow. But I haven't yet talked about methods for choosing examples to feature in your outlines. So, this chapter focuses on an outside-in method for writing scenario outlines. Chapter 3 defined *outside-in development* as a software development methodology that aims to create successful software through understanding the goals and motivations of stakeholders. In a nutshell, *outside-in outlines* focus on taking examples from the *outside* world (where stakeholders operate) *into* your product. In contrast, the previous chapter only taught you to use scenario outlines as a method to keep your specifications tidy, without the need to interact with anyone to get the job done.

I'll also talk about general rules for choosing meaningful examples for scenario outlines and how illustrative tests are different from exhaustive tests. As you progress, you'll learn that some kinds of tests should be performed in different tools than Cucumber or other Gherkin-compatible test runners.

5.1   *Example shopping application*

To retain a sense of continuity between the two chapters that talk about scenario outlines, chapter 4 and this chapter use the same example: an e-commerce shopping application similar to Amazon.

As explained in chapter 4, the company began by selling books, but it wants to be *the* online retailer of books, movies, music, and much more. It started expanding by adding products such as e-readers, tablets, and headphones, chosen to fit into the store's reading landscape. Next, the company entered the entertainment market by adding digitally distributed movies to its catalogue. Although there's still a lot of work ahead, the business is already diverse—and, fortunately, full of examples to work with.

5.2   *Writing outside-in scenario outlines*

As you already know, scenario outlines are templates for similar scenarios. But what you probably don't know—and what most people in the Gherkin community don't talk about often—is that the method you've been using to create outlines, based on merging redundant scenarios, is reactive instead of proactive. In this section, I'll show you a proactive way to write *outside-in* scenario outlines in Gherkin.

> **DEFINITION**   *Outside-in scenario outline*—A scenario outline written directly from examples gathered during an analysis phase rather than by merging similar scenarios

The outside-in method consists of two steps:

1   Collect real-world examples for your specification in the form of a table.
2   Write the scenario outline based on the table, adjusting the steps and parameters to the data.

This approach requires you to analyze examples first and write scenarios later. The table created in step 1 doesn't even have to be a Gherkin table—it can be a simple spreadsheet created in Excel by you and other stakeholders. The merging method described in chapter 4, on the other hand, assumes that you evolve scenarios into scenario outlines only if you notice any redundancy, and the specification becomes too difficult to manage easily. In that sense, the merging method is much more reactive than the outside-in method.

Generally, I prefer the outside-in method. Scenario outlines made from merging often look too programmatic, which makes business people reluctant to read them. I think it has something to do with *Don't Repeat Yourself* (DRY), which is the founding principle of the merging technique. The cost of elegant structure and reduced redundancy is often sacrificing Gherkin's natural language and putting too many things into brackets and parameters. In contrast, the outside-in method puts emphasis on a gradual evolution from a non-Gherkin table, which any nontechnical person can read, to a Gherkin scenario, which business owners don't have to read if they've already read the examples. The evolutionary process often makes the resulting outline look much more natural.

5.2.1 Collecting examples for outside-in scenario outlines

To derive a scenario outline from examples, you first need some examples. And to get examples, you need a new feature to implement. Luckily, your product owners can happily oblige. The company's current priority is to get more items into the store to expand its marketplace. Negotiating with big publishers and producers has proven to be difficult, so management wants to open the store to individual merchants who can sell both new and used items. The merchants will benefit from the company's advanced shipping infrastructure—and the company will take a cut from their profits.

After some analysis, sales and marketing have agreed on a pricing model that works according to the following rules:

- Merchants can create accounts and list new items for free.
- The company takes a cut after an item is successfully sold.
- The size of that cut depends on the purchaser's shipping location, because merchants have to pay for access to the global customer base available thanks to the company's shipping infrastructure.

So far so good. Let's settle on the pricing ranges and remake the list into a draft of the `Examples` table. The commission structure was designed based on shipping distances from the company's US operations base and infrastructure in each region (see table 5.1).

Table 5.1 Draft of a table with examples

Region	Commission
North America	10%
South America	11.4%
Europe	12.9%
Asia	12.9%
Africa	13.5%

Exercise 1
Rewrite the table of examples in Gherkin.

Such a table could easily be the result of a conversation between nontechnical stakeholders from sales and marketing and the delivery team of programmers, testers, and designers. No technical skill is required to create or understand it, because no Gherkin is involved yet. If you fear that scenario outlines are too technical, you can keep your examples at the nontechnical level during your specification workshops; there's nothing wrong with that.

5.2.2 *Writing outside-in scenario outlines from collected examples*

Now that you have the `Examples` table, you can write the `Givens`, `Whens`, and `Thens`. To do that, you need to find a scenario template that will work well with the structure of the table. For example, can you see that each entry in the `<region>` column is like a question and the corresponding `<commission>` entry is like an answer to that question?

- North America? You take 10% of the purchase.
- South America? The cut is 11.4%.
- Europe and Asia? That's 12.9%.
- Africa? Be ready to give away 13.5%.

From a technical point of view, the questions define the *state of the system* before you decide how much of a commission you take—and the answers define *an outcome based on the chosen state*. In chapter 3, I said that system states are described by `Givens` and that the outcomes should be written as `Thens`. So in a way, you already have two-thirds of the scenario ready to write down:

```
Given a purchase from <region>
 Then we should take <commission> of the price
```

That certainly looks promising. But because this is a scenario about sellers, not buyers, as in the previous scenarios, you can also add another `Given` specifying that a merchant is the main actor. Let's call the smaller shop Quick-Ship:

```
Given a merchant called Quick-Ship
  And a purchase from <region>
 Then we should take <commission> of the price
```

You only need one more step, which specifies the main action of the scenario:

```
Given a merchant called Quick-Ship
  And a purchase from <region>
 When Quick-Ship gets paid for the purchase
 Then we should take <commission> of the price
```

The last thing you need to do is combine the `Examples` table you prepared earlier with the Given-When-Then and add keywords like `Feature` and `Scenario Outline`.

Listing 5.1 Outside-in scenario outline derived from examples

```
Feature: Selling items through individual merchants

  Scenario Outline: Merchant commissions

    Given a merchant called Quick-Ship
      And a purchase from <region>
     When Quick-Ship gets paid for the purchase
     Then we should take <commission> of the price

    Examples:
        | region        | commission |
        | North America | 10%        |
        | South America | 11.4%      |
```

```
| Europe      | 12.9%     |
| Asia        | 12.9%     |
| Africa      | 13.5%     |
```

As you can see, with a little creativity, you've easily arrived at a complete scenario outline. Choosing examples from which to derive outlines is a separate art, though, and covering it appropriately will require a lot more space.

Now that you know how to write outside-in scenario outlines, I can talk in detail about collecting great examples. Section 5.3 talks about efficient methods for finding good examples. Section 5.4, on the other hand, is about examples you should avoid. By the end of this chapter, I'll have talked about every important aspect of writing exemplary scenario outlines, and you'll be ready to use that knowledge in the real world.

5.3 *Finding key examples for scenario outlines*

Good outside-in scenario outlines need good examples—that goes without saying. This section will teach you the general rules for choosing good examples. Then it will zoom in to explain particular techniques of collecting and refining examples. These techniques will help you

- Identify important business cases
- Make sure you cover all the relevant examples
- Spot troublesome examples that break often

Such techniques are also called *testing heuristics*.

> **DEFINITION** *Testing heuristic*—A set of rules of thumb, educated guesses, intuitive judgments, and common sense used by testers to generate new testing ideas

Testers and developers often aim to prevent or find as many bugs as they can. It's a great approach that increases test coverage and makes software more secure and easier to maintain. Thus, having more tests with more examples is, in general, considered to be "better." The most common indicator that can force delivery teams to simplify their tests are brittle, overcomplicated tests that cause performance issues. Other than that, the more the better.

But this isn't what Gherkin tests look like. As discussed in chapter 1, other indicators are in play, like readability and teaching principles. This section provides a simple framework you can use to distinguish between *exhaustive examples* and *illustrative examples*.

To understand the difference, imagine that examples in scenario outlines are like the contacts on your phone. An exhaustive list of examples is like a list of all the contacts you have on your phone. That's pretty much everyone you know and can think of along with emergency phone numbers in case a tragedy happens. With exhaustive examples, the goal is to *test safely* by detecting more defects with more tests.

> **DEFINITION** *Exhaustive testing*—An approach in which test coverage is measured based on how many checks and examples you have. The more examples, the better.

Illustrative examples, on the other hand, contain one key example from each of your important social circles: family, friends, work, and so on. A list like that is much shorter.

> **DEFINITION** *Illustrative testing*—An approach in which you use only the most representative examples and only as many as needed to understand the purpose of a test

An illustrative example of a contact list would be *a model simplified to represent the people you hang out with*. This simplified model would remove any phone contact that made the list more difficult to understand.

Exercise 2
Prepare a list of the most representative examples that will illustrate what your online shop is selling to someone who didn't read this chapter or chapter 4.

Choosing good illustrative examples is crucial to doing scenario outlines well. This section expands on the guidelines outlined in the previous paragraphs by discussing concrete candidates for illustrative examples. Reading it should help you come up with a table for any scenario outline more quickly and easily.

A specification should list only the key representative examples. This will help keep the specification short and easy to understand. The key examples typically include the following:

- *Each important aspect of business functionality*—Business users, analysts, and/or customers typically define these.
- *Each important technical edge case*—For example, technical boundary conditions. Developers typically suggest such examples when they're concerned about functional gaps or inconsistencies. Business users, analysts, and/or customers define the correct expected behavior.
- *Each particularly troublesome area of the expected implementation*—For example, cases that caused bugs in the past, and boundary conditions that may not be explicitly illustrated by previous examples. Testers typically suggest these, and business owners, analysts, and/or customers define the correct behavior.

This list of simple guidelines summarizes the most important points discussed in this chapter and will guide you when you begin collecting examples for your next requirement. The subsections that follow provide more information and insight about these areas. First, we'll look at representative business examples. Then we'll move on to examples with boundary conditions, ending the section with examples that highlight historically buggy functionalities.

5.3.1   Domain-specific examples

Domain-specific examples are inputs and outputs that are tied to your product's business domain extremely closely. In fact, you often need to be a domain expert—one who's extremely knowledgeable about the domain—to recognize and understand these examples at a glance.

Unfortunately, there are no quick and easy heuristics for spotting and managing domain-specific examples, because each business domain is unique. But there's something else I want to show to you.

An early reviewer of the book argued that a section about domain-specific examples seems a bit redundant, because unspecific examples are usually standardized and easy to understand. There's little value in documenting features such as restoring a password, changing basic settings, and so on—with some exceptions, such as generic examples that cause regular bugs. I agree—but I also want to argue that even the simplest functionality can have impactful domain-specific examples that sometimes may lead to discovering new, unexpected features. It's a fact that's overlooked by many developers, testers, designers, and managers.

The most domain-specific attribute for any e-commerce application is usually the *price*. Every e-commerce shop should experiment with its prices on a daily basis to subtly encourage customers to buy more. Many other factors can also influence the price of any item in the store: daily deals, coupons, fire sales, bundles, free shipping, and so on. That's a lot to convey in a single specification; but at this point in the chapter, you have all the tools you need to make that happen, such as parameters and multiple tables. Let's look at the result.

Listing 5.2   [GOOD] Specification full of domain-specific examples

```
Feature: Pricing

  Scenario Outline: Discounts

    Given items like <items> costing <price> in John's cart
      And a <discount> discount
    When John proceeds to checkout
    Then he should only pay <final> for the items in his cart

  Examples: Daily deals

    Daily deals are always 17% discounts.

    | items                       | price  | discount | final   |
    | "Writing Great Specifications" | $44.99 | 17%     | $37.34 |

  Examples: Coupons

    There are five different types of coupons available.

    | items                       | price  | discount | final   |
    | "Writing Great Specifications" | $44.99 | 5%      | $42.74 |
    | "Writing Great Specifications" | $44.99 | 15%     | $38.24 |
    | "Writing Great Specifications" | $44.99 | 30%     | $31.49 |
    | "Writing Great Specifications" | $44.99 | 50%     | $22.49 |
    | "Writing Great Specifications" | $44.99 | 75%     | $11.24 |
```

```
Examples: Bundles

  We offer "buy two, pay for one" bundles.

  | items                           | price  | discount | final  |
  | "Specification by Example" bundle | $44.99 | 50%      | $22.49 |
```

Using table briefs

Listing 5.5 is the first specification in the book to use table briefs. *Table briefs* are similar to specification briefs and scenario briefs, which you've been using throughout the book. They're free-flowing text sections between the table and the `Examples` keyword. You can use table briefs to expand on the context of the examples or provide additional information.

This is a good specification. The reader can easily see that there are three types of discounts and identify the discounted prices. But you can also do something more domain-specific here.

Your superior shipping infrastructure lets you sell and ship items more cheaply than your competitors. So, thanks to your margins, you can sometimes sacrifice short-term profits from single transactions for increased long-term volume. For example, research shows that when given various price options, 57% of consumers choose round, whole-dollar amounts ending in zero. Because of the straightforward nature of electronic payments, the most plausible explanation is that people prefer round prices. When a person buys a discounted book from your store for $23.23, the difference between that price and, say, $23.00 isn't much. So maybe you should discount prices even further, to whole-dollar amounts, to encourage more customers to buy and thus increase sales. In a high-volume store like this one that processes thousands of transactions each day, 23 cents doesn't make much of a difference. But if you could persuade an average client to buy two items instead of one during the same shopping session, that would result in a massive increase in revenue.

Listing 5.3 [GOOD] More complex discounting scenario

```
Scenario Outline: Discounts

  57 percent of consumers pick round, whole-dollar amounts
  ending in zero.

  Given items like <items> costing <price> in John's cart
    And a <discount> discount
  When John proceeds to checkout
  Then the order should technically be discounted to <discounted>
    But the final price should be discounted even further to <final>

  Examples:
    | items             | price  | discount | discounted | final  |
    | "Lord of the Rings" | $44.99 | 17%      | $37.34     | $37.00 |
    | [...]             | [...]  | [...]    | [...]      | [...]  |
```

This new discounting approach might be interpreted as overengineering, but my point is that even the simplest features have indiscernible, domain-specific quirks that can and should be covered by your executable specifications. You don't even have to dig that deep.

Another complex domain-specific example is a registration process in a custom employee-satisfaction application built for a company with thousands of employees. In addition to standard information like username, password, and email, you'll need to deal with a lot of inputs specific to the company. For instance, you'll have to add different departments, like Software Engineering and Sales; and branches, such as Los Angeles and New York. The onboarding flow for the app may look different for a software engineer from Los Angeles than for a salesperson from New York: if each city has a different satisfaction program, it will be pointless to ask New York employees whether they're interested in wellness programs that are only available in Los Angeles. To create a great onboarding experience, you'll end up with a complex registration form that needs to change and evolve for every employee. As an analyst, I like to look for domain-specific examples in processes that most people would consider *standard*, and I advise you to do the same in order to create a user experience that feels unique and tailored to your business domain.

If an example is highly domain specific, having it in an executable specification is of great help to the delivery team. The team can trust that the example is tested and up to date. They can even add more detail over time if they need to. And every time they implement new functionality, automated tests will remind them not to break these important examples.

5.3.2   *Counterexamples*

Balancing examples with counterexamples is another way to fill the `Examples` table in scenario outlines. By a *counterexample*, I mean a different combination of inputs, yielding another extreme outcome, in the same workflow. To see what I mean by *extreme*, let's talk briefly about a simple free-shipping example.

Let's say your online shopping application offers free shipping for orders that are more expensive than the average customer's average order. This is a popular e-commerce incentive to encourage customers to order more at a single time and simplify payment processing. You could illustrate the free-shipping behavior with this simple scenario.

Listing 5.4   [GOOD] Simple free-shipping example

```
Feature: Free shipping

  Scenario: Orders over $100 should be shipped for free

    Given items worth $100 in John's cart
    When John proceeds to checkout
    Then he should be offered free shipping
```

It's a good starting point, but it's simplistic. With a scenario like this one, you only know that a $100 purchase is in the range eligible for free shipping. You know nothing about less- or more-expensive purchases. You don't even know whether this is the lowest price point eligible for free shipping. In theory, the free-shipping threshold will be mentioned in the name of the scenario. But relying on that would mean assuming that all the people who need to see the scenario will read it from cover to cover. It's a risky assumption; most business people, programmers, designers, and testers will only *scan* text, because they're busy, on deadline, and looking for quick answers.

To improve this scenario, look for a visual way to highlight the contrast between orders that qualify for free shipping and orders that don't. A scenario outline can do exactly that.

Listing 5.5 [BETTER] Example contrasted with a counterexample

```
Feature: Free shipping

  Scenario Outline: Orders over $100 should be shipped for free

    Given items worth <purchase> in John's cart
    When John proceeds to checkout
    Then he should be offered <shipping>

    Examples:
      | purchase | shipping      |
      | $99      | $5 shipping   |
      | $100     | free shipping |
```

You could even throw in a third example showing a $101 purchase being offered free shipping. You'll see why and when a similar example can be useful in section 5.4.4, where I talk about classes of equivalence and the Goldilocks principle.

Exercise 3

When an item that's on sale is featured as a daily deal, what will a table with an example and a counterexample look like? Write a scenario outline with an answer. You can use the discounts from listing 5.6.

Counterexamples support the delivery team by drawing clearer boundaries between different combinations of inputs and outcomes. They can be used to illustrate edge cases, show contrasting areas of implementation, and define blank-slate states and extreme conditions. Readers benefit from counterexamples the same way pedestrians benefit from red and green lights: they know when they have a clear go and when they must stop and look around. It's a simple but effective heuristic.

5.3.3 *Exploratory outcomes*

Balancing examples with counterexamples isn't the only heuristic you can use to your advantage. I like to say that most engineers, analysts, designers, and testers are forced to be optimists due to the chaotic, uncertain nature of the software development process. If they truly care about a meaningful result, the journey requires at least *some* degree of optimism.

This optimism can blind you to less obvious or less probable examples and cause you to focus on positive outcomes only. Chapter 2 mentioned that testers often call scenarios with positive outcomes *happy paths* and that scenario outlines can account for a multitude of other paths including angry paths, scary paths, embarrassing paths, and forgetful paths. This chapter expands on the topic of these exploratory outcomes.

In general, *exploratory outcomes* pursue possible unhappy paths, leading to new testing ideas. They belong mainly to the analysis phase and can be used to stimulate group thinking and brainstorming during specification workshops or when a single person is analyzing a requirement.

I found the "go beyond the happy path" heuristic in the excellent book *Fifty Quick Ideas to Improve Your Tests* by Gojko Adžić, David Evans, and Tom Roden (Neuri Consulting, 2015). On a daily basis, you can use the following subsections as a checklist to generate new testing ideas. These questions can guide your conversations with stakeholders as you mine them for possible input.

THE HAPPY PATH

Find the main success scenario, usually describing the most straightforward example. What happens if everything goes all right? Should anyone be rewarded? What changes should be made in the system? Should the successful result be logged anywhere?

THE ANGRY PATH

Look for the main failure scenario: anything that will make the application throw errors, quit, or break. Maybe the angry path is a counterexample for the happy path. Or perhaps it's the most frustrating scenario imaginable, where only one thing goes wrong, but it breaks the entire process. An example could be a server error that appears when the user is completing a form six screens long and can't save their progress.

THE SCARY PATH

Think about the areas of highest risk. I usually try to imagine misunderstandings and errors that could get me or the end user fired. One of my projects dealt with sending a lot of paid text messages automatically. I was always scared that a bug would send thousands of messages at once that I would have to pay for. What failure scenarios and code would I, as the developer of the project, devise to relieve myself of my fear?

THE EMBARRASSING PATH

Write down all the things that, if they broke, would cause huge embarrassment on all fronts. Imagine you're the CEO, and you're giving a demo in front of investors or important customers. You're trying to create a new account, and you can't. Or you're trying to order something, and the payment can't be processed. "Maybe next time," you hear. Can you think of an example that would create a similar situation?

THE DELINQUENT PATH

Should the functionality be secured in any special way? Who is authorized to use it? Are any special permissions needed? Does any third-party regulatory body require legal compliance? If anyone saw the data produced by this functionality, would someone be in trouble?

THE STRESSFUL PATH

If scale, speed, and performance are important business aspects of the function or component you have to work with, give your projections for future changes of business volume. For example, a one-year business report could contain so much data that it might be impossible to download on the fly. Is there an example that would stretch your system to its limits?

> **NOTE** Scale, speed, and performance are nonfunctional requirements, and it isn't obvious whether those are a good fit for Gherkin and SBE. We'll get back to this issue in chapter 8.

THE GREEDY PATH

Select everything, tick every box, opt into every option, and order lots of everything. Sometimes, following the greedy path results in examples that apply to power users—excessive users who will try to use your application to the fullest. But other times, the greedy path will remind you about behaviors of casual users, such as those who wait until the last day of the last deadline and suddenly want your application to do 60 things at once. Will it be ready? Or will it break?

THE FORGETFUL PATH

Fill up all the memory available in the system, and check what happens. Leave a shopping cart full of items, but never finish the order. Be an admin user who forgets to approve new accounts. Nobody has a perfect memory. Can you find any forgetful examples and deploy appropriate countermeasures?

THE DESOLATE PATH

What does your functionality look like before the user uses it for the first time? What happens when users don't want to provide required input? What if they can't? They may not have the necessary information yet. On the desolate path, provide your feature with examples of nothingness. Give too little information. Don't upload enough photos. Write nothing.

THE INDECISIVE PATH

I'm an indecisive user every time I have to publish anything. I check all the tabs in the editor, rewrite all the headlines multiple times, add and remove tags, and reposition images. Are you sure your feature will work correctly with similar users?

EXAMPLE EXPLORATORY OUTCOMES

If you were to apply the exploratory-outcomes method to your e-commerce shopping application, you might use it to build a scenario outline for checking out. The checkout process is a good candidate because it involves many moving parts—payments, cart management, and shipping—and each of these parts can break at any moment, yielding a different outcome.

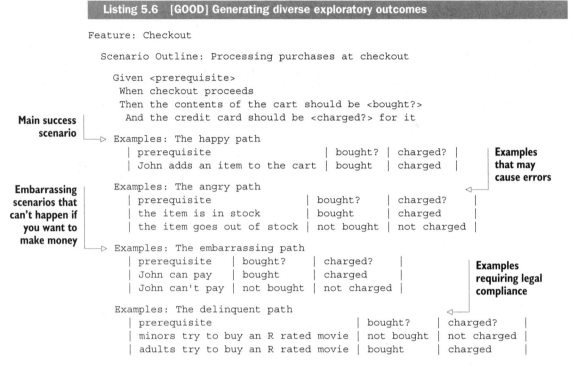

Listing 5.6   [GOOD] Generating diverse exploratory outcomes

```
Feature: Checkout

  Scenario Outline: Processing purchases at checkout

    Given <prerequisite>
    When checkout proceeds
    Then the contents of the cart should be <bought?>
    And the credit card should be <charged?> for it

  Examples: The happy path
    | prerequisite                | bought? | charged? |
    | John adds an item to the cart | bought  | charged  |

  Examples: The angry path
    | prerequisite            | bought?    | charged?    |
    | the item is in stock    | bought     | charged     |
    | the item goes out of stock | not bought | not charged |

  Examples: The embarrassing path
    | prerequisite | bought?    | charged?    |
    | John can pay  | bought     | charged     |
    | John can't pay | not bought | not charged |

  Examples: The delinquent path
    | prerequisite                     | bought?    | charged?    |
    | minors try to buy an R rated movie | not bought | not charged |
    | adults try to buy an R rated movie | bought     | charged     |
```

Main success scenario

Embarrassing scenarios that can't happen if you want to make money

Examples that may cause errors

Examples requiring legal compliance

TIP   You may have noticed that listing 5.6 features a `<prerequisite>` parameter that's substituted for an entire `Given` step. This is possible because test runners go through the parameters before execution and literally generate new scenarios out of the scenario outlines—and only then are the scenarios executed. In this case, a test runner like Cucumber will generate as many `Givens` as there are examples in the table for the `<prerequisite>` parameter, making the outline possible.

To make things clear at a glance, each table has examples that describe only one business rule. And, as discussed earlier, each table has both an example and a corresponding counterexample to clearly show boundaries.

  You could also use techniques like outcome questioning and context questioning, which you learned about in chapter 3. That way, you could see whether any of the tables could create more standalone examples, by asking, "Is there another outcome that also matters?" or "Is there a context that, for the same event, produces a different outcome?"

TIP   Exploring outcomes can help elicit better requirements, too. Asking for alternative examples can make whoever is asking for a feature think twice about whether the proposed solution is the best one. And you don't even have to write any Gherkin to ask this question early in the process.

Exploratory outcomes help the delivery team view the feature they're working with from multiple angles. They can also help discover troublesome edge cases. But not all outcomes have to generate meaningful corresponding examples. It's valuable to go through the list with most new features; such a checklist can come in handy in stressful, time-sensitive situations. In *The Checklist Manifesto* (Metropolitan Books, 2009), Atul Gawande talks about the risks of routine and repetitive tasks in a complex environment, where experts are up against the deficits of human memory and attention. Under pressure, people tend to skip some steps. A checklist with possible testing ideas, ingrained in your development process, can help you avoid that and can result in better coverage.

5.3.4 Boomerangs

Boomerangs are functionalities that keep breaking every now and then, returning from production to development despite your team's best efforts to fix the broken code for good. They negatively affect budgets, deadlines, and morale, because the team wastes time returning to the same functionality while other features have to wait. Boomerangs are also important to identify and contain because they clearly highlight areas where you lack domain knowledge and where there are communication issues. It's not as easy to prevent boomerangs as is it to identify them, but executable specifications can help you decrease the risk of a boomerang appearing.

Boomerangs can appear in the following situations:

- Functionality deals with complex domain rules that are difficult for industry outsiders to understand.
- The team didn't identify a major stakeholder who had a say in the decision-making process.
- The team underestimated such a stakeholder's requests and didn't satisfy the stakeholder.
- The team allowed for a bus factor of one. A bus factor is the number of people who need to get hit by a bus for the project or team to stop functioning. Therefore, a bus factor of one is the riskiest. If a feature that used to be fine becomes a boomerang only after somebody's departure, it means some knowledge disappeared along with the person.
- Customers aren't satisfied with the solution, even though it was implemented exactly as it was designed.

Executable specifications with examples can help you reduce the likelihood of most of these issues.

Some boomerangs can be prevented before they happen. For instance, collecting examples directly from end users and customers can increase the probability that your product will answer real customer needs. Examples can also help you understand complicated domain processes, as you saw in previous chapters—in chapter 3, for example, which talked about outside-in development. Other boomerangs can't be prevented before they happen—but executable specifications can still help you make sure they won't reappear.

Let's focus again on the scenario outline for free shipping. I used it to explain the rule for using counterexamples in section 5.1.2.

Listing 5.7   [GOOD] Scenario outline for free shipping

```
Feature: Free shipping

  Scenario Outline: Orders over $100 should be shipped for free

    Given items worth <purchase> in John's cart
    When John proceeds to checkout
    Then he should be offered <shipping>

    Examples:
      | purchase | shipping     |
      | $99      | $5 shipping  |
      | $100     | free shipping |
```

At the time you wrote it, this was a good outline: simple to grasp and self-explanatory, with two contrasting examples. But as soon as the coding was finished and the functionality hit production, the delivery team learned that they forgot about a simple yet crucial example.

After the release, it turned out that free shipping is location-restricted to customers based in the United States. Business stakeholders said the company couldn't afford to offer free shipping to other countries. You rework the scenario outline as follows, to reflect that decision.

Listing 5.8   [BETTER] Reworked boomerang scenario outline

```
Feature: Free shipping

  Scenario Outline: Orders over $100 should be shipped for free

    Given items worth <purchase> in John's cart
    And shipment to <country>
    When John proceeds to checkout
    Then he should be offered <shipping>

    Examples: Restrict free shipping to the USA
      | country | purchase | shipping      |
      | US      | $99      | $5 shipping   |
      | US      | $100     | free shipping |

    Examples: Other countries don't have free shipping
      | country | purchase | shipping    |
      | Canada  | $99      | $5 shipping |
      | Canada  | $100     | $5 shipping |
      | Poland  | $99      | $5 shipping |
      | Poland  | $100     | $5 shipping |
      | Egypt   | $99      | $5 shipping |
      | Egypt   | $100     | $5 shipping |
      | Japan   | $99      | $5 shipping |
      | Japan   | $100     | $5 shipping |
```

Analyzing boomerangs in depth

Spotting, analyzing, and fixing boomerangs is extremely important when it comes to eliciting better requirements. One technique you can use to understand the root causes of misunderstood requirements is the *Five Whys* technique.

Five Whys is an iterative interrogative technique used to explore the cause-and-effect relationships underlying a particular problem. The primary goal of the technique is to determine the root cause of a defect or problem by repeating the question "Why?" Each answer suggests the next question.

Here's a classic example of using Five Whys to analyze a problem. The issue is that a vehicle won't start:

1. Why? The battery is dead.
2. Why? The alternator isn't functioning.
3. Why? The alternator belt has broken.
4. Why? The alternator belt was well beyond its useful service life and not replaced.
5. Why? The vehicle was not maintained according to the recommended service schedule.

As you can see, this technique, even though it's simple, can be used to deeply investigate the problems that cause boomerangs.

Some analysts use the Five Whys technique not only to prevent defects, but also to elicit new requirements by asking why a requested feature is needed. Asking why something is needed can sound like a challenge and may put the other person in a defensive position, especially in larger organizations; instead, you can ask for a high-level example of how a feature would be useful, to start a discussion without challenging authority.

Five Whys was first developed by Toyota Motor Corporation. If you're interested, you can find more about it in most teaching resources about lean methodologies.

Sometimes, boomerangs return multiple times. The more often they return, the more prominence they deserve—more tests and more examples, which then become documentation. Chapter 1 talked about how a specification suite can become a living documentation system and a single source of truth. Being a *single source of truth* means that when stakeholders prepare to implement a new user story or repair a bug fix, they can use the suite to read relevant scenarios and check important examples. Relying on long-term, written knowledge instead of fallible human memory can help you spot inconsistencies and troublesome areas sooner and more easily. That's why boomerangs, should they appear, deserve a prominent place in your scenario outlines. We'll return to the topic of boomerangs as part of a living documentation system in chapter 7.

5.4   *Avoiding scenario outline anti-patterns*

Scenario outlines are like programs. They can help you automate. But one of the basic rules of technology is that automation, when applied to an efficient operation, will magnify the efficiency—but automation applied to an inefficient operation will magnify the inefficiency. So scenario outlines can hurt you, too, if you aren't careful. This section discusses examples that you *shouldn't* test with Gherkin; automating them would only magnify the inefficiency of the entire specification suite.

5.4.1   *Typical data validations*

Inputs in your application need to be validated against model rules, database-consistency constraints, I/O rules, and other parameters that depend on the type of data provided. These rules don't belong to your domain only; they're general data-validation rules. Should you include examples like these in your specifications?

For example, when dealing with numbers, should you write automated tests for accepting numerical formats such as `1,234,567`, `1.234.567`, `1234567`, and `1 234 567`? Or, with strings, should you deal with entering accented characters, like ð? Or, with dates, should you add examples of invalid dates, such as February 30 and September 31?

Executable specifications are only one part of the entire test suite a software application can have. The main role of scenarios is to provide a communication framework for talking with stakeholders that lets you build a living documentation system. You shouldn't try to use a specification suite to replace other kinds of tests—if you do, it will quickly become cluttered. Executable specifications should only optimize for three simple things: being clear, self-explanatory, and readable for both technical and nontechnical team members.

Usually, data validations are too low-level to satisfy these three criteria. You can easily validate this statement by trying to get business stakeholders to read scenarios with technical examples. Decision makers don't have time to read about strings or date validations. They want to read about their businesses. They want to make sure the scenarios cover cases needed by their sales teams to satisfy contracts that they want to sign with clients.

5.4.2   *Simple combinatorial outcomes*

Sometimes a functionality has to accept many different inputs that generate hundreds of outcomes. If you try to write a scenario to cover all the inputs and outputs, the `Examples` table will grow so large that it will be unreadable. Let's think about what to do in such a situation. Do you use all the examples and accept a scenario that's hard to read, or do you keep the `Examples` table short and possibly leave an important edge case without a test?

For example, suppose your website has a complex filtering system to help customers find new products more quickly. The shopping search engine has to deal with many attributes, such as keywords, author, title, ISBN, publisher, subject, format, language, and publication date—and these are just for books. Your shop also sells video games, groceries, gift cards, pet supplies, and so on, and each of these categories has its own filtering options.

Imagine a scenario outline like this (I intentionally left the Examples table empty):

```
Feature: Search

  Scenario Outline: Filtering

    Given books:
      | title      | genre     | author          | release |
      | "Sorrow"   | adventure | Damion Melville | 1994    |
      | "Setup"    | humor     | Beyhan Topuz    | 2000    |
      | "Recruits" | adventure | Fionna Walker   | 2005    |
      | "Aliens"   | sci-fi    | Phan Uoc        | 2013    |
      | "Invent"   | horror    | Stela Vánová    | 1988    |
    When Simona searches for <filter>
     And she wants to find <value>
    Then she should see <results>

    Examples:
      | filter | value | results |
      | [...]  | [...] | [...]   |
```

How many different combinations could you test here? How many would be meaningful? How many would you be including in the scenario *just in case?*

In this example, the business domain is simple. But the temptation to write examples exhaustively instead of illustratively increases when even the *simple* outcomes for a product are complicated—for example, when the team is new to the domain. Self doubt leads to scenarios with too many examples—examples that are too simple and boring for the business stakeholders and domain experts to read, but, at the same time, are too confusing and difficult for the delivery team to maintain. In my experience, this is the number-one reason teams become discouraged with SBE. Instead, you can reap the benefits of an approach called *pairwise testing*.

> **DEFINITION** *Pairwise testing*—A testing heuristic based on the observation that most faults are caused by a combination of at most two factors. Pairwise examples are shorter than exhaustive ones, but they can still be effective in finding defects.

Pairwise testing is an effective heuristic that should let you pay attention to both readability and preventing defects. Let's fill the Examples table with pairs to see if that's true.

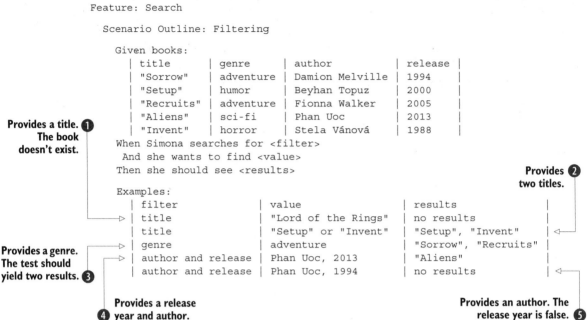

Listing 5.9   [GOOD] Using pairs of factors to generate outcomes

```
Feature: Search

  Scenario Outline: Filtering

    Given books:
        | title       | genre     | author          | release |
        | "Sorrow"    | adventure | Damion Melville | 1994    |
        | "Setup"     | humor     | Beyhan Topuz    | 2000    |
        | "Recruits"  | adventure | Fionna Walker   | 2005    |
        | "Aliens"    | sci-fi    | Phan Uoc        | 2013    |
        | "Invent"    | horror    | Stela Vánová    | 1988    |
    When Simona searches for <filter>
     And she wants to find <value>
    Then she should see <results>

    Examples:
        | filter             | value                  | results              |
        | title              | "Lord of the Rings"    | no results           |
        | title              | "Setup" or "Invent"    | "Setup", "Invent"    |
        | genre              | adventure              | "Sorrow", "Recruits" |
        | author and release | Phan Uoc, 2013         | "Aliens"             |
        | author and release | Phan Uoc, 1994         | no results           |
```

Provides a title. ❶ The book doesn't exist.

Provides ❷ two titles.

Provides a genre. The test should yield two results. ❸

Provides a release ❹ year and author.

Provides an author. The release year is false. ❺

Each example tests a different combination of two factors:

❶ Combines searching by a title and an empty set of results to test whether it's possible to create a failing query

❷ Combines *two* alternative titles to check whether advanced OR filtering works

❸ Combines two books belonging to the same genre to test whether the genre filter will return all possible results

❹ Combines an existing author and a correct release year to make sure filtering by two distinct attributes is possible

❺ Combines an existing author with an incorrect release year to check whether the advanced logic behind the two-attribute filter yields correct results

Exercise 4

Prepare a list of pairwise examples for another search scenario in which Simona looks for a new smartphone.

If you think there may be more possible edge cases, you're right. But remember that the process of collecting examples and refining executable specifications is continuous. It starts before anyone writes the first line of code, and it doesn't end with production deployment. I guarantee that this table will change—growing *or* shrinking—throughout the product's lifetime. You don't have to get it all right on the first try; you only have to do *enough* to begin writing code. You can always improve the model later.

5.4.3   Database models

A *database model* is a type of data model that determines the logical structure of a database. It can be a representation of all the attributes you need to store in the database to allow your application to persist data. For example, when a new user signs up, you need to store their username and password, but also their last sign-in date, number of sign-ins, and their IPs. Databases like Postgres and MySQL store data in tables, just as Gherkin does, so some programmers and testers are tempted by their old habits to write Gherkin just like SQL.

To see an example of such an approach, let's look at a feature file for a standard reviewing functionality. Every time a customer buys something, they can rate the item afterward, which can help you promote popular, high-quality items on the website and remove bad items from the store. When an item gets bad reviews, you should ask whether buyers want to tell you how you could improve their experience in the future. And if an item is rated well, you should try to persuade happy customers to recommend it to their friends.

Here's a scenario showing what happens when the author doesn't care about making the specification readable for nontechnical readers.

Listing 5.10   [BAD] Gherkin tables that look like SQL

**Publishers and authors are in the specification only because
they're required to save a book in the database; without them,
the book object wouldn't pass necessary internal validations.**

```
Feature: Reviews

  Background:
    Given customers:
        | id | name          | email             |
        | 1  | Dominic Advice | doad@exmaple.com |
    And items:
        | id | name                        | price  | type |
        | 1  | Writing Great Specifications | $44.99 | book |
    And publishers:
        | id | name                |
        | 1  | Manning Publications |
    And publications:
        | publisher_id | item_id |
        | 1            | 1       |
    And authors:
        | id | name          |
        | 1  | Kamil Nicieja |
    And book authored by:
        | author_id | item_id |
        | 1         | 1       |
```

Because both Postgres and MySQL are RDBMS databases, based on the relational model of data, you need to explicitly define relationships between the book and its author, and between the book and its publisher, by linking item_id and author_id or publisher_id.

```
Scenario Outline: Reviewing sold items by customers

  Given customer <user_id> bought item <item_id>
  When the customer gives the item <rating> stars
  Then we should <outcome>

Examples:
  | item_id | user_id | rating | outcome                 |
  | 1       | 1       | 0      | ask_how_can_we_improve  |
  | 1       | 1       | 1      | ask_how_can_we_improve  |
  | 1       | 1       | 2      | ask_how_can_we_improve  |
  | 1       | 1       | 3      | do_nothing              |
  | 1       | 1       | 4      | ask_for_recommendation  |
  | 1       | 1       | 5      | ask_for_recommendation  |
```

There are two major problems with this specification:

- It's full of technicalities that *aren't in any way related to what is being specified.*

- Instead of specifying the business context, it's mostly concerned with setting up the database in a way that won't break the test suite on execution.

You can see that many lines of the specification aren't necessarily connected to the topic of reviews. For example, are the price and type of a reviewed item required to understand how reviews work? They're important if you want to talk about marketing—but not from an implementation perspective. All these lines are probably included because the author decided to reuse steps written for another scenario where prices, authors, and publishers were relevant. But that's just lazy writing.

Now, look at the Background section at the beginning of the specification. These tables are included only to create required relationships between database objects. Because the author chose a book as the item that's being reviewed, you're forced to read about its publisher and author. You can only guess that without the publisher and the author, the book object couldn't be saved in the database, making the tests unable to proceed. Instead of solving the problem in the automation layer, the author decided to write steps that would make it easy to manipulate the testing code directly from the specification layer.

In general, technical stuff like managing database models should always be handled in the automation layer. Sometimes, though, delivery teams forget about the need for a healthy balance between the specification layer and the automation layer—they decide to handle database modeling in the specification layer to reduce redundancy and simplify step definitions.

Here's how to write the previous specification if you handle technicalities in the automation layer.

```
Listing 5.11  [GOOD] Scenario outline without unnecessary technical detail
```

```
Feature: Reviews

  Scenario Outline: Reviewing items by customers

    Given Dominic bought "Writing Great Specifications"
    When he rates it with <rating> stars
    Then we should <ask> for <feedback>

    Examples:
      | rating | ask       | feedback               |
      | 0      | ask       | tips to make it better |
      | 1      | ask       | tips to make it better |
      | 2      | ask       | tips to make it better |
      | 3      | don't ask | no feedback            |
      | 4      | ask       | a recommendation       |
      | 5      | ask       | a recommendation       |
```

The specification is much easier to read, you got rid of the artificial Background tables, and readers can easily see that the only thing being tested in this simple scenario outline is the numerical scale of ratings that need to be implemented in the system.

> **WARNING** Writing outlines that look like SQL tables is an anti-pattern. As a rule, you should always solve technical difficulties in the automation layer, instead of trying to solve them in the specification layer of your specifications.

Gherkin is, by definition, a *business-readable, domain-specific language*. There's nothing business-y, readable, or domain-specific about database rows. I think the confusion comes from the fact that some people don't treat Gherkin as a wrapper for automating conversations about requirements. Instead, they want to use it as a wrapper that makes writing tests easier, without having to write new testing code all the time. This may sound like a strong opinion, but I think this is a lazy, technology-oriented way to use executable specifications that should be—at all costs—avoided.

5.4.4   *Classes of equivalence*

Classes of equivalence are examples such as "X is less than Y," as in the following step:

```
Given a user who is less than 18 years old            ⟵┐  Class of
  When the user tries to buy a violent movie or game     │  equivalence
  Then the purchase should be blocked                   ─┘
```

A step like this can be used, for example, to make sure young users can't purchase violent movies or games. I don't recommend using classes of equivalence, though, because they can create an illusion of shared understanding, which is the gravest mistake an executable specification can make. Every class of equivalence is, in fact, a *set*, and mental operations on sets don't come naturally to most people. If you talk about sets expressed as domain-specific examples, the difficulty is twofold. When reading such a specification, your short-term memory has to maintain both the boundaries of the set *and* the new business domain concepts that the specification is trying to teach you. In such circumstances, mistakes come easily.

Examples that use classes of equivalence should be rewritten using a testing heuristic called the *Goldilocks principle*. This principle is derived from the children's story "The Three Bears," in which a little girl named Goldilocks finds a house inhabited by three bears. Each bear has its own food and bed. After testing all three choices of both items, Goldilocks determines that the first is to one extreme—too hot or too large. The second is to the opposite extreme—too cold or too small. But the third, she determines, is "just right."

> **DEFINITION**   *Goldilocks principle*—A principle that requires at least three testing samples whenever possible. The samples should include an average (or acceptable) example and two or more extreme examples (edge cases).

The Goldilocks principle is a good heuristic to convey classes of equivalence in scenario outlines. You can even use it if you don't have three clear-cut boundary examples. For example, you could rewrite the previous snippet something like this:

```
Given a user who is <age> years old
 When the user tries to buy a violent movie or game
 Then the purchase should be <blocked>

Examples:
    | age | blocked     |
    | 17  | blocked     |
    | 18  | not blocked |
    | 19  | not blocked |
```

Three examples illustrate the rule. The middle example in the table is the boundary condition: the age of majority. The first example is there to illustrate that 18 isn't the only age that's blocked from purchasing restricted content, so the reader can expect that the same applies to ages below 17 as well. The last example shows what should happen when you successfully cross the boundary condition specified in the middle example.

> **Exercise 5**
>
> Rewrite the following `Given` so that it will use a parameter, similar to the `<age>` parameter in the previous snippet, and a table with three Goldilocks examples:
>
> ```
> Given a discount that is higher than 10% and lower than 12%
> ```

You always need to be extremely careful when dealing with boundary conditions. Wherever you find yourself trying to express an example as a class of equivalence, rewrite it using the Goldilocks principle with concrete examples of the boundaries. It may seem like too much trouble at first, but it's a good, safe habit that can spare you many misunderstandings.

5.5 *Answers to exercises*

EXERCISE 1   Rewrite the table of examples in Gherkin:

```
Examples:
  | region        | commission |
  | North America | 10%        |
  | South America | 11.4%      |
  | Europe        | 12.9%      |
  | Asia          | 12.9%      |
  | Africa        | 13.5%      |
```

EXERCISE 2   Prepare a list of the most representative examples that will illustrate what your online shop is selling to someone who didn't read this chapter or chapter 4:

```
Examples:
  | item                        | category   |
  | "Sorrow" by Damion Melville | paperback  |
  | "Setup" by Beyhan Topuz     | hardcover  |
  | "Recruits" by Fionna Walker | e-book     |
  | "Aliens" by Phan Uoc        | audiobook  |
  | "Invent" by Stela Vánová    | audio CD   |
  | Kindle Paperwhite 3         | e-reader   |
  | Apple iPad                  | tablet     |
  | Beats Solo 2                | headphones |
  | "Inception"                 | movie      |
```

EXERCISE 3   When an item that's on sale is featured as a daily deal, what will a table with an example and a counterexample look like?

```
Examples:
  | item                | discount   | price    |
  | Kindle Paperwhite 3 | N/A        | $119.99  |
  | Kindle Paperwhite 3 | Daily Deal | $99.59   |
```

EXERCISE 4   Prepare a list of pairwise examples for another search scenario in which Simona looks for a new tablet:

```
Examples:
  | filter                 | value             | results              |
  | manufacturer and line  | "Samsung", "S2"   | Galaxy Tab S2        |
  | manufacturer and line  | "Samsung", empty  | Galaxy Tab S2, Tab E |
  | year and manufacturer  | "2013", "Apple"   | iPad Air             |
```

EXERCISE 5   Rewrite the Given so that it will use a parameter, similar to the `<age>` parameter in the previous snippet, and a table with three Goldilocks examples:

```
Given a <discount>

Examples:
  | discount     |
  | 10% discount |
  | 11% discount |
  | 12% discount |
```

5.6   *Summary*

- Outside-in scenario outlines are written directly from examples gathered during an analysis phase rather than by merging similar scenarios.
- Illustrative examples are tests that only test the key inputs and outputs. They're different from exhaustive tests that test every possible combination of inputs and outputs to maximize test coverage.
- Scenario outlines work well with representative examples illustrating each important aspect of business functionality.
- Examples should always be illustrated with counterexamples in order to show clear boundaries between business rules.
- The Goldilocks principle states that in a given sample of tests, there may be entities belonging to extremes, but there will always be an entity belonging to the average.
- Boomerangs are difficult areas of implementation, troubled with production bugs, and they also make good candidates to include in scenario outlines.
- Examples that prevent data-type attacks, such as testing input field validations, are usually too low level to be included in executable specifications.
- Examples created by combining all possible inputs often make executable specifications unreadable, brittle, and slow.
- You should always solve technical difficulties in the automation layer, instead of trying to solve them in the specification layer of your specifications.

The life cycle of executable specifications

6

This chapter covers

- Working with an executable specification throughout its life cycle
- Understanding requirements' precision level
- Using examples in different development phases
- Understanding what happens after implementation

In its original meaning in systems theory, *feedback* is the exchange of data about how one part of a system is working—with the understanding that one part affects all others in the system—so that if any part heads off course, it can be changed for the better. In SBE, a specification suite is the system, every executable specification is a part of that system, and the delivery team is the recipient of the feedback.

As anyone who works in a corporate environment knows, there are two kinds of feedback:

- *Supporting* that lets people know they're doing their job well
- *Critiquing* that's meant to correct the current course of action

The same rules apply to the systems of feedback in SBE. Back in 2003, Brian Marick wrote a series of blog posts about the concept of an agile testing matrix.[1] The series is also one of the oldest articles about modern testing methods I know of that suggested dropping the name *tests* and replacing it with *examples* for business-facing testing.

Marick organized his quadrant into distinct quadrants with two axes (see figure 6.1). The vertical axis splits the matrix into business-facing tests, such as prototypes and exploratory testing, and technology-facing tests, such as unit tests and performance tests. Unit tests deal with low-level testing; they make sure small components of code run well. Performance tests determine how a system performs in terms of responsiveness and stability under workload.

Our area of interest lies in the upper half of the matrix, though: it's split into tests that *support the team's progress* and tests that *critique the product*. Tests that support the team help the team write new code before they have a working product. Tests that critique the product look at a finished product with the intent of discovering inadequacies. As you can see, this is similar to the feedback system that powers any human organization.

The question we'll explore throughout this chapter is when examples should support the team's work and when they should critique the product. You'll see how examples and automation can give delivery teams feedback of both kinds. And you'll come to understand how feedback forces at the core of every executable specification suite work much like a development manager: constantly evaluating the job done by

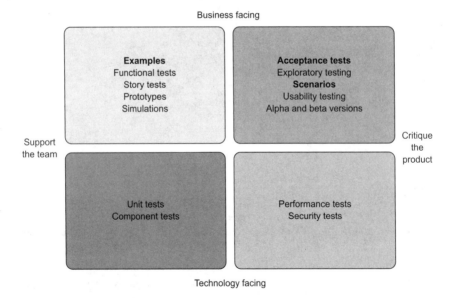

Figure 6.1   The agile testing quadrants. I've highlighted the tests that will be important in this analysis.

---

[1] See Brian Marick, "My Agile Testing Project," on his blog, "Exploration Through Example," August 21, 2003, http://mng.bz/TkO1.

programmers, analysts, designers, and testers; praising the team for their successes; and pointing out failures.

To see how feedback loops in SBE help uncover contradictions and uncertainty that can hide even in well-analyzed requirements, I'll also talk about the life cycle of an executable specification. In product design, *life cycle* can be defined as the process of bringing a new product or a new feature to market and then maintaining it over time.

Chapter 1 said that all software development processes follow similar phases as a functionality progresses from conception to release, such as planning, building, releasing, and getting feedback. These phases are also a called the *software development life cycle*. I also said that, traditionally, specifications belong to the planning phase because that's when delivery teams first interact with new requirements (as presented in figure 6.2).

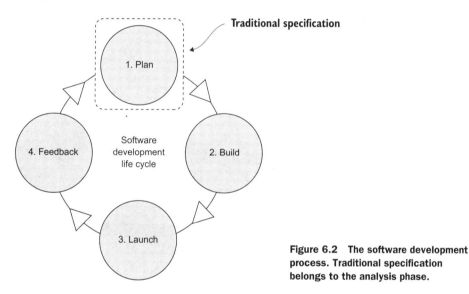

Figure 6.2   The software development process. Traditional specification belongs to the analysis phase.

SBE is different because it doesn't see specification as a singular phase but rather as a process that spreads across multiple phases as requirements evolve and change (see figure 6.3). Specifications become tests; and tests, as you'll see in chapter 7, become documentation.

By *evolving requirements*, I mean that the precision level of your requirements changes throughout the life cycle of an executable specification. Every requirement starts as a vague goal with a high level of uncertainty. As you implement it, uncertainty decreases, because the requirement gradually becomes working code. As you'll see, SBE and Gherkin have a different feedback loop at each stage of the life cycle, which helps decrease uncertainty even further than in other software development processes.

To understand this process thoroughly, we'll track how a raw requirement *becomes* a Gherkin specification—from a broad concept to a working implementation. This time

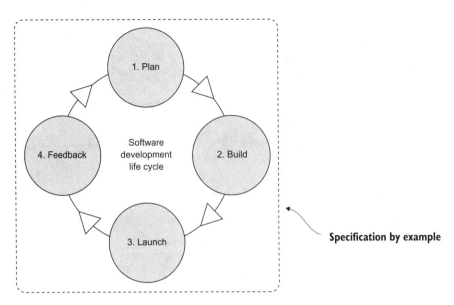

Figure 6.3   SBE in the software development process. Specification spreads throughout multiple phases.

around, you'll specify a new feature in a simple mapping application called Mapper. Maps are by definition instruments of changing precision. You can use one to look at continents and countries from a high-level view, but you can also buy a local map of your city and use it to find your home. A map is a great metaphor: just as there are low-resolution and high-resolution maps, there are low-resolution requirements and high-resolution executable specifications.

6.1   *End-to-end overview of the process*

In this and the next section, we'll look at a full overview of what *life cycle* and *precision level* mean. Every software feature goes through several development phases such as analysis, design, implementation, testing, and maintenance. This is what a life cycle is. As discussed in chapter 2, Gherkin specifications are also called *features*, and they go through similar phases.

At its core, every executable specification is the result of a five-step process (see figure 6.4):

1   Understanding business goals
2   Analyzing the scope of requirements through examples
3   Designing the solution by deriving scenarios from acceptance criteria and examples
4   Refining scenarios until you can implement the behaviors from the specification
5   Iterating the specification over time

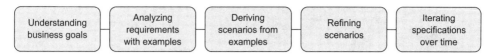

Figure 6.4   The life cycle of executable specifications

As you cross each threshold, the precision level of your analysis increases (see figure 6.5). The more precise you are, the better you understand the implications of implementing a requirement.

Business goals are broad directives that sometimes don't provide a specific solution. Requirements are less abstract; they define what needs to be built for whom in order to achieve the high-level goal. Solutions are precise plans for features, interaction flows, and user interfaces. Because software is comprised of thousands of moving parts, no solution is fully precise until it's implemented as working code. And only after the code is released to production do you get the feedback needed to asses whether a business goal has been met, which removes any remaining ambiguity.

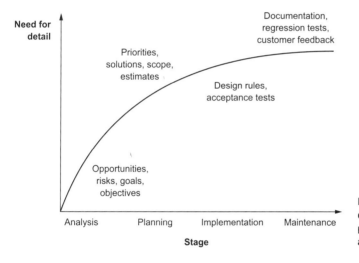

Figure 6.5   As the need for detail increases, so does the precision of artifacts that appear during development.

6.2   *Understanding business goals*

To see how the precision level increases throughout the life cycle of an executable specification, we need to start with the least specific phase: discussing business goals (see figure 6.6). For this example, assume on the Mapper project, your responsibility is to lead a team of developers, designers, and testers. Management is looking for a way to increase Mapper's presence among small businesses and get smaller enterprises to pay to be featured on your online maps. Right now, your maps feature only a few of the most popular outlets of international companies located at prominent locations, but management would like to include more firms. Your team has been tasked with making that change happen.

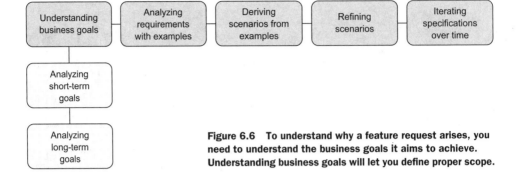

Figure 6.6   **To understand why a feature request arises, you need to understand the business goals it aims to achieve. Understanding business goals will let you define proper scope.**

TIP   When you're trying to elicit requirements, raising the discussion to the level of business goals lets you deal with scope and priorities more efficiently. As you raise the discussion to the level of goals, the number of things you have to talk about decreases. That makes it easier to focus on the essentials.

You and management agree on actionable goals that the team should aim to meet in the next six months; see table 6.1. You have to understand both the short-term and the long-term contexts. If you knew only the short-term goal, you'd devise a temporary solution. For example, your team could add new businesses to the platform manually and still achieve the goal. Because the absolute number of businesses featured on Mapper is low at the moment, doubling that number would take only a few minutes of work.

Table 6.1   **High-level goals for the next six months**

Perspective	Goal
Short-term	2x increase in businesses featured on Mapper's platform
Long-term	Establish presence in the unsaturated segment of small businesses in order to seek growth

Only when you also look at the long-term goal you can see that the company is looking for a solution that will let it achieve sustainable growth in a new market segment. Meeting such a goal will require you to take different actions.

Other resources for strategic planning
Impact mapping is one of the best methods I know for creating medium-term strategic plans. An *impact map* is a visualization of scope and underlying assumptions, created collaboratively by senior technical and business staff. It's a mind map that's grown during a discussion that considers the following four aspects:

- *Goal*—Why are we doing this?
- *Actors*—Who can produce the desired effect? Who can obstruct it? Who are the consumers or users of our product? Who will be impacted by it?
- *Impacts*—How should our actors' behavior change? How can they help us to achieve the goal? How can they obstruct us or prevent us from succeeding?
- *Deliverables*—What can we do, as an organization or a delivery team, to support the required impacts?

I like impact maps because they make assumptions hierarchical and testable. What does that mean? Let's say you have an impact map with a goal to grow mobile advertising for a website.

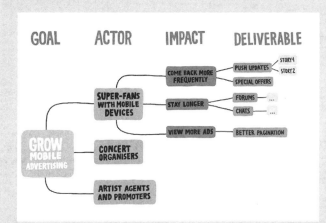

Example of an impact map from www.impactmapping .org/drawing.html

First, you define the success metrics for your goal. Then, you identify several actors who can help reach you that goal, including super-fans with mobile devices. One possible impact could be that they stay longer on your website and increase advertising exposure. You figure that features such as forums and chats, among others, might help achieve that impact.

Let's say that after implementing several deliverables, you realize that you were wrong in thinking that forums and chats would increase engagement. You may have several other, similar deliverables on your map, but now you know that this branch of the map isn't as impactful as you thought it would be—so you might discard that impact or even discard that actor. If you did the latter, all the other deliverables for super-fans with mobile devices would be automatically discarded as well, because the map is hierarchical. Thus you can treat the map as an easy-to-maintain, visual, testable product backlog that keeps changing its shape as your knowledge about the world grows.

You can read more about impact maps in *Impact Mapping* by Gojko Adžić (Provoking Thoughts, 2012).

6.3   *Analyzing requirements with examples*

As you may recall from chapter 1, an SBE process starts with deriving scope from goals. The previous section provided you with a goal. Now you need the scope. There are several methods to derive scope (see figure 6.7). In recent years, user stories have risen to become the most popular method for defining and discussing scope among agile teams; this section will guide you through the process of creating user stories, illustrated with examples.

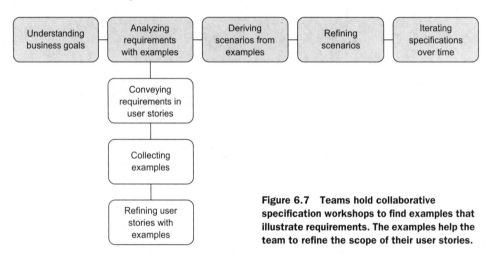

Figure 6.7   Teams hold collaborative specification workshops to find examples that illustrate requirements. The examples help the team to refine the scope of their user stories.

6.3.1   *Conveying requirements as user stories*

A user story lets you convey a glimpse of a requirement as a product backlog item. The item becomes a *ticket for a future conversation*. Through user stories, you can negotiate the priority of any given requirement, discuss possible solutions and scope, and make some estimates. They're used for *planning*.

The previous section talked about short- and long-term business goals. Even if you acknowledge both contexts that are important to your company, that's only one side of the story. Customers don't care about the goals of businesses; they want businesses to bring them value. Customer-oriented firms know that and use user-centered tools to align their strategies to their customers' interests.

That's what user stories are for. Writing a user story lets you restate your business objective as a customer benefit.

Listing 6.1   [OK] Your first user story

```
In order to let new customers discover my company
As an owner of a small business
I want to add my company to Mapper's platform
```

TIP I talk more about user stories in chapter 8. You'll learn alternative formats to express your stories so that you'll be able to aim for understanding rather than strict conformance to any single format. Stay tuned! Right now, you only have to focus on the three key elements that all user stories share— *who*, *what*, and *why*.

Thanks to your knowledge about your market, you know that making Mapper a new distribution channel will encourage small businesses to add themselves to the platform. They will essentially do the job for you, if you help them find new clients.

User stories are crucial to increasing precision to the level an executable specification needs. But stories and scenarios are separate creatures, as shown in table 6.2. User stories have acceptance criteria. Executable specifications have acceptance tests. Without the criteria, there can be no tests. A delivery team derives new executable specifications and new scenarios from user stories.

Table 6.2 A comparison of user stories and executable specifications

User story	Executable specification
Discarded after implementation	Kept after implementation
A unit of change	An effect of the change
Has acceptance criteria	Is an acceptance test
Produces short-term results, such as cards or tasks	Produces long-term, living documentation

At this stage, you already suspect that your team will have to build some kind of a form that will allow companies to sign up and mark themselves on your maps. You know that because analyzing business goals and writing the user story increased the precision level of the requirement to the point that you can begin to devise a specific *solution*.

Placing the responsibility for a solution on the development team is a great way to obtain the right scope for a goal. The executive team may already have ideas about the solution, derived from their intuitions and expertise; but they made you the product owner, so you're the decision maker.

When a requirement or a business objective contains implementation details, it usually means somebody's trying to slip in a predetermined solution, binding it unnecessarily with the problem your organization is trying to solve. It could be a team member, a manager, someone from marketing and sales, or even a bossy customer.

Henry Ford famously said, "If I had asked people what they wanted, they would have said faster horses." Visionaries use this quote as a beaten-to-death excuse for ignoring customer feedback. I think customers clearly told Ford what they wanted: they told him that speed is the key requirement for transport. But because they weren't engineers, they weren't able to say that cars would satisfy the requirement.

People will always use solutions to help themselves imagine consequences of any given requirement, because it's a natural way of thinking. But as someone who works with technology, you should strive to extract unbiased, pure requirements from their solutions. Only when you decide what will work best for the company should you move on to writing down an executable specification.

Storing user stories in a product backlog

A user story is only a token for a future conversation. It's a reminder that when the right time comes, you'll have to discuss the such-and-such requirement with your stakeholders in order to implement it correctly.

Even though user stories shouldn't by any measure *replace* conversations, you can prepare notes in advance that will help you get up to speed after you pull a story out of the product backlog. (A backlog is a lot like a freezer: some stories don't age well.) You don't want to be overly specific, of course. Specificity at this stage could constrain your flexibility in the future. You should never treat user stories as a to-do list. They're more like a list of guidelines: directions that you suspect you might explore in the future. But stories can stay in the freezer for months, so you may want to provide *some* details to remind you of its purpose back when you put that particular story in the backlog.

To specify my stories, I use a four-element template based on a simplified story-elements template first shown to me during a workshop by David Evans, who is a veteran of agile testing and an active member of the agile community. For each story, I write down the following:

- *Stakeholders and their interests*—Along with the primary actor who has the most interest in the story and is featured in the story, I sometimes list other stakeholders who could be affected by the story.
- *A trigger*—The event that causes the new behavior to be initiated or invoked by a user or by the system itself.
- *The main success scenario*—Intentions and outcomes that should guarantee the primary actor's success (remember not to over-specify UI or implementation details!).
- *Acceptance criteria*—Two to five one-line descriptions that sufficiently identify each testing condition for the story to be verified.

I put these notes in the description of the story in the backlog.

You can see that each of the four notes will help me prepare Gherkin scenarios more quickly after I pull the user story from the backlog. I'll already know the primary actor. From the trigger, I'll have some idea about the Givens. The main success scenario will help me imagine the Whens and Thens. And from the list of acceptance criteria, I'll be able to estimate how many scenarios an executable specification for this user story will have.

Sometimes notes don't age well. Requirements can change over time. But notes can still help you in such situations: you can always compare your past notes with your current direction. The difference between the former and the latter will be the sum of the learning your team has accomplished during the freezer time.

The template can also be useful when you gain new insights about the story, but it's still not the right time to implement that story—for example, when you gather new customer feedback, but have other priorities at the moment. Updating the template can preserve your new insights for the future discussion.

6.3.2　Collecting examples

You now have a user story that you can put in your team's backlog. You also have a rough sense of the amount of work you'll face: you know what's expected of you, and you've shared the news with the engineers, who told you their first impressions and initial ideas of what could be done to meet the requirements. What happens next?

Chapter 1 taught you that after you derive scope from goals, you should start *specifying collaboratively* to *illustrate requirements with examples*. Specifying collaboratively means domain experts, product managers, developers, testers, and designers working together to explore and discover examples that will become Gherkin scenarios. Let's assume that in the Mapper example scenario, you decide to organize a workshop.

> **TIP**　It's your job to be a facilitator and to extract relevant information from whatever is said. Starting by asking for rules is okay as long as you don't expect the rules to be a fully developed list of acceptance criteria. They'll be messy and, probably, contradictory or inconsistent. As a technologist, you should constantly challenge and refine the requirements your team takes on.

During the workshop, your team comes up with examples of small businesses based in your town that would be most likely to join Mapper's platform (see table 6.3). You also add a few ideas of how particular businesses may use Mapper to lead new customers through their conversion channels.

Table 6.3　Examples of relevant small businesses

Business name	Business type	Features for lead generation
Deep Lemon	Restaurant	Showing customers business hours
The Pace Gallery	Art gallery	Advertising expositions
French Quarter Inn	Hotel	Booking rooms
Green Pencil	Bistro	Showing customers business hours
Radio Music Hall	Concert hall	Advertising concert programs
City Cinema	Movies	Showcasing new films and ticket prices
Christie's	Pub	Showing customers business hours

What a diverse bunch of businesses! Having them sign up to Mapper would lead to a lot of healthy growth. The difficult part is that they would require different features in order to find the platform valuable, and some of those features would be as complex as integrating with external booking systems and payment processors. But for now, Mapper's customers will have to deal with the limited scope that we'll implement in this chapter.

At the analysis stage, delivery teams use examples to understand the business context of their requirements—just as you did when you illustrated your business goals with examples of use cases that might help you achieve those goals. Delivery teams can also use examples to check whether the designers, programmers, and testers are in sync with the domain experts—again, just as you did during your specification workshop. This is clearly the *supporting role of examples* that I talked about when I introduced the agile testing matrix in figure 6.1. Is there a relationship between the two critical diagrams in this chapter—the matrix from figure 6.1 and the life cycle diagram from figure 6.5? As you can see in figure 6.8, you could easily rework the life cycle diagram to show the supporting role of examples in the early stages of development.

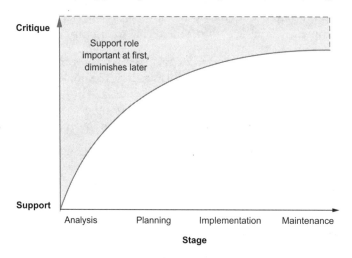

Figure 6.8 Before they're automated, examples support delivery teams in understanding the scope of requirements—which is important at the beginning of the life cycle.

The supporting role of early examples means delivery teams can use them to *support writing new code* when they work on new functionalities. In a way, the right examples *provoke* the right code, guiding the development process.

But as the requirements become more precise, the supporting role becomes less important than the critiquing role (see figure 6.9). By *critiquing*, I mean that examples begin to *challenge the requirement*. For example, what if the examples collected by the delivery team are wrong? Some surely will be.

Examples at the critiquing stage usually have something they didn't have earlier: an actual iteration of working software. When working software becomes available, it's

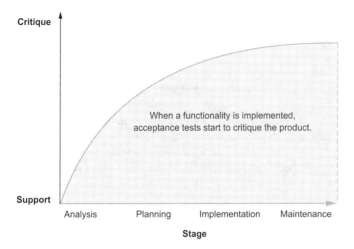

Figure 6.9   As requirements get more precise, examples are challenged by the working product.

easier to verify whether your initial analysis was right. Sometimes, the business expert will forget things that real users will need. They may also be misguided or may champion a preferred solution due to a personal agenda. And sometimes, you can end up overengineering the solution and worrying about too many examples that aren't useful in the real world.

6.3.3   *Refining user stories with examples*

Let's assume that building a feature for so many kinds of businesses proved to be too difficult for Mapper. Having a deadline to meet and limited resources you can use, you decide to reduce the scope. To choose a customer segment that will allow you to easily expand to other businesses in the future, you must look for a *carryover customer*.

> **DEFINITION**   *Carryover customer*—An example of a real customer who shares behavioral traits with as many other customers as possible and becomes a model for an average consumer. If you design a product or a feature for the right carryover customer, other segments of the market should find it valuable, too.

Did you notice that all of the gastronomy businesses in table 6.3 share the same feature— showing customers business hours—that would drive their conversion rates? Other businesses, such as shops, pubs, and clubs, share this trait, too. After some discussion, the Mapper team agree that restaurants and bistros make good carryover customers.

Listing 6.2   [BETTER] Refined user story

```
In order to let my customer know where and when they can come in
As an owner of a gastronomy business
I want to add my company to Mapper's platform
```

You believe that implementing this user story will fulfill the short-term business goal you were tasked with. While you test the waters with gastronomy, the user stories for other businesses will wait patiently in the backlog for their turn.

> **TIP** Features can usually be split only based on *technology*. This is a limiting approach. For example, if you wanted to split a report-generating feature into smaller portions, your first instinct would probably be to split it based on its *technological* ability to generate reports in different formats such as .pdf, .csv, and .xls. User stories and requirements, on the other hand, can be split by *value*. In your analysis of Mapper's platform, you choose the most valuable customer segment and split a small capability that would bring this segment a lot of value without a lot of effort on your side.

You wouldn't be able to make a confident decision without the validation provided by the examples you collected. That's their power.

Collecting, analyzing, and refining examples creates a powerful feedback loop within any project that uses SBE. Examples helped you define the scope of the features and split user stories into smaller, more precise backlog items. Even though you're yet to see an executable specification that your Mapper team could use, it should already be clear why examples lie at Gherkin's center.

Eliciting better requirements with Feature Injection

The process you've been using throughout the chapter to elicit requirements is similar in design to *feature injection*: a technique that iteratively derives scope from goals through high-level examples.[a] In feature injection, teams first "hunt for value" by creating a model for delivering business value and listing underlying assumptions instead of trying to describe the value with simple numbers such as revenue goals. You created a simple model for value delivery when we discussed Mapper's short-term and long-term goals, why the goals are important, how they influence Mapper's business model, and which stakeholders demand that you achieve the metrics.

Once a model is defined, you do more than just evaluate whether to accept or reject a suggested feature. You can proactively create a list of features that drive toward delivery of business value based on your models. You did that when you wrote your first user story and refined it to better fit the value model.

Injecting features provides a set of *happy paths* to create the outputs that will deliver the business value. But doing so doesn't provide all possible variations of input that can occur and that may affect the outputs, or all cases that need to be considered for successful delivery. You may recall happy paths from section 5.3.3, where I talked about exploratory outcomes. *Exploratory outcomes* pursue possible unhappy paths, leading to new testing ideas. When new examples are generated, you can put them together in an executable specification—which is what you're about to do for Mapper.

_____

[a] Feature injection was created by Chris Matts and then expanded with Rohit Darji, Andy Pols, Sanela Hodzic, and David Anderson over the years 2003–2011. For more information, see "Feature Injection: Three Steps to Success" by Chris Matts and Gojko Adžić, *InfoQ*, December 14, 2011, http://mng.bz/E5fS.

6.4 Deriving scenarios from examples

In this section, you'll step over another precision threshold as the user story you chose (listing 6.2) finally transforms into a draft of an executable specification. To do so, you'll finally write your scenarios (see figure 6.10).

> **TIP** A story becomes an executable specification when you're sure it's worth investing time and effort in it.

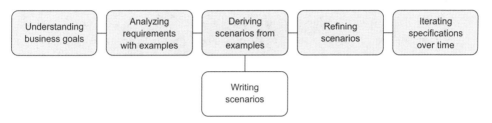

Figure 6.10 Examples serve as a basis for all scenarios to come. Over time, the team should optimize scenarios for readability and remove confusing, redundant examples.

From the examples you collected, you derive a list of acceptance criteria for the user story:

- Every new business should provide a name and a location to display on the map.
- Every business should provide business hours for each day of the week.

Let's take the relevant examples of pubs, restaurants, and bistros from the previous section to write the first draft of an executable specification.

Listing 6.3 [OK] First draft of an executable specification

```
Feature: New businesses

  Scenario Outline: Businesses should provide required data

    Given a restaurant <business> on <location>
    When <business> signs up to Mapper
    Then it should be added to the platform
    And its name should appear on the map at <location>

    Examples:
        | business      | location                       |
        | Deep Lemon    | 6750 South Street, Reno        |
        | Matt's        | 9593 Riverside Drive, St. Louis |
        | Back to Black | 8114 2nd Street, Stockton      |
        | Green Pencil  | 8583 Williams Street, Glendale |
        | Le Chef       | 3318 Summit Avenue, Tampa      |
        | Paris         | 2105 Briarwood Court, Fresno   |
        | Christie's    | 714 Beechwood Drive, Boston    |
        | The Monument  | 77 Chapel Street, Pittsburgh   |
        | Anchor        | 110 Cambridge Road, Chicago    |
```

Straightforward, isn't it? You take the first acceptance criterion from your list, rework it to fit the Given-When-Then template, and use a scenario outline to include all the relevant examples you collected during the previous phase of your analysis.

The increased precision level allows your team to spot a possible edge case: what if a restaurant has two establishments in two different locations in the same city? There might be one Deep Lemon in Reno at 6750 South Street and a second one at 289 Laurel Drive, for example.

Should you allow that in your application? And if the answer is yes, should you make that process easier? In the end, you decide there's nothing wrong with accepting multiple locations, but you don't have time to optimize the process. Users will have to make do with what they have. To finalize the decision, you add another example to the outline.

> **Listing 6.4   [BETTER] Second draft of the executable specification**

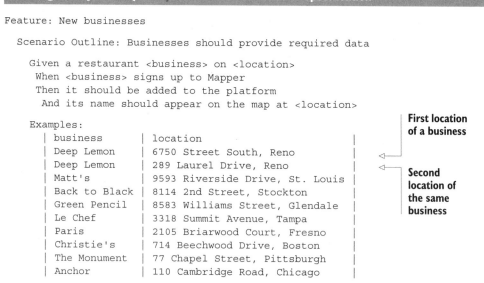

```
Feature: New businesses

    Scenario Outline: Businesses should provide required data

        Given a restaurant <business> on <location>
        When <business> signs up to Mapper
        Then it should be added to the platform
        And its name should appear on the map at <location>

        Examples:
            | business      | location                        |
            | Deep Lemon    | 6750 Street South, Reno         |
            | Deep Lemon    | 289 Laurel Drive, Reno          |
            | Matt's        | 9593 Riverside Drive, St. Louis |
            | Back to Black | 8114 2nd Street, Stockton       |
            | Green Pencil  | 8583 Williams Street, Glendale  |
            | Le Chef       | 3318 Summit Avenue, Tampa       |
            | Paris         | 2105 Briarwood Court, Fresno    |
            | Christie's    | 714 Beechwood Drive, Boston     |
            | The Monument  | 77 Chapel Street, Pittsburgh    |
            | Anchor        | 110 Cambridge Road, Chicago     |
```

First location of a business

Second location of the same business

This is a fine example of a typical SBE tendency: tests guiding implementation. Only when you get to the precision level of test cases can you see that you overlooked an important element of the design. That's because tests and requirements are essentially connected. In 1968, Alan Perlis wrote that "a simulation which matches the requirements contains the control which organizes the design of the system."[2] A test predefines "ideal" outputs and inputs up front; the application code must then be designed so that the *real* inputs and outputs match the ideal ones defined by the test. Otherwise, the test will fail.

---

[2]   *Software Engineering: Report on a conference sponsored by the NATO SCIENCE COMMITTEE, Garmisch, Germany, 7th to 11th October 1968*, eds. Peter Naur and Brian Randell (Scientific Affairs Division, NATO, 1969), http://mng.bz/jn3d.

Figure 6.11 Collecting, analyzing, and refining examples is a continuous, never-ending process that exists within a powerful feedback loop.

TIP Here's a rule of thumb: good code designs usually don't need complex tests. If your tests are too complicated, you may be missing an important domain concept or tackling a known concept the wrong way.

For the second time in this chapter, the feedback mechanisms of the SBE process have led you to discover something you missed in your initial analysis. You should expect to make such discoveries multiple times during any feature's development. You'll probably go back and forth multiple times during development or even after implementation (as represented in figure 6.11). SBE practitioners should adopt the mindset that there's no such thing as a single moment when a feature is finished—features only get *released*. These are two different things.

You can begin analyzing requirements either by looking for examples, as you did in Mapper's case, or by perfecting a list of acceptance criteria. Either way, feedback lets you spot inconsistencies more quickly and easily. You shouldn't expect to get everything right the first time; that's typical.

6.5 *Refining scenarios*

With a scenario now in place, your team can implement it. Implementing the behaviors described by a scenario is the stage with the highest possible precision before a feature is released to customers who validate its business value in the real world. This section will show you what happens when a raw scenario first meets working code, and how that meeting increases precision to a release-ready level.

In chapters 1 and 2, you saw that after you write the first draft of a new executable specification, you often need to *refine scenarios* and *choose key examples* to improve the readability of your executable specification (see figure 6.12). That happens when teams refine their specifications to merge similar examples, reject the ones that introduce noise, and choose the most meaningful or descriptive ones.

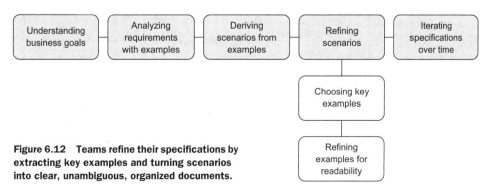

Figure 6.12 Teams refine their specifications by extracting key examples and turning scenarios into clear, unambiguous, organized documents.

Returning to Mapper, after your team begins to implement the behaviors from the scenario, they notice that the examples used in the previous section don't test any edge cases other than a business with two locations. The examples don't specify what happens when any attribute of a business is missing. All the examples in the outline end with the business successfully joining Mapper's platform. Why aren't there any counterexamples?

Let's think for a moment and look for a few counterexamples that would go astray from the happy path:

- The applicant might forget to fill out the input field with the business name on the registration form.
- The applicant might forget to mark the location on the map.
- The applicant might make both of the previous mistakes.
- The applicant might provide a location, but it might be inaccurate; for example, the user might mark the middle of a river as a location for their business.

Having defined new examples, you should now do two things. First, you need to remove redundant examples that don't bring any value to the specification. Second, add new examples and counterexamples that express the failure scenarios. You can also split the examples into multiple tables to improve readability.

Listing 6.5   [BEST] Executable specification with refined key examples

```
Feature: New businesses

  Scenario Outline: Businesses should provide required data

    Given a restaurant <business> on <location>
    When <business> signs up to Mapper
    Then it <should?> be added to the platform
    And its name <should?> appear on the map at <location>

    Examples: Business name and location should be required
      | business         | location | should?   |
      | UNNAMED BUSINESS | NOWHERE  | shouldn't |

    Examples: Allow only businesses with correct names
      | business         | location                 | should?   |
      | Back to Black    | 8114 2nd Street, Stockton | should    |
      | UNNAMED BUSINESS | 8114 2nd Street, Stockton | shouldn't |

    Examples: Allow businesses with two or more establishments
      | business    | location                | should? |
      | Deep Lemon  | 6750 Street South, Reno | should  |
      | Deep Lemon  | 289 Laurel Drive, Reno  | should  |

    Examples: Allow only suitable locations
      | business | location                     | should?   |
      | Anchor   | 110 Cambridge Road, Chicago  | should    |
      | Anchor   | Chicago River, Chicago       | shouldn't |
      | Anchor   | NOWHERE                      | shouldn't |
```

Annotations:
- **Failure scenario with no name or location** → points to `| UNNAMED BUSINESS | NOWHERE | shouldn't |`
- **Failure scenario with no name** → points to `| UNNAMED BUSINESS | 8114 2nd Street, Stockton | shouldn't |`
- **Failure scenario with no location** → points to `| Anchor | NOWHERE | shouldn't |`
- **Failure scenario with an inaccurate location** → points to `| Anchor | Chicago River, Chicago | shouldn't |`

TIP   You may have noticed that in listing 6.5, UNNAMED BUSINESS and NOWHERE are uppercase. To be honest, this isn't a Gherkin convention; but the capital letters make these examples stand out, which improves readability.

The reworked outline is much easier to read and has more-comprehensive scenarios. You need only to glance at it to recognize what it tests and why. It clearly distinguishes between success examples and failure examples. To my eye, the precision level of this scenario looks like it's release ready. Congratulations!

6.6   *Iterating specifications over time*

You don't stop working on an executable specification after you write it (see figure 6.13). It's a continuous process. The team should validate the specification suite frequently to spot any integration errors as soon as possible, keeping the suite consistent at all times. This section will show you how.

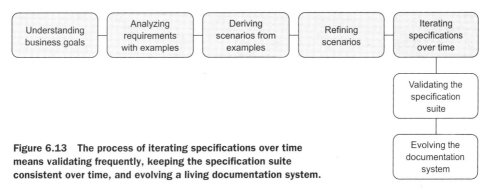

Figure 6.13   The process of iterating specifications over time means validating frequently, keeping the specification suite consistent over time, and evolving a living documentation system.

When the specifications are consistent and up to date, they evolve into a living documentation system that acts as a single source of truth about the system's behaviors. Everybody on the team can use the system freely to solve their disagreements. We'll enlarge on that, too.

6.6.1   *Validating the specification suite*

In the heat of the battle, while revising your scenario outline, you almost forgot that the user story you wrote at the beginning of this chapter specified two acceptance criteria:

- Every new business should provide a name and a location to display on the map.
- Every business should provide specific business hours for each day of the week.

So far, you've only taken care of the first criterion. Let's use what you've learned to write the second scenario.

Listing 6.6 Adding another scenario to the specification

```
Feature: New businesses

  Scenario Outline: Businesses should provide required data

    [...]

  Scenario Outline: Businesses should be able to set their hours

    Given a restaurant <business> on <location>
    When it schedules its hours to be <times> every day
    Then the hours should appear on the map at <location>

    Examples: Restaurants
      | business    | location               | times     |
      | Deep Lemon  | 6750 Street South, Reno | 7 AM-8 PM |

    Examples: Bistros
      | business    | location                | times     |
      | Le Chef     | 3318 Summit Avenue, Tampa | 9 AM-9 PM |

    Examples: Pubs
      | business    | location               | times     |
      | Anchor      | 77 Chapel Road, Chicago | 3 PM-3 AM |
```

After you agree on the shape of the scenario, the team proceeds to automate it. They write new application code and generate the step definitions required to test the code. Having done that, they run the test-execution engine to make sure the modified system works as they expect it to.

And that's when they find out that implementing the behavior from the new scenario breaks another scenario in the specification suite.

Listing 6.7 Broken scenario

```
Feature: Show sightseeing objects on the map

  Scenario: Tourists should be able to see sightseeing objects

    Given a sightseeing object:
      | name              | location   |
      | Memorial Monument | Oak Street |
    When Janet, who is a tourist, looks at Oak Street
    Then she should see Memorial Monument on the map
```

It turns out that the new attributes of business hours don't work well with other types of entities that Mapper features on its maps, such as sightseeing objects. Not all sightseeing objects—such as monuments—have opening and closing times.

Your team forgot about that, and the validations they added prevented sightseeing objects from being created in the database. To fix that, you decide to make the validations optional instead of required. As soon as you do, the system starts working again, and the feature is ready to be deployed to production.

Before we move on, let's dissect what happened. The specification suite has to be consistent. When the team implements the behaviors from a new executable specification, they should execute the existing specifications in order to check whether they still work. The team must test the existing specifications every time changes are introduced to the system.

If a scenarios breaks after you introduce a new feature, you can take only two actions:

- Update the broken scenario so it complies with the changes.
- Change the new feature so it won't break the scenario.

As you can see, whereas new scenarios influence old scenarios, the old ones can also affect new features (see figure 6.14). It's another feedback loop within the process of SBE. I've already talked about it in chapter 1, which listed *validating frequently* as one of SBE's key practices.

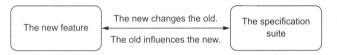

Figure 6.14   The feedback loop between new features and the existing specification suite

When you validate frequently, you once again operate in the product-critique quadrant of the testing matrix. As soon as you automate the critiques, the test-execution engine will check the application regularly against new examples, protecting the quality of your product (see figure 6.15). Modern development practices take advantage of that in various ways. For example, teams that employ continuous integration (CI) practices will integrate as often as possible, leading to multiple integrations per day. Each integration will then be verified by an automated build that can detect errors almost instantly. Some teams trust their specification suites so much that they let every change be automatically deployed to production if the tests pass—a practice known as *continuous deployment*.

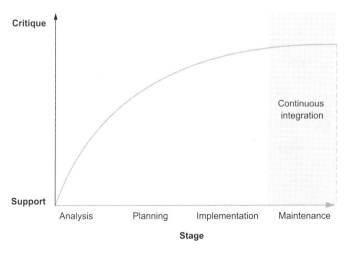

Figure 6.15   After release, examples become automated tests that critique the finished product, if they're validated frequently.

Most often, integration tests are followed by *user acceptance testing* (UAT). A popular argument for performing UAT manually is that getting your hands on the product activates a different type of perception and judgment than thinking about automation. Manipulation is different than cogitation. For example, when you test-drive a car, you notice things you wouldn't spot when poring over its specs, like the seats being too stiff or the leather not looking right.

> **DEFINITION** *User acceptance testing (UAT)*—The last phase of the software-testing process. During UAT, actual end users test the product to make sure it can handle the tasks required by the specifications.

But when business stakeholders trust in their executable specifications, they can replace simple, manual, boring checks with automated tests from the specification suite, streamlining the UAT process. (I'm not saying they should remove manual tests altogether; they can just have fewer trivial ones.) Such trust is an ultimate sign that you're doing SBE well and that the stakeholders understand why examples and scenarios are important.

6.6.2 *Evolving the documentation system*

After you deploy the feature to production, it starts living a life of its own. A bug may occur from time to time; you fix it, write a regression test, and move on. As with any other feature, when development ends, maintenance begins. This section covers what happens with an executable specification at the end of its life cycle, when it reaches the highest precision level.

The Mapper features turn out to be a success. Gastronomy businesses sign up like crazy. You hope that implementing the user stories about other types of businesses will happen in the future. For now, management is happy. You're proud of your team, too. The code is good; the specification looks fine.

At least, you think so, until your team comes back to the specification two months later. That's when Martha, a fresh hire on your team, takes on a new user story connected to small businesses. To implement it, she needs to understand the feature better, so she reads the specification the team created a few months ago. She still has some questions, though, so she talks to you:

"Hey," she says. *"What are popular hours?"*

"No idea. Why?"

"Here's a user story you created two months ago, before I joined the team. It only mentions that you might also want to consider letting gastronomy businesses specify popular hours."

"OK ... that does ring a bell. But I'm not sure ..."

"If it helps, I read the specification, and it already has a scenario that allows businesses to schedule some kind of hours. Maybe somebody already implemented that user story but forgot to mark it as done."

"Let's ask Gus. I think he was the last one to work with this feature. Hey, Gus, have you already implemented something called popular hours?"

"Didn't we do that two months ago? Or wait, maybe it was business hours, not popular hours. Let me check the code …"

You get the gist.

Two months ago, you made a frequent development mistake: mid battle, you thought the specifications you wrote were perfectly clear, because you still had all the domain concepts in your short-term memory. After the dust settled, you realized that your feeling of clarity was illusionary. Martha bravely brought a fresh perspective that helped you realize that issue. You cringe at the thought of how many other decisions were made without clear distinctions between domain concepts like the one she noticed.

You decide to rewrite the scenario in question and include some clarifying definitions.

Listing 6.8   [BETTER] Executable specification with clarifications

```
Feature: New businesses

  Scenario Outline: Businesses should provide required data          Added
                                                                  definition
    [...]                                                        for business
                                                                      hours
  Scenario Outline: Businesses should be able to set relevant hours

    BUSINESS HOURS define when a business opens and closes.         <──

    Businesses provide POPULAR HOURS to help their customers     Separate
    decide when it's the best time to come in.                   definition for
                                                                 popular hours
    Given a restaurant <business> on <location>                  that explains
    When it schedules <hours> to be <times>                      the difference
    Then the <hours> should appear on the map at <location>

    Examples: Restaurants
        | business    | location               | hours          | times     |
  ──> | Deep Lemon  | 6750 Street South, Reno | business hours | 7 AM-8 PM |
        | Deep Lemon  | 6750 Street South, Reno | popular hours  | 3 PM-5 PM |  <─┐

    Examples: Bistros
        | business    | location               | hours          | times     |
        | Le Chef     | 3318 Summit Avenue, Tampa | business hours | 9 AM-9 PM |
  ──> | Le Chef     | 3318 Summit Avenue, Tampa | popular hours  | 8 PM-9 PM |  <─┤

    Examples: Pubs
        | business    | location               | hours          | times     |
        | Anchor      | 77 Chapel Road, Chicago | business hours | 3 PM-3 AM |
  └─> | Anchor      | 77 Chapel Road, Chicago | popular hours  | 9 PM-2 AM |  <─┘
```

Examples of business hours (annotation pointing to "business hours" rows)

Examples of popular hours (annotation pointing to "popular hours" rows)

Building and evolving a documentation system is the last step in the life cycle of any executable specification. Your work on a specification is rarely finished after you deploy the new feature to production. You'll likely come back to rewrite the steps, or change the structure of the scenarios, or, as in the case we just discussed, add clarifications to the specification layer. Chapter 7 goes into depth on these topics.

Gall's Law

Why do I keep talking about gradual evolution of requirements and domain concepts instead of trying to find the perfect system design from scratch? Gall's Law is the reason.

Gall's Law is a rule of thumb for systems design that comes from John Gall's book *Systemantics: How Systems Really Work and How They Fail* (General Systemantics Press, 2002):

> *A complex system that works is invariably found to have evolved from a simple system that worked. A complex system designed from scratch never works and can't be patched up to make it work. You have to start over with a working simple system.*
>
> —Gall's law

I'm a strong believer in the power of this law. That's why I keep repeating that you should look for simple things that work, in terms of both the requirements and the implementation, and then build on them. Moreover, SBE's feedback loops will help you spot systems that work, and thus never break, and systems that don't work, and thus break constantly.

As the application changes and you discover new requirements, you may realize that some of the scenarios you thought were distinct are parts of a bigger whole and should be combined in a single specification. Sometimes the scenarios you thought were connected will branch out into their own requirements. As the business evolves, your specification suite should evolve with it. Changes in a specification suite often directly reflect the changes in a delivery team's understanding of the business domain. It's a fascinating subject that we'll explore deeply in chapters 8–11.

Before we finish this chapter, figure 6.16 takes another look at the full life cycle of any executable specification. The next chapter focuses on the last box in this life cycle. As you may remember from chapter 1, fully fledged executable specifications are also called *living documentation*. Living documentation is always up to date because it changes alongside the system, thanks to the link between the documentation and automated tests. When an executable specification evolves into living documentation, its *active* life cycle ends. That doesn't mean the specification won't change anymore, of course, but it'll be more *passive* from now on. Usually, it'll be changed and influenced by new specifications that enter the specification suite as the product matures. In chapter 7, which talks about the details of building a living documentation system, I discuss techniques that help you manage and maintain specifications in the passive stage of their life cycle (see figure 6.16).

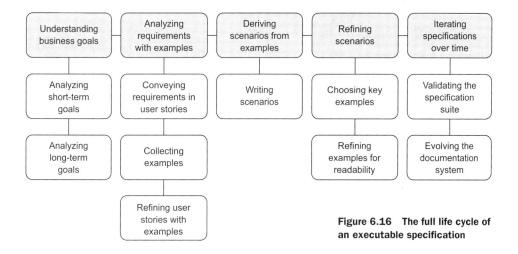

Figure 6.16   The full life cycle of an executable specification

6.7   *Summary*

- An executable specification evolves throughout a project's life cycle.
- As the project progresses, executable specifications become more precise. The later the life cycle's phase, the greater the need for detail.
- Exploring examples is a process of discovery: you start with little certainty about the examples' completeness, and as you contest them and improve the list, you become more certain that your understanding is sound.
- Key examples should be chosen to illustrate the acceptance criteria clearly and completely. As acceptance criteria change, the list of key examples evolves.
- Some examples support the team in their attempts to write new code, and some examples critique the product, aiming to improve its quality.
- New features add new specification documents to the specification suite, but the existing specification suite can also cause changes in new features. The new influences the old, but the old can also change the new.

Living documentation

7

This chapter covers

- Understanding living documentation
- Helping new team members with living documentation
- Defining domain concepts consistently
- Documenting product changes and troublesome areas

Everybody who's ever worked with software has probably dealt with documentation at some point. Documentation can be provided on paper or online, or on digital or analog media, such as audiotape or CDs. SBE introduces a different type of documentation.

> **DEFINITION** *Living documentation*—Documentation that changes along with the system it describes. Thanks to frequently validated acceptance tests, the living documentation system is aware of changes you make to the system; if the changes yield different results than the results expected by the living documentation system, running acceptance tests will yield an error.

SBE is actually a *system* of documentation. What I mean is that living documentation is a suite of acceptance tests written in a domain-specific language like Gherkin and

148

readable by nontechnical team members. Through acceptance tests, automated scenarios are tied to application code. This means scenarios that describe functional and behavioral requirements can be used to create a living documentation system that evolves every time the code changes.

Moreover, writing documentation isn't a separate activity or a standalone phase. The scenarios *are* the documentation. In chapter 6, you saw that every executable specification evolves during development, increasing its precision level throughout its life cycle. You start with high-level requirements that vaguely describe business goals, and you end up with a set of automated acceptance tests that are low-level and precise because they're actual working code. At the high-fidelity end of that spectrum, when the first drafts of scenarios are finished and approved, executable specifications become living documentation. Having already explored how to write scenarios in chapters 2 and 3 and how to write scenario outlines in chapters 4 and 5, it's high time we talk about creating high-precision living documentation from specification drafts.

Even though I didn't dwell on it, you used some of the techniques for building a living documentation system in previous chapters to do the following:

- Explain difficult domain concepts
- Highlight differences between dangerously similar domain concepts
- Document troublesome areas of implementation
- Give more context about business goals

Thanks to these activities, living documentation can be of great value to software companies:

- It allows team leads to get new hires up to speed much more quickly, because they can take advantage of documentation that is brief, concise, customer oriented, and always up to date.
- When teams validate frequently and make the specification suite part of a continuous integration system, they can easily trace an integration error back to its test and, beyond, to a scenario linked to the broken part of the application. Such scenarios can be used as documentation to repair the bug more quickly.

I talked about continuous integration in section 1.6.2: it's a software development practice where members of a team integrate their work frequently, and each integration is verified by an automated build to detect integration errors quickly. And throughout chapters 5 and 6, we investigated how valuable good, meaningful tests in scenario outlines can be in terms of product quality.

This chapter talks in depth about each of the activities needed to create great documentation that evolves along with the system. By the end of the chapter, you'll know what a minimally qualified reader is and why writing for a specific reader in your organization matters. A reader-oriented mindset will teach you to better document changes in the specification suite. You'll practice creating definitions for new concepts in the ubiquitous language of your projects. In the long term, this will help you manage the that language in a growing specification suite.

7.1   *Living documentation in action*

First, we'll look at living documentation from a practical perspective. Throughout this chapter, you'll be using as an example an application called HouseKeeper. House-Keeper is free property-management software for independent tenants and landlords. Let's suppose that thousands of property managers save time and money every month with HouseKeeper, whether they're managing one unit or hundreds. HouseKeeper handles online rent payment, tenant screening, and credit and background checks. This example will show you documentation practices in action in a domain that's both familiar and difficult.

One day, a coworker named Peter comes to you because he saw in the version control system that you were the last person who contributed to the specification document he's having trouble with. Peter is new to the team. He's also from Poland, where renting works much differently than in the United States; there are fewer legal obligations in Poland, and the market is less saturated, because most people buy their own apartments and the only renters are college students. Understandably, Peter is having a rough time with the transition, but he's trying his best to learn fast.

Peter mentions that he has some questions about the documentation—mainly the lack of it. You're surprised. Before you can get to the bottom of the problem, you read the scenario in question. It's about qualifying and scoring the best candidates when a property is vacant and no lease has yet been signed.

> **Listing 7.1   [BAD] Executable specification with no documentation**

```
Feature: Qualifying tenant leads

  Scenario Outline: Screening candidates

    Given a lead:
      | name            | credit used | total debt |
      | Simona Jenkins  | <used>      | <debt>     |
      And that the lead waits in the queue to the tenants pipeline
    When the candidate has a <score>
    Then we should <result> the lead

    Examples:
      | used | debt      | score               | result |
      | 40%  | $202,704  | credit score of 499 | reject |
      | 41%  | $202,704  | credit score of 500 | accept |
```

You then ask Peter what's wrong.

"I'm just confused," he says. "There's a lot of terminology that isn't explained anywhere. For example, what's a tenants pipeline?"

"It's a list of verified tenants that landlords get … but I see your point. Are there any other issues you've noticed?"

"Yes. Are screening and qualifying leads the same? And, while we're at it, are tenant leads and candidates the same? Or is a candidate some special kind of a lead? Or maybe it's the other way around."

"You're right, that might be confusing. They're actually the same. I suppose I didn't want to use the same expression so often."

"Yeah. By the way, is the credit score rating the entire screening process? If so, why can't it be called a credit report? Why invent an additional name?"

"Actually, the credit score is just one part of the screening process, which can involve other steps as well. We just don't support them right now."

"Oh, I see. That might not be obvious for some people, like me. And that might become a larger issue in the future, because I noticed that we're hiring more engineers from all over the world. And renting doesn't work the same everywhere!"

As you can see, there are several troublesome areas when it comes to the documentation aspect of your scenario outline:

- You need to make the naming consistent, making sure the same concepts are always referred to by the same name. Doing so should remove the trouble with *candidates* and *leads*, as well as *screening* and *qualifying*.
- When you first wrote the text, you had some assumptions about your team members' prerequisite knowledge, regardless of their experience. The *tenants pipeline* is an example. And even though screening is the main criterion for landlords considering tenant leads, it's not explained anywhere. That has to change.
- Some domain concepts, like screening and credit scores, may be new to some team members and difficult for them to understand. That means you didn't take into account the idiosyncrasies of your team when you wrote the scenario. It's out of touch.

What could you do to change that? Here are some ideas.

Listing 7.2 [GOOD] Documented specification with fixed issues

"Qualifying" is now called "screening" everywhere the concept is mentioned.

Definition of "screening" supplied in the specification brief

Definition of "tenant lead" supplied in the specification brief

```
Feature: Screening tenant leads

    SCREENING is the process of evaluating a tenant lead before
    signing a lease in order to choose the best candidate.

    TENANT LEAD is a potential tenant who applied to live in
    an apartment managed by our rental platform.

    Please note that the manual screening process is more complex
    than the one we currently support in our product. For example,
    in the future we might want to support checking criminal or
    eviction history, or even terrorist watchlist search.

    Scenario Outline: Screening tenant leads based on credit score
```

Explanation of the screening process's business context and your team's progress on implementing it

Candidates are now consistently called tenant leads.

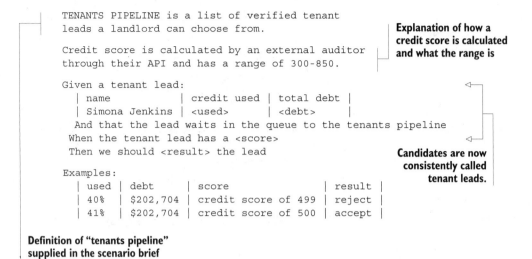

```
TENANTS PIPELINE is a list of verified tenant
leads a landlord can choose from.

Credit score is calculated by an external auditor
through their API and has a range of 300-850.

Given a tenant lead:
  | name           | credit used | total debt |
  | Simona Jenkins | <used>      | <debt>     |
  And that the lead waits in the queue to the tenants pipeline
When the tenant lead has a <score>
Then we should <result> the lead

Examples:
  | used | debt      | score                | result |
  | 40%  | $202,704  | credit score of 499  | reject |
  | 41%  | $202,704  | credit score of 500  | accept |
```

Explanation of how a credit score is calculated and what the range is

Candidates are now consistently called tenant leads.

Definition of "tenants pipeline" supplied in the scenario brief

Let's sum up the changes:

- You added a few short definitions that explain the most important domain concepts. This should ensure that every team member who reads the scenario, regardless of their experience, has more or less the same knowledge when they start working with the specification.
- You cleared up the naming issues so there's no way to confuse a domain concept with any other domain concept.
- You added notes about screening and the credit score that explain the business context of the feature. You let the reader know that you're at the beginning of a journey to create a great screening process; even at this early stage, you need help from other companies who do credit reports and background checks, because those aren't your company's area of expertise.

Note that although all of these changes could have been made earlier in the life cycle of the executable specification—when it was first written, for example—there's nothing wrong with the fact that the changes are only happening now, after Peter pointed them out. That's why we talk about a living documentation *system*. Such a system employs feedback loops to correct itself over time. These feedback loops can be manual—as in Peter's case, when he had to read the specification before tackling a bug error connected with that area of your product. But feedback loops can also be automated. For example, if a particularly nasty bug breaks your continuous integration system periodically, you can progressively add more regression examples to ensure that the system doesn't break again. That, too, is documentation.

You saw how such automated living documentation works in section 5.3.4, when we discussed boomerangs. Executable specifications can eventually stop boomerangs—functionalities that break every now and then—if you automate each new edge case as a regression example.

In chapter 6, you saw automated living documentation in action when we discussed iterating executable specifications over time. Section 6.1 showed that when a delivery team implements a new executable specification, they should also execute existing specifications in order to check whether they still work after changes are introduced to the system. Only in this way can the team verify that the specification suite is still consistent—and that the living documentation is up to date.

Because previous chapters covered many areas related to automation, I focus here on writing high-precision documentation instead of having up-to-date tests. In SBE, iterations are the common thread between automated documentation and manual documentation. Either way, manual or automated, the living documentation system works iteratively—so you can let go of the expectation that you should nail things down on the first try every time.

> **NOTE** When I say *living documentation* in the context of this book, I mean that the documentation changes along with the product; tests help to achieve this result, but they aren't the only component. Be aware that other authors may mean *regression tests*, discussed in chapters 6.

7.2 Writing documentation

The example in the previous section showed some documentation challenges and practical solutions to deal with them. Let's now talk in depth about each of these methods. You'll see how to use them effectively and what their major use cases are.

From a 50,000-foot view, Gherkin scenarios are high level and talk about the business instead of technology specifics; as a result, business stakeholders will read and contribute to them, which helps bridge the communication gap between delivery teams and the business. Because scenarios explain the most important user flows as well as the inputs and outputs of features, high-level documentation for a business can do two other important jobs:

- Document the business domain for people who are unfamiliar with it
- Document the delivery team's decision-making process for future reference

Without business domain documentation, scenarios will be difficult for anyone unfamiliar with the product to understand. For example, let's say I'm a product manager and you're a new hire on the team. I'm onboarding you to the product. I could start by telling you about the steps needed to make the application generate a tenants pipeline—you need to click here, write that, go there—but that doesn't guarantee you'll know what the pipeline is. Sometimes seeing doesn't equal understanding.

Living documentation can include decision making because executable specifications have a long life cycle that covers every phase of development. Scenarios can reflect decisions made in analysis, design, or development. The life cycle even expands beyond implementation. When acceptance tests that are part of the continuous integration process break, the specification suite prohibits integration or deployment, thus avoiding errors in production. Teams can use that to spot and document troublesome areas that break often. If any errors still slip through, they can be documented as regression tests later, after they're fixed. Why should you do that? Because documenting the decision-making process will let you and your peers recreate your thought process in the future and make sure future decisions are consistent with past ones.

Next, let's explore documenting domain concepts and documenting decisions.

7.3 *Defining important domain concepts*

The two most popular and practical uses of any documentation are these:

- Learning about things you don't know
- Recalling details you learned in the past but have forgotten

For example, if you hear somebody mention a domain concept called a *price index*, and you have no idea what that means, you can check the documentation. And if you work on that feature again in a few months, you'll check the docs again to refresh your memory. Defining new concepts and making the definitions easy to find under quickly searchable names is one of the most important jobs of any documentation.

7.3.1 *Writing lexical definitions*

Chapter 1 talked about the *ubiquitous language*: a common language for developers, business stakeholders, and end users. To illustrate the concept of such a language and the cost of mental translations, I talked about a public transport mobile app that suggested Edison *Street* to the user as a final destination, because it couldn't fetch Edison *Business Center*—the user's intended destination—from the database. The mistake happened because the user and the developers associated different domain concepts with the term *destination*. The delivery team thought of bus stops; but the user wanted to get to a specific place regardless of whether it was a bus stop, a street, or a building.

In that case, a wrong definition led to wrong code. To avoid similar mistakes, the team could add a refined definition to the executable scenario and use it as documentation for future reference.

In the example of the real estate application at the beginning of this chapter, you did a similar thing to clarify the domain concepts of *screening*, *tenant leads*, and a *tenants pipeline*. Here's a definition within a scenario outline:

```
Scenario Outline: Screening leads based on credit score

   TENANTS PIPELINE is a list of verified tenant
   leads a landlord can choose from.
```

You used the scenario brief to write a short note that explains what the pipeline is. (You also used the specification brief for the same reason with a second definition.) Truth be told, this isn't the most advanced definition in the history of definitions—it's a simple clarification that gives the reader more context. When it comes to the art of definitions, Gherkin favors a utilitarian approach: use anything that works for your team, and refine it in case of any misunderstandings.

> **TIP** Write lexical definitions in specification and scenario briefs when you want to explain a domain concept in your own words. Use specification briefs for *global definitions* that are important to the entire specification. Use scenario briefs for *local definitions* that are relevant to specific scenarios only.

Because specification and scenario briefs are free-flowing text sections in Gherkin's syntax, there's no specific way to format definitions. Many Gherkin practitioners use systems like Markdown, with its headings and text formatting. Personally, I favor common text files, using uppercase to define new domain concepts. The choice is almost entirely aesthetic, but I also like that it's the simplest possible way to make definitions stand out—you don't have to know a formatting system to see that a brief includes something important.

Exercise 1

Create a short definition that explains what a scenario outline is.

Using connotative definitions

Definitions used in this section are called *connotative definitions*. A connotative definition specifies the necessary and sufficient conditions for a thing to be a member of a specific set.

Here are two examples of connotative definitions:

- Triangle: a plane figure that has three straight bounding sides
- Quadrilateral: a plane figure that has four straight bounding sides

As you can see, *connotative meaning* relates to the associations, overtones, and feel of a concept, rather than what it refers to explicitly—which is what denotative definitions do.

In terms of logic, connotative definitions create a decision tree of questions whose answers can be used to state whether an objects fits the definition. For example, in the case of the definition of a triangle, you can ask two questions that let you define whether any object is a triangle. The first question is whether the object is a plane figure. If it isn't, it can't be a triangle. If the object is a plane figure, you need to ask the second question: whether the object has three straight bounding sides. If it does, it can't be a triangle—but only in terms of pure logic, of course. (And every person who has ever built software knows how difficult it can be to find perfect boundary conditions while also taking care of all the edge cases and exceptions.)

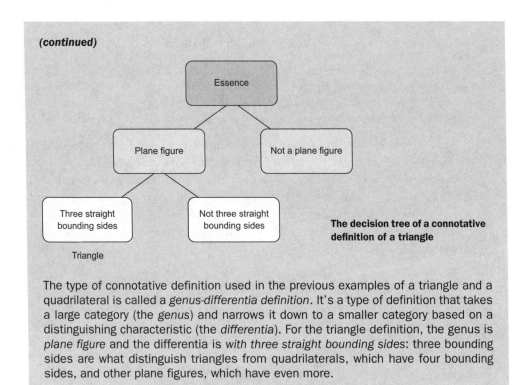

(continued)

Essence

Plane figure

Not a plane figure

Three straight
bounding sides

Not three straight
bounding sides

**The decision tree of a connotative
definition of a triangle**

Triangle

The type of connotative definition used in the previous examples of a triangle and a quadrilateral is called a *genus-differentia definition*. It's a type of definition that takes a large category (the *genus*) and narrows it down to a smaller category based on a distinguishing characteristic (the *differentia*). For the triangle definition, the genus is *plane figure* and the differentia is *with three straight bounding sides*: three bounding sides are what distinguish triangles from quadrilaterals, which have four bounding sides, and other plane figures, which have even more.

7.3.2   *Writing illustrative definitions*

Other ways to define a domain concept can also be considered. Sometimes, it may be too difficult to write a clear, concise definition that captures the essence of a problem. In that case, you can use the second popular way to create definitions: *illustrating*, listing examples that belong to the set you're trying to define. Gherkin works great with this method, because illustrating is Gherkin's core job. Even the term *specification by example* reflects that.

Let's look at how you can use a definition by example. Suppose the HouseKeeper app can work with multiple types of tenancies, by which I mean that some landlords want to rent an entire apartment, some want to rent a single bedroom, and others rent a single bed in a shared bedroom. You could try to define these tenancies under the umbrella term *housing unit,* and you could try to define *units* the same way you did with the previous definitions. For example, you might say that a unit is a place where the occupants live and eat separately from other residents in the structure or building. But is that the best approach? It sounds horribly abstract.

Instead, you can create an illustrative scenario that lists all the types of units. This way, the scenario itself becomes a definition of a domain concept. Here's how that might look.

Listing 7.3 Defining by example using a scenario outline

```
Feature: Units

  Scenario Outline: Defining types of units

    Given a <unit>
    When a new tenant moves in
    Then the tenant should have a lease on <rent>

    Examples:
      | unit           | rent                             |
      | apartment      | the entire flat                  |
      | room           | their room only                  |
      | shared bedroom | share the rent with a roommate   |
```

This scenario outline isn't a great test. It's simple, like the definitions you created before, and it doesn't test anything mission critical. But it does its job well: it illustrates by example a new domain concept better than you could define the concept with an abstract definition.

> **TIP** Use a definition by example when it's easier to imagine and understand the properties of a given set of items by listing the items within that set than by trying to capture the set's essence with a concise definition in the specification brief.

Exercise 2

Create a definition by example that will define the concept of Gherkin keywords like `Given`, `When`, and `Then`.

Using denotative definitions

Definitions by example can also be called *denotative definitions*. A denotative definition means a list that names the objects that belong to the set being defined; for example, "A plane figure is something like circles, triangles, squares, rectangles, and so on." Denotative definitions are practical; they state *what is, as is.*

They can be inefficient, though—for example, a complete list of plane figures will be long. A connotative definition creates a hierarchical decision tree of investigative questions, whereas a denotative definition creates a flat decision tree of all possibilities in a given set—a plane figure can be a circle *or* a triangle, *or* a square, *or* a rectangle, and so on. The listing is safer, because the only thing you have to do is to check whether an item belongs to the specified set, but it's also longer and more difficult to maintain in the long run. The list can grow or shrink; you have to keep it up to date.

7.3.3   *Using glossaries*

Although putting a definition in a scenario that required clarification in the first place comes naturally, it also has some downsides. The most obvious is that various scenarios can mention the same domain concepts multiple times throughout the specification suite. For example, the scenario outline used in this chapter's main example mentions a tenants pipeline, so you put the definition there; but if you had to deal with the complete specification suite of the HouseKeeper application, you'd probably have to mention the pipeline in many other feature files, too. Should you define each domain concept from scratch in every scenario that mentions it? If you did so, you'd quickly discover that having so many definitions is difficult to maintain over time.

One way to solve the dilemma is to define a domain concept only in the scenario in which it *originates*. In that case, you'll only have a definition for the tenants pipeline in the scenario outline about tenant leads from this chapter—because that's where the concept appears for the first time in the domain. This isn't the perfect solution, though, because it forces readers to search for the definition in other feature files. But formatting definitions in a consistent way may make searching the specification suite much easier.

Another approach is to quit writing definitions in the briefs and instead create a separate file in the specification suite that contains all the definitions. Such a file can function as the project's glossary. It doesn't even have to be written in Gherkin; if you write a simple .txt file (or perhaps a .md document formatted in Markdown), every test runner will ignore it during validation. I've used glossaries several times and been happy with the results, especially in projects with complex domains where concepts required frequent clarification. The downside of having a glossary is that maintaining it requires additional effort; a plain text file isn't connected to the automation system that keeps the living documentation up to date. Whenever you change a scenario in a way that redefines a corresponding domain concept, you must remember to update its definition in the glossary—which is more difficult because the definition is no longer in the same file and can't serve as an obvious reminder.

> **NOTE**   We'll come back to the concept of glossaries in chapter 11. The problem with glossaries is that they depend heavily on context. For example, a single term can have multiple meanings, depending on context. Such terms are called *polysemes*. In chapter 11, you'll learn how to deal with polysemes and create unequivocal glossaries.

7.3.4   *Naming important domain concepts*

Closely connected to the area of definitions is *naming*. Naming domain concepts appropriately is important because people involved in development may call the same concept by the same or different names, which can lead to potentially disastrous misunderstandings. You saw something like this in the HouseKeeper project, when Peter wasn't sure whether screening and the process of qualifying tenants were the same; he had similar doubts regarding candidates and tenant leads.

TIP A single domain concept should *always* be referred to by the same name. Even slight changes in naming can cause people to wonder whether they're dealing with an existing domain concept or a new one—is it the same, or similar but slightly different? There's no way to know without additional clarification.

Names have power. As the saying goes, "There are only two hard things in computer science: cache invalidation and naming things." A lot of the effort involved in writing Gherkin also concerns naming, because Gherkin is a domain-specific language that looks similar to plain, business-readable speech. And, as in any language, Gherkin writers must be careful when creating or giving names.

TIP Don't invent a new name if you're modeling a domain concept that exists in the real world outside of your application. Delivery teams should strive to understand and use the language of domain experts and not replace it with their own technical language. For example, don't call *screening* something like *validating candidates*, even if you think it's a better name for what's going on behind the scenes in the backend. (You can use your own names for domain concepts that the delivery team invented to help users do their jobs more quickly and easily.)

In Gherkin, naming has three crucial areas: naming actors, naming actions, and naming beginning and ending states.

NAMING THE ACTORS THAT APPEAR IN SCENARIOS

Let's say you have two scenarios that are unrelated to each other. The first scenario mentions Simona Jenkins, who is an admin in the application. The second scenario talks about Adam Johnstone but calls him a user with admin privileges. Are admins and users with admin privileges the same or different? The reader of the scenarios can only assume. And you know what they say about assuming …

NAMING THE ACTIONS IN SCENARIOS

I talked about naming actions with regard to screening and qualifying tenant leads. In the example domain, these two terms describe the same activity. They have different names, though, which made Peter think they might be two separate, although related, domain concepts.

NAMING THE STATES IN WHICH SCENARIOS BEGIN AND END

In the strictest sense of the word *state*, the subsection on naming actors inferred states: two actors were in the state of having an admin account. Similar inconsistencies happen so often that I wanted to talk about them separately. But there are also problems with naming other states.

For example, you should focus on maintaining consistency between initial states and expected states. The *initial state* is set in the Givens and talks about how things look at the beginning of a scenario. The *expected state* is the state at the end of the scenario, when the change described in the main action of the steps has taken place. Initial states and expected states are extremely important to the testing aspect of each executable specification. They tell testers and developers the intended consequences behind the scenario—the consequences they have to make sure take place. So naming the same state one way when it's an initial state and another way when it's an expected state can result in misunderstood features and rework.

> **TIP** You should favor simple names that are easy to search for. Doing so will come in handy when you have to find a single definition in a huge specification suite.

7.4 Documenting decisions using briefs

In section 7.2.1, you saw how specification and scenario briefs can contain useful information such as definitions. Specification and scenario briefs are versatile; they can contain any free-flowing information—and because the life cycle of an executable specification is long, starting in the analysis phase and expanding even beyond the implementation phase, you may want to include information in addition to definitions. For example, you could explain why you wrote a scenario the way you wrote it, or you could give some context about the scope of the feature. These decisions can also be documented in briefs, in several ways.

7.4.1 Using warning notes to highlight problematic areas

A *warning note* is meant to highlight troublesome areas of any given specification. A warning can indicate, for instance, difficult testing or implementation issues that shouldn't be missed if the delivery team decides to rework the feature.

Here's an example of a warning note. You may have seen it before, because it's a popular joke, but it always makes me smile:

```
Once you are done trying to 'optimize' this routine,
and have realized what a terrible mistake that was,
please increment the following counter as a warning
to the next guy:

total_hours_wasted_here = 42
```

This warning note was originally a code comment, which makes it ineligible for a business-level specification suite, but I mention it because you can have similar warnings for domain concepts and requirements. For instance, section 5.3.4 discussed boomerangs (functionalities that break repeatedly) as a good source of examples for scenarios. A warning note in the table brief would be perfect to explain the context behind any given boomerang and maybe give some tips to the maintainers about how to avoid repeating mistakes the team made in the past.

7.4.2 Using context notes to deepen the business context

Context notes explain the details of a feature's business context. You can use them to elaborate on the current scope of the functionality, talk about industry standards, make a quick analysis of similar features used by competitors, or describe the circumstances of taking on the feature in the first place.

The HouseKeeper example uses a context note when the specification brief explains the minimized scope of the screening feature, which, in this case, only covers credit score reports:

```
Please note that the manual screening process is more complex
than the one we currently support in our product. For example,
in the future we might want to support checking criminal or
eviction history, or even terrorist watchlist search.
```

7.4.3 *Using maintenance notes for internal purposes*

By *maintenance notes*, I mean notes that aren't related to the functionality itself. Instead, they help readers navigate the specification suite and maintain it in the long term if they choose to edit a scenario or add a new Gherkin file.

A maintenance note is a meta-note. It doesn't elaborate on any particular step in the scenario; it talks about the scenario itself. For example, it can explain where certain scenarios are located or why they were split between various Gherkin documents in a certain way:

```
Since screening is a huge functionality, this
specification file describes only the most important
high-level scenarios.
You can find more detailed scenarios in the rest
of the files inside the "screening" folder in the
specification suite.
```

7.5 *High-level overview of the documentation process*

So far, this chapter has taken you on a whirlwind tour of the most important documentation techniques an SBE practitioner may want to use. But when you're working day to day with real teams, knowing the techniques may not be enough. Knowing that you can document product changes using notes is different than knowing *when to* document these changes and *when not to* document them. Both of these questions can be equally important, and the answers can vary depending on the particular team. Some teams may need more documentation; some teams need less. Every team needs *different* documentation. In this section, I'll talk about how to understand your team's idiosyncrasies, choose the best strategy to achieve your documentation goals, and tweak the content of your scenarios so everyone on your team can benefit from the documentation.

From a high-level perspective, the main purpose of documentation is communication. Documentation can communicate relevant instructions and applications, dangerous bottlenecks, potential issues, and proven solutions.

In communications theory, a *message* is the smallest unit of communication. Every message is made out of three elements:

- Sender
- Receiver
- Content

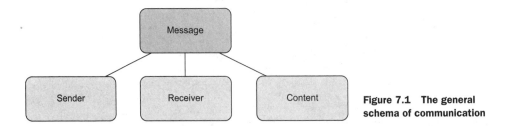

Figure 7.1   The general schema of communication

Figure 7.1 illustrates these three elements.

We can translate such a diagram to the domain of SBE as follows:

- A *sender* is anybody who writes documentation.
- A *receiver* is anybody who reads the documentation, intending to use it in work.
- *Content* means Gherkin scenarios that are refined and precise enough to be used not only as short-term specifications but also as long-term documentation.

I've already talked about the techniques you can use to create fine documentation content. You were able to do so thanks to a well-defined example. The example, though, is always just an example; it's a static snapshot of an imaginary application that's designed to be easy to digest in order to facilitate learning. The real world is messier.

While working with your documentation, you may feel the urge to jump straight to writing the content of your scenarios, as you did earlier. This isn't always a good idea. In this section, I'll argue that senders and receivers can greatly influence the final shape of living documentation, and—if these elements aren't given enough care—not always in a positive way. Even a crafted message can be met with a dismissive shrug if the message isn't tailored to the audience, highlighting passages they're most likely to agree with. On the other hand, sometimes a good message with a well-defined audience misses its mark because the sender wasn't the right person to drive its point home. Think of a politician who runs on a platform of getting rid of corrupt officials in a country where corruption is the number-one issue—but at the same time, that politician has a history of corruption scandals.

To create great documentation, you need three elements: people who can create a meaningful message, a well-defined audience, and engaging content that's full of helpful tips (see figure 7.2). I covered the topic of engaging content at the beginning of this chapter, when describing useful documentation techniques, and in the other chapters, when I talked about writing great scenarios. Now let's look at writers and readers.

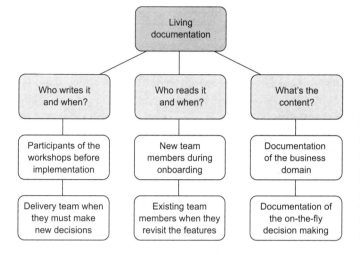

Figure 7.2   When working with a living documentation system, you must take into account three aspects: the people who create the documentation, the people who will read it, and the kind of content that should be created by the former to satisfy the latter.

7.6   *Who creates living documentation?*

Traditionally, professionals whose field of work is documentation are technical writers and corporate communicators. A technical writer is a professional writer who produces technical documentation. Technical writers can sometimes be domain experts who know the ins and outs of the business they're writing about. Most of the time, though, they collaborate with domain experts, engineers, and—if documentation is publicly available—end users to create full documentation.

Why are communication and collaboration important? Melvin Conway had a good answer. He was the computer programmer behind *Conway's Law,* which is an adage introduced in 1968: "Organizations that design systems are constrained to produce designs that are copies of the communication structures of these organizations." In other words, healthy communication produces healthy designs—and dysfunctional communication produces dysfunctional designs.

With Gherkin, documentation is a result of the entire team's work and is everybody's responsibility. Every engineer, designer, analyst, and tester can write Gherkin documentation, just as anyone can write or edit scenarios. It's not only encouraged; sometimes it's necessary. SBE is a process that by definition requires interdisciplinary collaboration. Most of the time, analysts and designers can provide the correct behavior—but developers and testers know the best way to write a test so that it's easy to automate later and fits into the rest of the living documentation system.

If analysts or designers worked alone, they would most likely write brittle tests. If developers and testers worked alone, they would probably optimize for automation too much and write scenarios that were difficult for nonprogrammers to understand. Balance is key.

7.6.1   Creating documentation through all-team specification workshops

Section 1.5.3 talked about how SBE encourages you to specify collaboratively by inviting stakeholders to specification workshops or holding smaller, more regular meetings within the delivery team. Because automated tests let specifications become documentation, the same workshops can be used to work on the most important aspects of future documentation: for example, clarifying difficult domain concepts.

Big, all-team workshops can help teams that have recently started working with SBE. They're intense domain- and scope-exploration exercises. Although most of the time in workshops is spent collecting relevant examples and building the short-term understanding required for the delivery team to kick off development, you can just as easily design exercises to facilitate long-term learning that later pays off in documentation.

For example, one of the most effective exercises I've ever seen has participants write in their own words a definition for a particular domain concept—while forbidding them to talk to each other. Comparing differences in definitions almost always yields interesting results and gets everyone on the same page.

Another interesting exercise is to delegate one person to be a note taker and later use the notes in creating documentation. Having a single delegate often frees the other participants to fully immerse themselves in the workshop, although having more people taking notes is also fine.

> **TIP** If you need more inspiration for conducting workshops, read *Gamestorming: A Playbook for Innovators, Rulebreakers, and Changemakers* by Dave Gray, Sunni Brown, and James Macanufo (O'Reilly Media, 2010). The book includes more than 80 games to help you break down barriers, communicate better, and generate new ideas, insights, and strategies. The authors have identified tools and techniques from some of the world's most innovative professionals, whose teams collaborate and make great things happen.

7.6.2   Creating documentation through Three Amigos meetings

Teams who've been doing SBE for a while don't need as much time or as many people in their workshops. They often opt to hold smaller meetings and include only the people who are required. For example, a team may choose to delegate a developer, a tester, and a designer or an analyst to represent each of the key roles required to ship the right software.

Such meetings are typically called *Three Amigos meetings* and are run when the domain still requires frequent clarification, but the most important stakeholders aren't available on demand. Such meetings yield most of the benefits of big, all-team workshops while being much leaner, faster, and easier to organize; but they require additional effort to get the delivery team and the business stakeholders on the same page if a stakeholder representative such as a product owner isn't present.

At the same time, the Three Amigos have to be careful not to force their ideas, perspectives, and experiences on others by remembering that they only represent the delivery team. For example, it can be easy for the Amigos to document one area well because they find it interesting, while leaving other areas unexplored because they understood them intuitively. It's a good idea not to have the same people be the Amigos repeatedly and instead to change the squad from time to time.

If you choose the right participants, workshops—both big and small—can be a great step to fight information asymmetry. Chapter 1 defined *information asymmetry* as a situation where one party has more or better information than another. Such asymmetry can sometimes drastically impair the delivery team's ability to make independent decisions in the face of a crisis. Good workshops naturally reduce information asymmetry among the participants; but the best workshops leave a long-term imprint, usually in written form, that can help people who weren't present during the meeting.

7.6.3 Creating documentation through individual people

Documentation can also be written by a single individual chosen by the team. That may be, for example, the most experienced developer on the team or the only analyst who has direct access to the client because of the way the organization is structured and managed. I played such a role in some of the projects I worked on; I worked on preparing detailed examples and documenting new domain concepts ahead of the team.

This isn't necessarily a bad practice, even though it may sound like it. After all, isn't SBE all about collaboration? It is—but having a single person work ahead of the team doesn't rule out collaboration. That person can speed up development by laying a foundation for future work while the rest of the team is still working on the current iteration.

A problem emerges when the person becomes a *single source of truth* about requirements by controlling the flow of information between business stakeholders and the delivery team. For example, they may want to present *their* perspective on a particular domain concept as the only way to understand it correctly. In such a case, the single source of truth can easily become a single source of failure. Both the person who's working ahead and the delivery team must be aware of that.

> **NOTE** Keeping the rest of the team in the loop and reviewing the new domain concepts shortly after the initial analysis is done are good steps toward eliminating the possibility of a single point of failure, but reducing bottlenecks is more of a management topic and beyond the scope of this book. If you're interested, you can read *Elastic Leadership: Growing Self-Organizing Teams* by Roy Osherove (Manning, 2016); chapter 3 in the book, "Bus Factors," talks about bottlenecks and how to eliminate them.

Sometimes a single person can write documentation *after* development, too. Chapter 6 examined SBE as an iterative process that starts when the delivery team is still highly uncertain about implementation detail. Writing documentation in such conditions, at the beginning of the process, can be wasteful because the delivery team is probably wrong about some things. For example, a delivery team working with a corporation's legacy software can be sufficiently sure of the requirements even early in development, because a big company has established processes. But almost every time you work on something new, whether for a corporation or a startup, things will be less certain. A team may hold workshops and draft some scenarios without worrying about long-term definitions and notes; these can be added later, as the living documentation evolves along with the feature.

Unfortunately, in the real world, most teams can't afford the luxury of holding another workshop with several participants to work on documentation after a feature is implemented. Teams that can't work on documentation collaboratively early in the process must train designers, testers, programmers, and analysts to write documentation iteratively. Let me give you an example of what I mean when I say *iteratively*. Let's say a programmer was delegated to fix a bug that resulted from a misunderstanding of a domain concept. That programmer may work on the bug alone. The programmer should be able not only to fix the bug but also to fix the scenarios by clarifying the relevant domain concept and, therefore, making sure nobody repeats the same mistake in the future. They must either write the documentation with enough empathy to keep less technical teammates in mind or be communicative enough to find and engage other viewpoints as they make the changes, thus making the effort more collaborative.

7.7   *Choosing the right audience for living documentation*

Before you can start thinking about writing documentation, you need to consider *who* you want to document for. Do you remember the last time you read well-written documentation? As you were reading, did the text seem to know most of the questions you were going to ask, and address most of the doubts in your mind? That's how it should be if the authors considered their audience. This section talks about techniques that can help you become such an author.

A single warning before we start—when you hold specification workshops frequently, you may think you're covered in terms of including diverse perspectives in your documentation. That may be true with regard to technical skill if testers, designers, developers, and analysts collaborate during the workshops. But there are other aspects you may want to consider. For example, I think we can agree that it's reasonable to choose senior personnel to run Three Amigos meetings and write new scenarios. After all, they're the most likely to analyze requirements correctly due to their experience and skill. The problem is, they may write scenarios for junior and mid-level personnel and lose track of what other team members need from the specification. The reason is the same as the reason you chose them in the first place—their experience and skill. Their seniority may cause them to underestimate some issues and focus on others, which they consider interesting or worth tackling.

7.7.1   *Who's a minimally qualified reader?*

Among its many useful purposes, documentation is a teaching tool. By documenting features, user stories, and code, you teach readers everything they need to know to get the feature to work. It seems logical, then, to draw some inspiration for creating better living documentations from the realm of education. But in school, everyone learns at a different pace—for example, students who are curious may already know some of the material from other sources. Even if we come from similar backgrounds, everybody's knowledge base is a little different. Yet the textbook is the same for all students.

To do their jobs well, authors who write textbooks must first establish a baseline of knowledge and skills that *every* student must possess in order to successfully complete the course. Only if they do so will they know which skills need to be covered in detail, forming the main body of the text. If they don't, the results will be catastrophic. To understand why, let's consider an average student in an average class. Being average means half of the students are doing worse than the chosen student and half of them are doing better—which means if the textbook was written for the average student, at least half of the kids will find it more or less difficult to read. That's why textbook authors spend a lot of time thinking about the right *minimally qualified reader* (MQR) and write as if for that person only, keeping in mind what that person likely does and doesn't know.

> **DEFINITION**   *Minimally qualified reader (MQR)*—The persona of a typical student with the basic skills needed to benefit from the information. Knowing the MQR means understanding what that person already knows, and teaching what that person doesn't yet know. Defining the reader is an essential part of making good, useful living documentation.

7.7.2   *Finding the perfect MQR in an organization*

Just like students, people on teams and in organizations aren't uniform. For example, let's consider a junior-level engineer, straight out of college, who joined the team a few months ago; an analyst who's fairly senior but as a new hire hasn't yet fully grasped the business domain; a mid-level designer; and a senior tester who has been around forever and knows the ins and outs of the system. They all have different work experiences and skills. How can you write documentation for all of them?

Each profession—engineer, analyst, designer, and tester—already has its own documentation. Engineers can document their work with code comments or architecture diagrams. Analysts also use diagrams, and they can write user stories or use cases. Designers build design systems that explain their decisions and make sure elements and styles are used consistently. Testers document their work by building matrices for manual tests, refining acceptance criteria, and writing down bugs and errors by creating regression tests.

Engineers write documentation for other engineers, analysts write for other analysts, designers write for other designers, and testers write for other testers. But living documentation is documentation that can and should be *written by* all the team members. The content is different, too. Gherkin scenarios talk about business features, the business domain, and broad-concept examples, which may be new and difficult for the delivery team to understand, regardless of their role and technical skill.

So living documentation can be *written by* all the team members as well as *written for* all the team members. But if everyone on the team is the audience, how do you choose the MQR? In the previous section, I told you that it's a good practice to write as if for that person only, keeping in mind what that person likely does and doesn't know. In my experience, it's best to choose an actual person in your organization as the MQR, because you can always run your scenarios past that person, watch the reaction, and then revise accordingly.

How do you spot that person? What criteria should you look for?

The MQR should

- Be experienced enough to be confident in their craft, so you don't feel the urge to explain any universal solutions, either in design or in technology.
- Have at least some technical understanding due to working with a technical team, but programming skills aren't necessary.
- Be new to the business domain. It's expected that the MQR doesn't know the terminology, business-related concepts, industry standards and regulations, company workflows, or competitive advantages.

TIP The MQR should be a mid-level new hire who knows the basics of their craft but doesn't yet understand the business domain of the project. The ideal person is a basic, solid programmer, designer, analyst, or tester who maybe has a couple of years on the job.

Exercise 3
Find a good MQR in your organization. Can you think of anyone? They may be a coworker sitting at the desk next to you.

Thinking about the MQR, you can also consider creating a list of prerequisites to explicitly define the areas of knowledge your team members must have before working with the specification suite. Creating such a list is usually unnecessary when you're dealing with easier business domains that the team thinks they know well, but sometimes such a list can be of help in projects that are more difficult.

Exercise 4
Based on the HouseKeeper example, make a list of three to five domain prerequisites for your team in your latest project. Are you sure the MQR will know all of them?

When dealing with any particular feature, you may want to think about the takeaways you want future readers to understand. Defining the takeaways up front will let you decide on the best method for teaching the reader each skill. Some takeaways will require their own scenarios; some will work well as examples within other scenarios; and others just need a short note in the specification brief or the scenario briefs.

Exercise 5

Make a list of takeaways for the screening feature from listing 7.2.

7.8   *Answers to exercises*

EXERCISE 1   Create a short definition that explains what a scenario outline is:

A scenario outline is a scenario that can take multiple examples at once.

EXERCISE 2   Create a definition by example that will define the concept of Gherkin keywords like Given, When, and Then:

A Gherkin keyword is any special word like Given, When, Then, But, And, Scenario, Feature, *and so on. Keywords are always placed at the beginning of a new line.*

EXERCISE 3   Find a good MQR in your organization:

It's tricky to provide an answer for this exercise, but I'll try. A good MQR in my last medium-sized project was Mark, a great programmer who recently joined the company but had no idea about the products we were working with, because we were an agency and had multiple rotating clients. Mark, if you're reading this—hello!

EXERCISE 4   Based on the HouseKeeper example, make a list of three to five domain prerequisites for your team in your latest project:

- What property management is
- Rental process differences in the countries you support
- The details of signing a lease

EXERCISE 5   Make a list of takeaways for the screening feature from listing 7.2:

- A reader should know what the screening process is.
- A reader should know what you're screening for.
- A reader should know what you don't screen for and why.
- A reader should know what a credit score is.
- A reader should know when a candidate is accepted.

7.9   *Summary*

- Living documentation is documentation that changes along with the system it describes.
- Gherkin can document the business domain for people unfamiliar with it or document the delivery team's decision-making process for future reference.

- A lexical definition explains domain concepts in specification briefs and scenario briefs.
- A definition by example is a list naming the objects that belong to the set being defined.
- A single domain concept—such as an actor, an action, or a state—should always be called by the same name throughout the specification suite, to avoid confusion and misunderstandings.
- Specification briefs and scenario briefs can be used to document various decisions made during the development process for future reference, including business context, warnings, and maintenance notes.
- Creating Gherkin documentation is an iterative process that starts during team workshops. The documentation is progressively refined as the feature evolves.
- A minimally qualified reader (MQR) is a persona of a person in your organization with the basic skills needed to benefit from the documentation on their own.
- A good MQR is a mid-level new hire who knows the basics of their craft but doesn't yet understand the business domain of the project.

Part 2

Managing
specification suites

This part of this book is a four-chapter series about managing specification suites. Chapter 8 talks about organizing scenarios into specifications. Chapter 9 examines refactoring large specifications into smaller ones, chapter 10 discusses designing domain models in a specification suite, and chapter 11 talks about managing multiple domain models in large projects.

Unlike in part 1, each chapter in part 2 discusses the same example: Activitee, an online platform for Fortune 500 companies that want to achieve better business results by improving employee engagement. Whether a company is looking to enhance health and wellness or foster team building, the HR department can tap into Activitee's extensive library of suggested events or charge up existing internal team events—like company retreats and annual staff picnics.

Organizing scenarios into a specification suite

8

This chapter covers

- Organizing scenarios into specifications
- Organizing specifications by outcome and stakeholder
- Working with functional and nonfunctional requirements
- Choosing among features, abilities, and business needs

I remember one particular specification my team and I worked on. The scenarios were meant to describe a highly personalized management panel for the organization's key performance indicators (KPIs). We started with a few KPIs and no option to combine them to create custom reports. Putting the scenarios in a single feature file seemed an obvious choice back then—but in the end, that turned out to have been a bad decision.

The file kept growing as new KPIs appeared. At the time, we didn't recognize the difference between exhaustive and illustrative examples, so we tested too many combinations. The specification ended up being unreadable. It had 508 lines of text—about 10 times as many as the longest ones you've seen in this book so far. When we finally rewrote the specification, we found that we had specified the same option in two separate scenarios because we hadn't noticed that a similar example already existed. If we'd had a different, more focused organization system, we would have been able to consider the granularity of our scenarios from the start.

These are the types of issues discussed in this chapter, and for good reason. If all of the 50 or so scenarios in part 1 were written for the same project, you'd end up with a respectable specification suite. But real projects can have hundreds or even thousands of scenarios, depending on the size of the product. They have to be organized some-how—a real specification suite is never just a single feature file. I've blissfully skipped over such challenges so far, because each chapter in part 1 deals with a single feature file. Such conditions exist only in training exercises, though.

The sections to come focus on the topic of organizing scenarios into specifications. We'll analyze two methods:

- *Organizing scenarios by features*—Cucumber-flavored Gherkin's default method of organization
- *Organizing scenarios by user stories*—The default for other SBE tools, but only an unofficial (although popular) method in the Gherkin community

In this chapter, we'll determine that the second method is better when it comes to spec-ifying requirements. We'll also discuss choosing the correct granularity level for specifications based on user stories, to make sure your scenarios don't get out of control.

To create a more complete theory of organizing requirements, we'll expand the discussion by adding some notes about working with functional and nonfunctional requirements. (I realize that some experts see this terminology as a minefield—we'll discuss that, too.) And we'll also talk about two new keywords that will let you organize your specifications in a systematic manner: `Ability` and `Business Need`.

The example discussed in chapters 8–11 concerns Activitee: an online platform for Fortune 500 companies that want to improve employee engagement. Let's say that you and I are a part of an Activitee team. Encouraged by chapter 7's praise of collabo-rative specification, we decide to hold a specification workshop. Because it's our first workshop together, we purposely choose a simple area to specify: the capabilities of an HR administrator role in Activitee's employee-management module. We want to answer this question: what are the behaviors that HR admins can perform that casual employees can't?

Assume that the following are some of the scenarios we come up with. Don't worry about the Given-When-Then aspects of these scenarios—the names are sufficient for the purpose of this story:

- Editing employee profiles
- Removing former employees
- Managing other HR administrators

- Seeing the list of all employees
- Approving new employees
- Assigning a new employee to a company branch
- Assigning a new employee to a department
- Syncing Activitee's organogram with an external source
- Onboarding new employees
- Emailing employees with important announcements
- Granting limited admin access to team leaders
- Creating common interest groups

Some of these scenarios relate to employee management, and others specify self management between HR administrators; there's even a scenario about email announcements, which will become yet another area of implementation. If we keep brainstorming, we could easily come up with more ideas.

This process of starting with multiple disorganized ideas that are later organized into more coherent material is common in all specification meetings. But how should we organize our new scenarios coherently? We already suspect that we won't be able to put them all in the same feature file. We wouldn't even be sure what to call it. Would *Feature: Admins* be an expressive name for a specification? It sounds more like a catchall.

If keeping the results in the same file isn't a viable option, then the only possibility is to split the scenarios into several specifications. But *how* should we split them?

As you write scenarios, such questions constantly arise. Which scenarios should be in which specifications? Should we establish a hierarchy of feature files, or will a flat structure, such as putting everything in a single directory, work? Even the simplest question—how long a standard specification should be—doesn't have an obvious answer. So far, the specification documents in this book have been short. But short documents may only have been a consequence of the simplicity of the exercises. And even if keeping specifications short is a good practice to follow—which it is—how should you split scenarios when dealing with large functionalities like modules?

8.1 Is organizing scenarios by features a good idea?

Cucumber-flavored Gherkin *does* offer a default way to organize scenarios into specifications. Every time you wrote a specification in previous chapters, you started with the `Feature` keyword, indicating that you were specifying system features. The files that contain scenarios are called *feature files*, which is official Cucumber nomenclature that isn't used in other tools for making executable specifications. (We'll get to that later.)

In the case of the long list of scenarios for Activitee, you'd normally create a feature file like this:

```
Feature: Employee management

    [...]
```

You'd put all the scenarios in this feature file and call it a day.

I have a couple of issues with features, though:

- *Anything* can be a feature. A single button, like the Share button in Facebook, can be a feature. A new screen, such as a user profile, can be a feature, too. Even a brand-new module (like a simple payment system) can be a feature. The word *feature* is often nothing more than an umbrella term for anything that's being added to the product.
- A reasonably sized feature can change as the product evolves. If a feature turns out to be more important than you initially thought, it will grow larger—and so will its feature file. The question is, how do you split it? Unfortunately, there's no clear answer, because, once again, *anything can be a feature.* Without a clear methodology in place, your team may split features differently each time a similar problem appears. (Goodbye, consistency.)

Nonetheless, it's easy to understand why Cucumber-flavored Gherkin uses features as the default option. If anything can be a Gherkin feature, people who only recently started using the language will be less intimidated by it. At first, this choice can facilitate faster learning. (It's also the reason previous chapters used the Feature keyword. I warned you in chapter 2 not to become too attached to it!) But as you write more scenarios, and your specification suites become larger, you'll realize that organizing scenarios by features may not be the best idea. Let's look for something better.

8.2   Organizing scenarios by user stories

If features aren't the best choice, do we have other options? Earlier, I said that other test runners that execute specifications don't use the terms *feature* or *feature file*. Let's examine one such tool: JBehave, a Java testing framework for behavior-driven development.

JBehave calls executable specifications *stories*. In chapters 1 and 2, I described scenarios as short stories about the behaviors of particular actors. But JBehave takes the metaphor even further: each story file can have an optional *narrative* section at the top of the specification brief. Here's an example from JBehave's official tutorial:

```
Narrative:
In order to communicate effectively to the business some functionality
As a development team
I want to use Behaviour-Driven Development
```

It's not only a "narrative"—it's a user story! User stories are one of the most popular methods among technical teams for defining and discussing scope. It makes sense that stories should be able to define the scope of a specification, too. In section 6.3.1, you wrote a user story in a similar format when you were working on the Mapper application and wanted to see how executable specifications fit into a real-world process of delivering software; so the concept of narratives should be more or less familiar to you by now.

With stories, JBehave presents a different answer to the dilemma of organizing scenarios. You can organize scenarios according to the user stories that brought them to life, which results in a more chronological model of organization. Because each file is a separate user story and the implementation of each story can be placed in time, you can track which user stories created which scenarios and when. In a way, you can see how the product evolved from the first user story the team implemented to the last one. This already sounds like a more exciting possibility than features for organizing specification suites. The rest of this section look at other benefits.

Unfortunately, unlike JBehave, Cucumber doesn't support the `Narrative` keyword. Instead, a new `Ability` keyword will replace the sometimes-troublesome `Feature` keyword.

8.2.1 *Introducing the Ability keyword*

The `Ability` keyword is simple to use. To keep changes minimal, you only have to replace the `Feature` keyword at the beginning of each Gherkin specification with `Ability`. No changes are needed in the automation layer, and you should keep the .feature extension for your files.

> **NOTE** Strangely, although features and abilities are synonymous, you won't find a word about `Ability` in Cucumber's official documentation. I stumbled on it when looking at Cucumber's source code. I later learned that the keyword is listed in a table that appears if you type `cucumber --i18n en` in a command shell.

This section takes a somewhat more elaborate route to show how to link abilities with user stories. By setting scope boundaries, you can make a user story answer the question of which scenarios belong together in the same specification. Let's begin by creating a simple feature. You'll then rewrite it as an ability. Here's the user story I chose as an inspiration:

```
In order to increase my engagement
As an employee
I want to see relevant events and courses in my news feed
```

> **NOTE** I wrote this story in feature injection format. Section 8.2.2 will talk more about different formats.

After an HR admin assigns an employee to the correct branch and department, the employee should be able to see events, courses, and discussions from interest groups that are relevant to their job title. Employees from New York shouldn't see events at the Atlanta branch; likewise, engineering employees won't be interested in training workshops meant for the sales department. But sometimes an engineer from Atlanta *may* be interested in an engineering course that takes place in New York. Here's the specification.

Listing 8.1   [OK] Specification derived from a user story as a feature

```
Feature: Branches and departments

   Scenario Outline: Employees should only see content relevant to them

      Given <person> from <branch> who works in <department>
      When <person> looks at the company dashboard on Activitee
      Then <person> should see <type> <content>

      Examples: Employees should see after-
      work content only from their location
         | person | branch   | department  | type                 | content |
         | Jane   | New York | Engineering | New York after-work  | events  |
         | Mike   | New York | HR          | New York after-work  | posts   |
         | Tom    | Atlanta  | Sales       | Atlanta after-work   | events  |
         | Ramona | Atlanta  | Engineering | Atlanta after-work   | posts   |

      Examples: Employees should see work-related content from all locations
         | person | branch   | department  | type                 | content |
         | Mike   | New York | HR          | Atlanta HR           | events  |
         | Jane   | New York | Engineering | Atlanta engineering  | posts   |
         | Jane   | New York | Engineering | New York engineering | events  |
         | Tom    | Atlanta  | Sales       | Atlanta sales        | events  |
         | Ramona | Atlanta  | Engineering | Atlanta engineering  | posts   |
         | Ramona | Atlanta  | Engineering | New York engineering | events  |
```

Each employee has a few examples that specify the different types of content they should be allowed to see. Only people from New York will see New York after-work activities such as bowling and collective outings. When it comes to work-related events and discussions within departments, people from all locations can participate. But, most important, this specification uses the Feature keyword. Let's attempt to replace it.

REWORKING FEATURES INTO ABILITIES

Let's begin by replacing the Feature keyword with the Ability keyword.

Listing 8.2   [BETTER] Feature reworked into an ability

```
Ability: Branches and departments
```

That's a good start. The second step is to write down the expected business outcome.

Listing 8.3   [BETTER] Ability with an outcome

```
Ability: Engage with content I like
```

Next, let's clarify which stakeholder has this capability.

Listing 8.4   [BETTER] Ability with a stakeholder and an outcome

```
Ability: Employees can engage with content they like
```

To complete the translation process, you should also specify the proposed technical solution: it was the last part of the user story and will help you achieve your objective.

Listing 8.5　[BEST] Ability with stakeholder, outcome, and technical solution

```
Ability: Employees can engage with content they like in their news feeds
```

NOTE　For a fully working content management system, you also need a specification that takes care of assigning events to particular branches and departments. Chapter 9 discusses that.

The line now looks slightly different than the original story. The reasons are simple:

- To keep the line short and easy to read.
- To make it fit well with the `Ability` keyword.
- Different user stories can be written in different formats, as discussed in section 8.2.2.

ORGANIZING THE SPECIFICATION SUITE WITH ABILITIES

Similar to this example, you can group scenarios into abilities in a specification suite based on the following, in this order:

1　Stakeholders
2　Business capabilities of these stakeholders
3　Reasonably small common outcomes

Figure 8.1　The progression from left to right indicates hierarchy. First is the `Ability` keyword, which creates a space for user stories in the specification suite. Then come different stakeholders. In the end, stakeholders can achieve concrete outcomes.

If you used the system in figure 8.1 to organize the specification suite, you'd end up with something like figure 8.2. Note that neither figure includes a proposed technical solution, even though that's typically part of every user story. The figures only include the expected abilities of stakeholders—for example, the ability to update a map (even though a map can be updated many different ways). That's because each specification specifies the technical solution in the scenarios, so you don't have to include it again in your system of hierarchy.

Figure 8.2　A specification suite organized according to figure 8.1

NOTE　You'll create a more complex example of a specification suite based on abilities in chapter 9.

Here's a short cheat sheet summing up everything you need to know in order to use abilities in practice:

- Two scenarios for two different stakeholders are, by definition, two different requirements—so they should be two different abilities.
- Two scenarios that describe two different business outcomes are probably two different requirements—so they, too, should be split into two abilities.
- If behaviors that look similar at first yield different outcomes in the end, they should be put into separate abilities, because they're probably from two different domains. For example, a simple behavior like a `company can join the Activitee platform` could yield two or more outcomes like these:
  - The employees should be invited to create their `Activitee` accounts (an employee management behavior)
  - `Activitee's` sales department should be notified about a new company on `trial` (a sales behavior)

  In the end, you'd need to split these scenarios into two separate abilities.

Following these rules will yield a specification suite full of short feature files, especially if you decide to use scenario outlines as you did in chapters 4 and 5. Each scenario outline would be a different ability for a different stakeholder, with similar outcomes grouped in a few tables with examples. I also like to keep one to three edge cases as additional scenarios in the same feature file if they're small variations of the behavior from the outline. (You can find such edge cases by using techniques like context questioning and outcome questioning, which we discussed in sections 3.3.3 and 3.3.4.) You'll probably end up with a specification that's 50–100 lines long, which is a good length for an executable specification; any reader will be able to understand its general purpose at a glance.

CHOOSING THE RIGHT LEVEL OF GRANULARITY FOR ABILITIES

In the list of rules in the previous section, I mentioned that the common outcomes should be *reasonably small*. Let's expand on what that means and look at another example.

Some companies on the Activitee platform have so many events that the application will be unusable without a good search engine to find those events. To create such a search engine, the engineering team has to deal with many filters: searching by name, department, branch, event type, participants, and so on.

Listing 8.6   [BAD] Searching for events

```
Feature: Event search

  Scenario Outline: Filtering events

    Given events:
      | name          | department | branch   | type         | users         |
      | Sales 101     | Sales      | New York | work-related | Mike, John    |
      | Weekly status | HR         | New York | work-related | Simona, John  |
      | Bowling       | -          | Atlanta  | after-work   | Jane          |
```

```
When Simona searches for events by <filter>
 And she wants to find <value>
Then she should see <results>

Examples:
   | filter     | value          | results                      |
   | name       | "Staff picnic" | no results                   |
   | department | "Sales"        | "Sales 101"                  |
   | branch     | "New York"     | "Sales 101", "Weekly status" |
   | type       | "After-work"   | "Bowling"                    |
   | user       | "Mike"         | "Sales 101"                  |
```

Exercise 1

Make a [BAD] specification a [GOOD] one by rewriting the `Feature` line from listing 8.6 into an ability with a clear outcome and a stakeholder.

You could obviously think of more search filters on the spot:

- Add `AND` and `OR` filters.
- Filter by date and time.
- Filter by organizers.
- Filter by distance from location.

The real question is this: in terms of granularity, should you add more scenarios to the same specification, or split scenarios for different filters between different abilities? It's an interesting dilemma. There are reasons to consider putting these scenarios in the same feature file. The behavior would probably stay the same, regardless of the type of filter. Inputs and outputs would differ a little, but they would be acceptably similar. The differences between filters would be solved in the automation layer. But due to the number of scenarios, the resulting feature file would be so long that its length could affect readability.

This is why I mentioned *reasonably small common outcomes*. In this case, I can think of two possible solutions:

- Split the scenarios into several abilities based on the rule of thumb provided earlier, which says that a single file should generally contain a single outline and a few scenarios for possible edge cases. Thus, you'd give each filter its own feature file.
- Redefine what *key examples* means for this particular case. I like this solution better. You should probably have only one example for each filter instead of multiple repetitive scenarios.

Either way, this is what I mean by *reasonably small*: when other rules fail, split your scenarios in a way that's not overwhelming.

8.2.2   Understanding the structure of user stories

This section deals with user stories. The chapter has used them already, but I haven't explained much about them.

The user stories we've analyzed so far were written in the feature injection format:

```
In order to [achieve a business outcome]
As [an actor or a stakeholder]
I want [a technical solution]
```

This format was first proposed by Chris Matts, an agile business analysis thought leader. You first used feature injection in chapter 6, to derive scope. Teams "hunt for value" by creating a model for business-value delivery and listing underlying assumptions instead of trying to describe the value model with simple numbers. (That's why "achieving a business objective" is on the first line of the template.) A well-phrased user story that's illustrated with high-level examples and that yields a fruitful discussion about expected business value can help create such a model.

The assumption is that if you create a value model first and only then "inject" a functionality derived from the model, you'll eliminate pet features, and the functionality will more likely be accepted by users and deliver real value. Therefore, abilities based on user stories will be more likely to deliver value, because they enable you to connect your specification process with feature injection and to derive scenarios directly from the value model.

The feature injection format isn't the only format; most agile coaches can come up with four or five. It isn't even the most popular format for user stories. The most popular is the Connextra format:

```
As [an actor or a stakeholder]
I want [a solution]
So that [I can achieve a business benefit]
```

The general format we presented for abilities is a mix of the feature injection format and the Connextra template. It doesn't follow them exactly, so it should be familiar to people who've used either one. If you don't like it, feel free to tweak it so it looks more like your format of choice. The specific format isn't important—what matters is understanding the value-delivery process for a requirement. Any user story that will bring you and your team closer to understanding this model is a good story, regardless of the format. Just make sure the template is easy for everyone to understand—even people who weren't present during implementation.

> **TIP**   If you're looking for more resources about user stories, I recommend reading *Fifty Quick Ideas to Improve Your User Stories* by Gojko Adžić and David Evans (Neuri Consulting LLP, 2014) and *User Stories Applied* by Mike Cohn (Addison-Wesley Professional, 2004).

8.2.3 *Analyzing the relationship between user stories and executable specifications*

Organizing a specification suite by user stories engenders an important question: are executable specifications extended user stories? Making abilities look similar to user stories only makes the issue more difficult. This section explores the similarities and differences between user stories and executable specifications.

If user stories and executable specifications are one and the same, you'd expect that every user story would become an executable specification and that your projects would have as many stories as specifications. In practice, this isn't true. A typical project has many more stories than specifications. There must be differences between them, despite their similarities.

SIMILARITIES BETWEEN USER STORIES AND EXECUTABLE SPECIFICATIONS

We'll start with the similarities. In 2001, Ron Jeffries—the creator of Extreme Programming—wrote that "user stories have three critical aspects. We can call these Card, Conversation, and Confirmation." He considers the textual artifact—the card—nothing more than a piece of text to put on a Trello board or hang on the wall as a sticky note. The card only captures a glimpse of the requirement behind the user story. It doesn't matter how refined it is; you still need to discuss acceptance criteria, tests, and success and failure scenarios, as well as define confirmation metrics to produce a working capability. In short, you must take care of the conversation and confirmation. That's why experts often call the card only a *ticket for a conversation.*

In this sense, an executable specification is similar to a fully realized user story. Gherkin scenarios often consist of recorded conversations between stakeholders, and the underlying tests confirm and validate the acceptance criteria automatically. If you phrase the abilities similarly to how you phrase user stories, you'll even have a link between every card and the title of the user story's Gherkin ability.

DIFFERENCES BETWEEN USER STORIES AND EXECUTABLE SPECIFICATIONS

Even with all their similarities, there are some crucial differences between user stories and Gherkin specifications, as outlined in table 8.1; I talked some about them in section 6.3.1, when you wrote your first user story. Unfortunately, these differences mean that ultimately you can't treat stories and specifications the same way.

Table 8.1 Comparison of user stories and executable specifications

A user story...	An executable specification...
Is discarded after implementation	Is kept after implementation
Is a unit of change	Is an effect of the change
Has acceptance criteria	Is an acceptance test
Produces short-term results, such as cards or tasks	Produces long-term living documentation

User stories have acceptance criteria—but executable specifications are acceptance tests. Obviously, without the criteria, there can be no tests—but that doesn't mean executable specifications and user stories are the same thing. They only share some underlying core similarities that spring from the fact that they're both tools to talk about requirements.

The main difference is that user stories

- Represent the *future* scope of work (see the right side of figure 8.3)
- Discuss *changes* that have to be made to the system
- *Expire* if they stay in the product backlog too long

Whereas, executable specifications

- Represent the scope of the work that *has been done so far* (see the left side of figure 8.3)
- Discuss *the current state* of the chosen part of the system
- Become more precise as time passes, thanks to automated tests and feedback loops like those you saw in action throughout chapters 6 and 7

Figure 8.3   Executable specifications represent requirements that have been implemented so far or are currently being implemented. User stories represent the future scope of work and are often used as reminders for a future conversation about the requirement.

Although it may have seemed at the start of the chapter that I was encouraging you to consider user stories and specifications as equal, we should take a more conservative approach and say that new executable specifications and new scenarios are only *derived* from user stories. What I mean is that even though user stories can generate new scenarios, they can also change or remove existing scenarios. A model of organization based on user stories can't assume a 1:1 relationship between a single story and a single specification. Any single specification will most likely be changed by multiple user stories as the product evolves. If you assume that specifications are extended stories, you'll end up creating a false equivalence between stories and specifications.

8.2.4   *Iterative dangers of organizing scenarios by user stories*

Why would an equivalence between stories and specifications be false? Because user stories *are* requirements—just like executable specifications are requirements—but user stories are often requirements *only for the current iteration.*

For example, in Scrum, the backlog holds all the user stories; at the beginning of every sprint, the development team and the product owner select the user stories for the current sprint. Scrum requires the development team to deliver a fully functional iteration of the product at the end of each sprint. So for some bigger features, you'll end up simplifying the solution, only to make it more complex iteratively. A blogging platform might at first introduce a full-text search that only lets readers search by title, and then add a capability to search by body text in the next iteration. The second capability would become a separate user story, but it would still have to build on a previously completed story. Should you create two specifications because there are two user stories? Or should you treat the second story as an expansion of the first story?

> **TIP** To those who argue that every user story must be independent—and that thus you can't have a story that builds on another story—I say you can implement a title search or body search in any order, so there's no dependency between the stories. Nonetheless, some stories inevitably build on previously implemented solutions.

From a technical point of view, a user story can only be a complete requirement when it introduces a brand-new capability to the system. If a user story changes an existing capability, the requirement is now formed from two user stories: the one that introduced it in the past and the one modifying it right now.

User stories don't have to be full units of the requirements. They're often only units of *change* in the requirements. They're like commits in Git or any other version control system. Every story is a new layer of changes you introduce to the application. To recreate requirements from them, you'd have to juxtapose all stories related to a single functionality chronologically and reason the final shape of the requirement currently in effect out of the changes made to the original story by newer stories. That's way too much effort.

Thinking of user stories in terms of geometry and geography

I like thinking about user stories and executable specifications in spatial ways. A user story is like a Euclidean vector: it has a direction (in which the delivery team wants to go) and length (a scope estimate). A story is merely a *planning tool* that helps teams organize themselves in order to get from point A to point B. When you want to get from A to B, you know that your current plan is temporary—the same route that got you from A to B won't automatically get you from B to C, and so on.

An executable specification, on the other hand, is more like a two-dimensional plane. It's an overview of what the vectors created. It's like a *map* that your team has charted along the way during your journey. It shows your current knowledge about the requirements. You'll probably improve the map as you venture into new territories. But because most of the hard work is already done, you can be more thoughtful about the long term and organize the map in a way that won't get you lost in the woods in the future.

The iteration problem is why putting user stories in the specification brief is a problematic method that I don't advise practicing. Which of multiple user stories influencing the specification should the brief contain? All of them, in chronological order? (I was surprised to learn that JBehave embraced this pattern back in the day.) How can you do better than that? Here are a few thoughts:

- Don't store user stories in specification briefs. Instead, extract desired business outcomes from your stories, and name specifications after the outcomes. Mention stakeholders to put actors in context.
- Make brand-new executable specifications only from user stories that imply brand-new business outcomes.
- If a user story implies a change in the behavior of an existing outcome, review the existing specification to see if the new scenarios are important enough to warrant a change in the contents of the `Ability` keyword.
- Sometimes a change in behavior is so significant that adding new examples or scenarios isn't enough. In this case, check whether the change results in creating a brand-new capability for an existing actor or a new actor; if the answer is yes, split the old ability into two new, separate specifications.

8.3   *What about nonfunctional requirements?*

By default, abilities imply capabilities of specific actors. We can say that such and such a user should *be able to* do such and such a thing. But what about requirements that don't apply to particular actors? Think of security, usability, testability, maintainability, extensibility, scalability, and so on. Trying to specify an ability that makes sure every functionality in your system is fast could result in a feature file with hundreds of scenarios, rendering your effort to create small specifications pointless. Such requirements are often called *nonfunctional requirements*.

> **DEFINITION**   *Nonfunctional requirement*—A requirement that defines a general quality that the entire system must stick to horizontally

If you decide to use the nonfunctional terminology, you can also say that a requirement that defines a capability of an actor is a *functional requirement*.

> **DEFINITION**   *Functional requirement*—A requirement that defines a function of a system as an ability to solve a problem or achieve an objective at hand

Whereas functional requirements define the utility of a system, nonfunctional requirements define its architecture. They aren't related to any particular vertical functionality. So, if we said that a specification suite is like a map of requirements, should nonfunctional requirements be on the map, too? The answer isn't unequivocal. In this section, we'll look at the question from two angles:

- How to handle nonfunctional requirements according to SBE's key patterns
- The difficulty of writing nonfunctional requirements in Gherkin

I have to admit that conveying nonfunctional requirements in Gherkin isn't an established practice. I haven't seen any Gherkin thought leaders advising this approach. Other than one practical use case, which you'll see in section 8.3.4, most of the ideas outlined in this case are theoretical. So if you're only interested in learning practical techniques, go straight to section 8.3.4.

I was even advised to drop the terms *functional* and *nonfunctional requirements*, because the differences between them can cause confusion. I decided to keep the terminology intact, because I assume that many readers are already familiar with it. There's no point in pretending the terms and the controversy don't exist. This is also an interesting topic to explore. With some hesitation, I decided to include it here so that you can build a more complete understanding of requirements in your specification suites.

> ### Exercise 2
> Can you identify more nonfunctional requirements?

8.3.1 *Dealing with nonfunctional requirements according to SBE*

Teams that use SBE illustrate requirements using concrete examples to build a better mental model of whatever they're about to do. Although illustrating functional requirements with examples comes naturally, because each behavior needs concrete inputs and outputs, most people intuitively think that nonfunctional requirements don't fit this process pattern as well. For example, some nonfunctionals aren't discrete. Think of a fun requirement for a game: how could you specify *fun*?

To illustrate nonfunctional requirements with examples, you need to adopt a beginner's mindset and stop thinking about *your* system, which you do when you work with functionals. Instead, you should think about *other* systems that you know of and can use as an inspiration, a standard, or a benchmark. For example, for a security requirement, you could find examples of the most secure systems in your product category and see whether you could replicate what they did. In the case of a usability requirement, you could ask your UX designers to showcase some useful patterns from products they like, and UI requirements could be illustrated with low-fidelity mockups or interactive prototypes and animations. For a performance requirement, you could look at your competitors if they're better than you; or, if they aren't, make a list of products from other industries that the team should look at as gold standards. And finally, for the problematic fun requirement, you could find examples of game mechanics that you or your players enjoyed in the past.

Unfortunately, nonfunctional requirements are usually difficult to automate, except for security tests or performance tests. (For example, performance requirements are usually discrete, which makes automation easier: "The system has to process X GB of data within Y hours on a Z hard drive.") But lack of automation doesn't mean you can't use these examples to discuss such requirements with business stakeholders or during specification workshops and reap the benefits.

8.3.2   *Can Gherkin specify nonfunctional requirements?*

Throughout the book, I've treated Gherkin scenarios as behavioral requirements. As behaviors, scenarios should by definition be functional requirements. But the relationship between behaviors, functional requirements, and nonfunctional requirements is more complicated than it may seem. For example, security requirements may imply a two-factor authentication function; in this case, a nonfunctional requirement is generating a functional requirement. And some nonfunctional requirements can be phrased as behaviors, like this scenario:

```
Given a search form
 When the user submits a query
 Then the user should see the result in less than 100 seconds
```

I'll agree that, in this case, the nonfunctional requirement sounds like it's being forced into the template. That's because I mixed two domains—the search domain and the performance domain—while trying to write the scenario in the outside-in style you've been practicing throughout the book. Unfortunately, only the search domain fits the outside-in style meant for stakeholders; the performance domain, which is the main domain of this scenario, must be written in another style. But is that possible? I'm playing devil's advocate right now, but let's think about that for a moment.

As we examined advanced techniques for writing scenarios in chapter 3, you saw that every scenario must be written from the perspective of an actor. Because anything that influences an action or a process taking place in the system under design can be an actor, three kinds of actors come to mind: stakeholders, organizations, and systems. As I mentioned, scenarios in which the actor is a stakeholder are written in the outside-in style. But that leaves out organizations and systems.

I'll argue that you *could* rewrite the previous example scenario without using the outside-in style and with the system in the role of an actor. You could even use good technical practices from performance testing, such as averaging query run time to get better results. Here's the same nonfunctional requirement written from the system's perspective:

```
Given a search query
 When the system runs the query 100 times
 Then the average execution time should be less than 100 seconds
```

The system style matches performance much better, because they're both technological at heart, whereas the outside-in style required a more empathetic approach. But better phrasing doesn't get rid of all the issues:

- You can't use the Goldilocks principle (discussed in section 5.4.4) and get rid of the class of equivalence from the Then step (less than 100 seconds) due to the nondeterministic nature of the requirement.

- The scenario is more technical and may seem boring to nontechnical stakeholders. This could possibly be solved with good stakeholder management: for example, you could show the system scenarios only to technical stakeholders who are interested in the performance domain, and keep the outside-in scenarios for the nontechnical stakeholders. It's an interesting idea that we'll talk about in section 8.3.3.
- The scenario only tests the average execution time of search *queries*, without testing whether the results are rendered on the screen quickly enough.
- If you decided to simulate a full user experience in order to test whether the search was fast enough from a user perspective, you'd need to test every screen where a user could execute a search query.

Even though we still have many unanswered questions, let's set them aside for a moment and say that we *will* try to use Gherkin to specify this requirement. But how do we do that?

8.3.3 *Introducing the Business Need keyword*

Theoretically, if you *wanted* to specify a nonfunctional requirement with Gherkin, you could. Syntax would be problematic, though. Keywords like `Feature` and `Ability` seem out of place. Performance isn't a feature. It *could* be an ability, but that would sound as phony as the initial scenario that mixed the empathetic outside-in style with the technical performance domain. Fortunately, Gherkin has a third keyword that's similar to these two: `Business Need`. Here's how it looks in practice:

```
Business Need: Performance
```

Like abilities, business needs don't influence the automation layer, and you store them in files with the .feature extension. Here's the search scenario, phrased as a business need.

Listing 8.7 Performance requirement phrased as a business need

```
Business Need: Performance

  Scenario: Searches must run faster than 100 seconds

    Given a search query
      When the system runs the query 100 times
      Then the average execution time should be less than 100 seconds
```

Adding business needs to figure 8.1, which outlined the structure of functional abilities, yields the diagram shown in figure 8.4.

Figure 8.4 Requirements in a specification suite. Abilities specify functional requirements, and business needs specify nonfunctionals. Instead of stakeholders and outcomes, business needs talk about required quality measures.

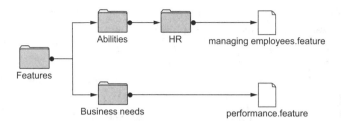

Figure 8.5   A specification suite organized according to figure 8.4

Figure 8.5 shows the example specification suite when it includes the business need for performance.

Impatient readers may say that dedicating an entire section to the mostly theoretical concept of business needs in Gherkin was extravagant. They're probably right—but I had an ulterior motive, which I'll reveal in the next section. In my opinion, if a specification suite were to truly become a map of requirements for an entire product, it *would have to* include nonfunctional requirements. And in some cases, it can do so more easily than in our previous problematic example.

8.3.4 *Using the Business Need keyword to identify new stakeholders*

As I said at the beginning of section 8.3.2, the relationship between functional and nonfunctional requirements is more complicated than it seems at first. I used the example of a security requirement that might imply a two-factor authentication function to show that, sometimes, nonfunctional requirements create functions and behaviors that *can* be described in Gherkin—and *even in the outside-in style*. We'll now examine such situations in depth. When do they occur? And are there consequences you should be aware of?

MEETING THE CHAMPIONS BEHIND REQUIREMENTS

To keep things simple, we'll stay in the security domain introduced by the two-factor authentication example. But to discuss the issue fully, we'll need something more: a story.

Let's say it's Monday, and you're at the weekly status meeting where you discuss the stories your Activitee team chose to implement during this iteration. The product owner unexpectedly adds a new story to this week's backlog. The story is about making passwords in the system more secure. The team decides that the simplest way to achieve results this week, given the team's current capacity, is to force users to create passwords that are harder to crack.

Together, the team creates a list of acceptance criteria for new passwords:

- Passwords should have a minimum of eight characters.
- Don't use repetitive or sequential characters.
- Usernames, first names, surnames, and so on shouldn't qualify as passwords.

The team then collects a list of examples and drafts a scenario that checks whether each example is strong enough to pass the security measures. A few weeks ago, the team would probably have added this scenario to an existing feature file connected to account management; but let's say you've just read the first half of this chapter and know that Gherkin specifications can be organized as requirements and that nonfunctional requirements, such as security, can be specified using the `Business Need` keyword.

```
Listing 8.8  Business need for security

Business Need: Security

  Scenario Outline: Passwords should be secure

    Given Simona has to set a password
    When she tries to set the password to <password>
    Then the password should be considered <secure>

    Examples: Too short
       | password | secure   |
       | shorty   | insecure |

    Examples: No repetitive or sequential characters
       | password | secure   |
       | aaaaaaaa | insecure |

    Examples: No usernames, first names, or surnames
       | password      | secure   |
       | simonajenkins | insecure |

    Examples: Good password
       | password           | secure |
       | nevergonnagiveyouup | secure |
```

It's a classic case of a functional behavior that the end user can interact with. To make the examples easy to read, you put them in a scenario outline. Each acceptance criterion has its own table—isn't that what you'd do with any other requirement? In a way, this is a standard Gherkin specification. But if you remember that it was created from a nonfunctional requirement, some interesting questions appear. For example, what prompted the security requirement to emerge in the first place? (Yes, I know. I, too, am sure that a real-world delivery team would ask this question *before* writing the specification. I admit that I structured the story so I could ask the question dramatically now. Sorry about that!) In a software development agency, the request for the security requirement would come from the clients—but who or what planted it in their heads in the first place? The same goes for in-house teams, where the requirement might be handed off to the product owner by someone from management.

Requirements listed as nonfunctional usually imply that there's a stakeholder whom the team hasn't yet explicitly identified. For example, the company might have hired a chief security officer, who, unbeknownst to the team, ordered a security audit. The request for stronger passwords may be only the first step, if the functional behavior for forcing stronger passwords was just the easiest fix on the CSIO's list. In that case, you can assume that more security requirements will emerge in the future.

Another reason for the security requirement to appear might be that the company signed a contract with an enterprise client that cares about security. Some stakeholders work behind the scenes for a long time and become more active only when an issue that interests them is on the table—they're identified when new nonfunctional requirements crop up, seemingly out of nowhere. Even if business needs can't create a complete map of nonfunctionals, you can use them to mark potentially dangerous areas from which you suspect new stakeholders may emerge.

Exercise 3

Think of some other examples of behavioral functions that could be derived from non-functional requirements. You can use the requirements you prepared in exercise 2.

APPLYING A FRAMEWORK TO WORK WITH BUSINESS NEEDS OVER TIME

I suggest the following simple framework to work with requirements like those just discussed:

- Include nonfunctional requirements in the specification suite if they can be specified as functional behaviors, such as a two-factor authentication scenario in a security requirement.
- Mark nonfunctional requirements as business needs with general names such as Security, Usability, and so on.
- Let each business need grow naturally by adding new functional scenarios over time.
- If one of the business needs grows too large and has too many functional aspects, consider splitting it into several smaller abilities. By now, you should have enough functional scenarios to justify doing so.
  - If you haven't already, work to identify the stakeholder behind the business need that had to be split, and try to include that stakeholder in your software development process.
  - Having identified the stakeholder, move the acquired abilities under the abilities filesystem tree.

You'll see this framework work in practice in chapter 9.

Exercise 4

Add a two-factor authentication scenario to the business need for security as another quality measure.

Exercise 5

Split the business need for security into two abilities: one for secure passwords, and another for two-factor authentication.

8.4 *Answers to exercises*

EXERCISE 1 Make a [BAD] specification a [GOOD] one by rewriting the `Feature` line from listing 8.6 into an ability with a clear outcome and a stakeholder:

```
Ability: Employees can find events by using advanced search filters
```

EXERCISE 2 Can you identify more nonfunctional requirements?

- Testability
- Maintainability
- Extensibility
- Scalability
- Reporting

EXERCISE 3 Think of some other examples of behavioral functions that could be derived from nonfunctional requirements. You can use the requirements you prepared in exercise 2:

> *A nonfunctional reporting requirement can imply functions such as generating reports, downloading reports, archiving reports, and so on.*

EXERCISE 4 Add a two-factor authentication scenario to the business need for security as another quality measure:

```
Scenario Outline: Use two-factor authentication for more security

  Given <authentication> for Simona
    And Simona's desire to log in
  When she provides her username
    And she provides her password
    And she enters <code>
  Then she should be <authenticated>

  Examples: Two-factor authentication
      | authentication  | code             | authenticated  |
      | two-factor auth | the correct code | logged in      |
      | two-factor auth | the wrong code   | not logged in  |

  Examples: Make sure single-factor authentication still works
      | authentication  | code    | authenticated  |
      | traditional auth | no code | logged in      |
```

EXERCISE 5   Split the business need for security into two abilities: one for secure passwords, and another for two-factor authentication:

```
Ability: Users can secure their account with strong passwords

  Scenario Outline: Passwords should be secure

    Given Simona has to set a password
    When she tries to set the password to <password>
    Then the password should be considered <secure>

    [...]

Ability: Users can turn two-factor authentication on for more security

  Scenario Outline: Use two-factor authentication

    Given <authentication> for Simona
      And Simona's desire to log in
    When she provides her username
      And she provides her password
      And she enters <code>
    Then she should be <authenticated>

    [...]
```

8.5   *Summary*

- Cucumber organizes Gherkin scenarios into specifications through feature files.
- Even though the default way to organize scenarios in Cucumber-flavored Gherkin is through the `Feature` keyword, features are difficult to organize consistently because anything can be a feature.
- Testing tools like JBehave use user stories to organize scenarios; but more often, executable specifications are only *derived* from user stories, because they can not only add, but also change or remove existing scenarios.
- If you don't use user stories, you can organize your scenarios by any other kind of functional requirement.
- A functional requirement defines a function of a system as an ability to solve a problem or achieve an objective at hand.
- You can specify user stories or functional requirements as abilities of particular stakeholders.
- Be careful with user stories that are iterative!
- Nonfunctional requirements define general qualities that the entire system must stick to, such as security, usability, and testability.
- You can specify nonfunctional requirements as business needs that define particular quality measures.
- Some nonfunctional requirements can imply functionality.
- Requirements listed as nonfunctional usually imply that there's a stakeholder whom the team hasn't yet explicitly identified.

Refactoring features into abilities and business needs

This chapter covers

- Managing functional and nonfunctional requirements
- Refactoring features into abilities
- Recognizing and refactoring business needs
- Identifying new stakeholders with business needs

This is the second chapter in a four-chapter series about managing large specification suites. Chapter 8 focused on organizing scenarios into specifications, discussing the optimal length of an average executable specification and the theoretical aspects of deciding to put a scenario into one specification or another. In this chapter, we'll put the theory into practice by refactoring larger executable specifications into smaller ones that will be easier to manage.

We'll continue to work with Activitee, an online platform for Fortune 500 companies that want to improve employee engagement. Chapter 8 introduced two new types of executable specifications: abilities and business needs. They replaced the Feature keyword because they're easier to organize. But it's one thing to know a theory and another to apply it in practice. In this chapter, we'll deal with two core aspects of the Activitee experience—events and application security—in order to determine which is an ability and which is a business need.

9.1   Analyzing user stories: a practical example

Before you can talk about abilities and business needs, you need to learn about the requirements in question. This section looks at two Activitee teams who are getting to know the scope of work ahead of them. Imagine that the two teams have just finished their previous iterations. They're ready to take two new user stories from the top of their backlog, which has recently been prioritized by Activitee's product management.

The first team—which I'll refer to from this point on as the *events team*—will work on a user story connected with Activitee's core value proposition: organizing and managing events. The user story introduces a new capability for team leaders to create events with an attendance fee:

```
In order to organize informal company outings online
As a team leader
I want to create events that let people pay for attendance on Activitee
```

The use case for paid events is to let team leaders organize informal team outings without involving the entire HR department. The team may just want to go bowling after work—and Activitee should let employees organize and pay for the event up front online. Section 9.2 covers the actions of the events team.

The second team, which I'll call the *application security team*, will work on a user story that deals with security:

```
In order to meet my company's security policy
As a Fortune 500 company employee
I want to increase my account security
```

As of this moment, the team doesn't have a lot of information about this story, which popped up in the backlog recently and was quickly prioritized to the top. Activitee's primary clients—Fortune 500 companies with thousands of employees—always have their own security policies. It makes sense that Activitee should work on its security measures in order to meet their standards; but right now, the team has to wait to see what kind of solution will be required. We'll look at that in section 9.3.

As the teams talk about requirements with relevant stakeholders and draft new Gherkin scenarios in response, they must determine what kinds of requirements they're dealing with. Chapter 8 provided frameworks for working with two types of requirements in Gherkin: defining system functions using abilities, and using business needs to define functional aspects of general system qualities like security and performance. You may already suspect which keyword will help with which Activitee user story.

9.2   Refactoring features into abilities

Let's examine how the events team works with the user story about paid events. The story introduces a new *capability* for team leaders to create events with an attendance fee. It's fitting, then, to suspect that the team will use the `Ability` keyword to define such a requirement.

Throughout the rest of this section, you'll see the challenges of organizing functional scenarios over time, how they can accumulate into executable specifications that are too long to manage without significant effort, and what steps are necessary to break such specifications into smaller parts. As you'll see, we can't talk about these issues without touching on the topic of the legacy `Feature` keyword, too—but let's not get ahead of ourselves just yet.

9.2.1 Deriving new scenarios from user stories

In the case of the events team, finding relevant stakeholders and discussing the user story with them isn't difficult. Most of Activitee's HR and team leadership use the company's own product. The team gathers a few team leaders in a conference room, and together they come up with a scenario that they think will satisfy both their own needs and the needs of their clients.

Listing 9.1 Events team: scenario derived from the user story

```
Scenario: Users should be able to pay for events online

  Given an event created by team lead Mike for his team:
    | name            |
    | 2nd Bowling Night |
  And an attendance fee of $25 set by the team lead
  When Jane pays for the event online
  Then she should become a confirmed attendee
```

Activitee's specification suite has grown significantly since the company adopted SBE and Gherkin. So, the team must decide where to put this new scenario.

9.2.2 Starting with simple features

After reading the previous paragraph, you've probably thought about finding an existing ability or creating a new one. But remember that when teams begin using Gherkin, they almost always define new system functions using the `Feature` keyword, which is Cucumber-flavored Gherkin's default way of defining requirements. Activitee's very first executable specification is no different (see the following listing).

Listing 9.2 Activitee's first executable specification

```
Feature: Creating events

  Scenario: HR admins should be able to create company events

    Given a Fortune 500 company like Coca-Cola
      And James, an HR admin in that company
    When James organizes a company-wide event:
      | name              | date       | time  |
      | Annual staff picnic | 10-03-2017 | 10 AM |
    Then the employees in other departments should be notified
```

As it happens, the current events team is the same team who worked on this scenario, back when Activitee was still striving to launch its product. They imagine that their new scenario will seamlessly fit into what they remember as a one-scenario feature about the catchall topic of creating events. We'll soon see if they're right.

9.2.3   Adding scenarios over time

The event system lies at the heart of Activitee's value proposition. Over time, multiple teams have been tasked with delivering new functionalities in the events space. They took artistic license with the initially simple feature by adding new scenarios as they saw fit. The word *feature* is an umbrella term, so anything can be a feature—if a hammer is the only tool you have, everything looks like a nail.

The current events team is surprised by how many different scenarios have been added. You can imagine the questions that pop into their heads when they read the latest version of the specification (shown in the following listing): How are these scenarios related? What's going on? Will we break anything?

Listing 9.3   [BAD] Feature with loosely related scenarios added over time

```
Feature: Creating events

  Scenario: HR admins should be able to create company events          ◁─┐

    Given a Fortune 500 company like Coca-Cola                     Basic success
      And James, an HR admin in that company                      scenario for
    When James organizes a company-wide event:                  creating company-
      | name          | date       | time  |                      wide events
      | Annual staff picnic | 10-03-2017 | 10 AM |
    Then the employees in other departments should be notified

  Scenario Outline: Managing invited participants                     ◁─┐
                                                                Scenario outline that
    Given James drafted a new event                             deals with managing
    When he invites <invitee>                                   participants
    Then only <invitee> should be notified about the invite
      But <uninvited> should not be notified

    Examples: Invites to one-on-one events such as annual reviews
      | invitee | uninvited |
      | Simona  | Jane      |

    Examples: Invites to local events in specific locations
      | invitee           | uninvited           |
      | Atlanta employees | New York employees  |

    Examples: Inviting one department, but not the other (all locations)
      | invitee   | uninvited   |
      | engineers | salespeople |

    Examples: Inviting a specific department from a specific location
      | invitee           | uninvited                     |
      | Atlanta engineers | New York engineers, salespeople |
```

Scenarios that deal with time and date management ──▷ `Scenario Outline: Managing simple events and serial events`

```
    Given a company-wide event called <name>
      And that it takes place <date> at <time>
    When Simona wants to attend the event
    Then she should get a reminder <date> before <time>
```

```
  Examples:
```

name	date	time
Annual staff picnic	on 10-03-2017	10 AM
Yoga classes	every Monday	10 AM

Scenarios that deal with time and date management

```
Scenario Outline: Managing scheduling conflicts for company-wide events
```

```
  Given a company-wide event created by James:
```

name	date	time
Annual staff picnic	10-03-2017	10 AM

```
  And that Terry wants to organize another company-wide event:
```

name	date	time
The Move with Purpose Marathon	10-03-2017	10 AM

```
  When Terry does <action> that the scheduling conflict is OK
  Then the event should be <result>
    And the employees in other departments should get <email>
```

```
  Examples:
```

action	result	email
confirm	published	a notification
not confirm	not published	no notification

Scenarios that deal with time and date management

```
Scenario: Managing scheduling conflicts for local events
```

```
  Events from local branches shouldn't cause conflicts.
```

```
  Given an Atlanta event created by James:
```

name	date	time
Local staff picnic	10-03-2017	10 AM

```
  When Terry wants to organize another event in New York:
```

name	date	time
The Move with Purpose Marathon	10-03-2017	10 AM

```
  Then the event should be successfully published
    And the employees in other departments should be notified
```

NOTE Don't worry about the details of these scenarios right now. We'll discuss them at length soon.

This specification has 10 examples in a single file that spans more than 75 lines of text! These examples cover three important areas of implementation:

- *Creating and scheduling events*—The first scenario introduces the concept of company-wide events that are visible to all employees.
- *Managing participants by location and department*—These four scenarios discuss events that are either local or limited to particular departments or specific employees.
- *Managing participants by date and time*—These three scenarios introduce the third type of events, *serial events,* which can take place in multiple time slots (think of yoga classes that take place over several months).

Adding the scenario about paid events would enlarge the text to 6 scenarios and 84 lines, talking about 4 loosely connected areas of implementation. Given that an average scenario in this feature file has about 10 lines of text, adding just 2 more scenarios to each of these 4 areas would result in 80 additional lines, making the entire specification 164 lines long. Early reviewers of this book shared that the specification suites they encounter in their environments often deal with hundreds or even thousands of scenarios! There is a dire need for a more granular organization system.

When the Activitee events team tries to fit the new scenario into this overgrown feature, they come to the same conclusion. Fortunately, while they searching for a good solution, they stumble on the `Ability` keyword and decide to break their huge feature into several smaller abilities.

9.2.4 *Splitting huge features into small abilities*

The events team choose to split their feature according to the four areas of implementation specified in the previous section. This decision is driven by the fact that they were able to track the source of each area to a different user story in the archives of their backlog—just as we did back in section 8.2.1.

SPLITTING SCENARIOS BETWEEN ABILITIES

The first ability created by the Activitee team deals with company-wide events and the basic success scenario for creating events.

Listing 9.4 [GOOD] Ability allowing HR reps to create company-wide events

```
Ability: HR reps can organize their wellness programs through online events

   Scenario: HR admins should be able to create company events

      Given a Fortune 500 company like Coca-Cola
        And James, an HR admin in that company
      When James organizes a company-wide event:
        | name                | date       | time  |
        | Annual staff picnic | 10-03-2017 | 10 AM |
      Then the employees in other departments should be notified
```

This ability shows the basic flow of events being created and scheduled for entire companies by HR departments, which are Activitee's primary users. You can expect that the behaviors and examples from this ability will always be required to create the most basic type of event on the Activitee platform.

Soon after, the Activitee events team prepares the second ability for the user story that started the rewriting process in the first place: the paid informal events functionality.

Listing 9.5 [GOOD] Ability that lets team leaders create paid informal events

```
Ability: Team leads can facilitate teamwork by organizing team outings online

   Scenario: Users should be able to pay for events online

      Given an event created by team lead Mike for his team:
```

```
     | name              |
     | 2nd Bowling Night |
   And an attendance fee of $25 set by the team lead
  When Jane pays for the event online
  Then she should become a confirmed attendee
```

Once the events team deals with the newest user story, they can move on to reorganize the other requirements that have been added to the specification by different teams over time. They start with the scenarios that specify managing and inviting participants (see listing 9.6). There are four use cases:

- Inviting selected individuals
- Inviting all people from a specific location
- Inviting all people from a specific department
- Inviting all people from a specific department in a specific location

All of these scenarios deal with *targeting*. HR representatives want to target different events to different people. They don't want people from Atlanta to see events that are organized for the New York branch. They also know from experience that engineers may be interested in different after-work activities than employees in the sales department.

Listing 9.6   [GOOD] Ability for targeting event programs

```
Ability: HR reps can target wellness programs by choosing specific audiences

  Scenario Outline: Managing invited participants

    Given James drafted a new event
    When he invites <invitee>
    Then only <invitee> should be notified about the invite
     But <uninvited> should not be notified

    Examples: Invites to one-on-one events such as annual reviews
        | invitee | uninvited |
        | Simona  | Jane      |

    Examples: Invites to local events in specific locations
        | invitee           | uninvited          |
        | Atlanta employees | New York employees |

    Examples: Inviting one department, but not the other (all locations)
        | invitee   | uninvited   |
        | engineers | salespeople |

    Examples: Inviting a specific department from a specific location
        | invitee          | uninvited                      |
        | Atlanta engineers | New York engineers, salespeople |
```

The remaining three scenarios are related to scheduling issues, so the events team decides to group them together under managing the company's event calendar.

Listing 9.7   [GOOD] Ability for managing the event calendar

```
Ability: HR reps can manage their wellness program's calendar by scheduling events

  Scenario Outline: Managing simple events and serial events

    Given a company-wide event called <name>
      And that it takes place <date> at <time>
    When Simona wants to attend the event
    Then she should get a reminder <date> before <time>

    Examples:
      | name               | date           | time  |
      | Annual staff picnic | on 10-03-2017 | 10 AM |
      | Yoga classes       | every Monday   | 10 AM |

  Scenario Outline: Managing scheduling conflicts for company-wide events

    Given a company-wide event created by James:
      | name               | date           | time  |
      | Annual staff picnic | 10-03-2017    | 10 AM |
      And that Terry wants to organize another company-wide event:
      | name                          | date           | time  |
      | The Move with Purpose Marathon | 10-03-2017    | 10 AM |
    When Terry does <action> that the scheduling conflict is OK
    Then the event should be <result>
      And the employees in other departments should get <email>

    Examples:
      | action      | result        | email           |
      | confirm     | published     | a notification  |
      | not confirm | not published | no notification |

  Scenario: Managing scheduling conflicts for local events

    Events from local branches shouldn't cause conflicts.

    Given an Atlanta event created by James:
      | name              | date           | time  |
      | Local staff picnic | 10-03-2017    | 10 AM |
      When Terry wants to organize another event in New York:
      | name                          | date           | time  |
      | The Move with Purpose Marathon | 10-03-2017    | 10 AM |
    Then the event should be successfully published
      And the employees in other departments should be notified
```

The events team ends up with four small specifications split from a single long one. Each of the four new feature files deals with a specific area of implementation. Being smaller, they're also easier to comprehend, and they can be expanded in the future without losing their readability. The team also splits the scenarios among the stakeholders that are relevant to their content. Under the previous system, the feature talked about events created by both HR representatives and individual team leaders. Now, each stakeholder has their own specification with their own scenarios.

MANAGING THE HIERARCHY OF FEATURE FILES IN THE SPECIFICATION SUITE

The last thing we need to discuss before moving on to the second Activitee team is the hierarchy of feature files in the specification suite created as a result of the changes made to the suite in this section. In chapter 8, we established a hierarchy of feature files for abilities (see figure 9.1).

Figure 9.1   The progression indicates hierarchy. At the top is the `Ability` keyword, which creates a space for user stories in the specification suite. Next are different stakeholders. At the bottom are outcomes that stakeholders can achieve.

The events team uses that hierarchy to organize the four new executable specifications (see figure 9.2). They end up with a specification suite organized by abilities and stakeholders. Each stakeholder can achieve different outcomes valuable to them. Thus, the specification suite is now organized as a map of Activitee clients and the value the company delivers. As you'll learn in section 9.3, the system is also flexible and can be easily expanded to fit other requirements, such as functional aspects of nonfunctional requirements.

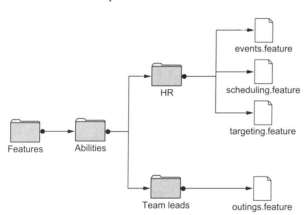

Figure 9.2   A specification suite organized according to abilities of stakeholders such as HR administrators and team leads

9.3   *Recognizing and refactoring business needs*

Now, let's move on to the application security team, who take on the user story about security:

```
In order to meet my company's security policy
As a Fortune 500 company employee
I want to make sure only I can access my account
```

This section focuses on specifying the functional aspects of the nonfunctional security requirement using the `Business Need` keyword. You'll also see how a business need can grow in size over time and how to react when that happens, by slicing the specification into smaller abilities—similar to what the events team did in section 9.2.

The goal of the application security team is to find and implement solutions that could increase the security of the Activitee platform according to industry standards. They didn't have to start from scratch. You may remember the business need shown in the following listing, which you wrote for Activitee in chapter 8. An Activitee product owner unexpectedly added to the backlog a new story about making passwords in the system more secure. The team decided that the simplest way to achieve results quickly, given Activitee's current capacity, would be to force users to create passwords that are harder to crack:

```
Business Need: Security

  Scenario Outline: Passwords should be secure

    Given Simona has to set a password
    When she tries to set the password to <password>
    Then the password should be considered <secure>

    Examples: Too short
      | password | secure   |
      | shorty   | insecure |

    Examples: No repetitive or sequential characters
      | password | secure   |
      | aaaaaaaa | insecure |

    Examples: No usernames, first names, or surnames
      | password      | secure   |
      | simonajenkins | insecure |

    Examples: Good password
      | password           | secure |
      | nevergonnagiveyouup | secure |
```

The password scenario looked like a good starting point. But the new user story implied a larger scope than just passwords. In order to decide on the most suitable solution, the team needed to understand the broader context of how the new story appeared in the backlog in the first place.

9.3.1   *Adding functional scenarios to business needs*

A quick investigation by the Activitee team determined the origin of the new security requirement. Activitee is a technology platform, and it works best with technologically savvy companies—but most of its early clients were less technologically oriented and had never used software for employee wellness. Such clients were easier to capture, but they also paid less and required more customer service. Most of Activitee's target customers already use some kind of wellness program. Activitee, as a new player on the market, had to catch up to its competitors.

When asked about the security requirement, the sales team confirmed that the company had reached the point that it could successfully compete with existing employee wellness solutions, and that the sales team had entered into contract negotiations with some desirable potential clients. But seducing technologically oriented customers meant the product would have to excel in areas where nontechnical clients were more forgiving—such as application security.

The application security team was pleasantly surprised to hear from the sales team that at this stage in the negotiations, the business value could be brought by preparing a few security scenarios showing that Activitee had something in the works. Enterprise sales often take months to close, so the team would have lots of time to implement the solutions they would suggest. Saying they were working on something and actually doing it wouldn't make much of a difference—the sales representatives just wanted a few scenarios to discuss during their sales pitches. Questions about security were popping up more often, and they needed some leverage. They said that an upcoming meeting with a potential client would be a good opportunity to try the scenarios.

The application security team decided to add new functional scenarios to the existing security business need. The first scenario was simple and was requested by the team's UX designer, who wanted to improve the experience of choosing a strong enough password by adding a password strength meter. The designer had wanted to address this omission for a long time, but there was always something more important. The team agreed that they could include it in the scope this time. The scenario outline was as follows.

Listing 9.8 Scenario outline for a password strength meter

```
Scenario Outline: Users should be able to see a password strength meter

  Given Simona has to set a password
  When she tries to set the password to <password>
  Then Simona should see that her password is <strength>

  Examples: Short passwords
    | password | strength |
    | shorty   | weak     |

  Examples: Longer passwords that are common dictionary words
    | password    | strength |
    | imagination | medium   |
    | countryside | medium   |
    | inimitable  | medium   |

  Examples: Long, non-obvious passwords
    | password          | strength |
    | nevergonnagiveyouup | strong |
```

The next scenario was suggested by the technical team. Increasingly, two-factor authentication is required for both enterprise-oriented and customer-oriented applications. The two-factor authentication the team agreed on would involve entering a combination of a password and a random code sent over SMS.

Listing 9.9   Scenario outline to introduce two-factor authentication

```
Scenario Outline: Users should be able to use two-factor authentication

  Given <authentication> for Simona
    And Simona's desire to log in
  When she provides her username
    And she provides her password
    And she enters <code>
  Then she should be <authenticated>

  Examples: Two-factor authentication
    | authentication | code             | authenticated |
    | two-factor auth | the correct code | logged in     |
    | two-factor auth | a wrong code     | not logged in |

  Examples: Make sure single-factor authentication still works
    | authentication | code    | authenticated |
    | traditional auth | no code | logged in     |
```

The third scenario the team decided to suggest was another industry standard: a reviewable login history. With a login history, a user would be able to see where and when their account was recently used. The team used a simple example of a hacker from a distant location who somehow got access to the account of an unlucky Activitee user. They also suggested that the user should be able to log out from all devices remotely in case of a security breach.

Listing 9.10   Scenarios for a login history

```
Scenario Outline: Users should be able to review their login history

  Given Simona's previous logins were from <country>
  When somebody logs in to her account from <login>
  Then her account should be considered <compromised>
    And Simona should be notified about the security breach

  Examples:
    | country | login   | compromised |
    | the USA | the USA | secure      |
    | the USA | the UK  | compromised |
    | the UK  | the UK  | secure      |
    | the UK  | the USA | compromised |

Scenario: Users should be able to log out remotely

  Given Simona was notified about the security breach
  When she confirms her identity via two-factor authentication
  Then she should be able to log herself out from all devices remotely
```

The team was happy with the scenarios they prepared. But when the sales representatives came back from the meeting with the prospective client, they didn't mention the scenarios. They were confused and had only one question: what is SSO, and why don't we have it?

We'll address that question in the next section.

9.3.2 *Identifying new stakeholders with business needs*

In chapter 8, I said that requirements listed as nonfunctional and defined as business needs usually imply that there's a stakeholder the team hasn't yet explicitly identified. For example, some stakeholders work behind the scenes and become more active only if an issue that interests them is on the table. Such stakeholders can be identified when new nonfunctional requirements appear, seemingly out of nowhere.

It turns out this was exactly what happened during the sales meeting that confused Activitee's representatives. The prospective client was interested in security because it had a very active Chief Information Security Officer who was responsible for the company's IT and computer systems. The CISO was involved in the process from the get-go, which was something Activitee's reps hadn't seen in less technologically savvy companies. The CISO turned out to be a competent, demanding stakeholder who was the ultimate decision maker but worked behind the scenes, leaving the negotiations to another executive. But as Activitee reps kept coming back with proposals that weren't satisfying, the CISO decided to become personally involved.

During the meeting, the CISO took for granted the scenarios presented by Activitee's sales team, which meant they officially became part of the future scope and not just proposals, as they were first pitched. Moreover, the CISO wanted Activitee to satisfy another requirement: that's right, the SSO thing.

> **DEFINITION** *Single sign-on*—A session- and user-authentication service that permits a user to use one set of login credentials (such as username and password) to access multiple applications

SSO stands for *single-sign on*. You use consumer-facing versions of SSO every time you use Facebook or Twitter to sign up on a website. In such cases, Facebook and Twitter play the role of identity providers that manage aspects of your accounts. For example, a website can ask the identity provider for your real name or profile picture and update it if you changed it on Facebook or Twitter.

Enterprises need SSO because every day their employees use dozens of applications to get the job done. I myself have mostly worked at small-to-medium agencies and startups, but even there I used 20 or 30 apps to manage my work—without SSO. It was a pain. For companies with thousands of employees, the pain must be a thousand times stronger. Enterprise identity providers like okta.com can help teams alleviate the pain and manage their application stack.

Having investigated the topic, the application security team came up with a few new scenarios to make the business need for security more complete.

Listing 9.11 SSO scenarios

```
Scenario: CISOs should be able to have the IT Security team set SSO up

  Given a valid SSO API endpoint provided by an IT Security team
    And a client ID
    And a client secret
```

```
    And a callback URL
  When IT Security team activates SSO
  Then the company's Activitee should start pointing to the Identity Provider
```

```
Scenario: SSO-enabled users should be authenticated and let in
```

```
  Given an SSO-enabled company
    And James, an employee who's logged in to the Identity Provider's system
  When he doesn't re-enter his credentials on Activitee when he logs in
  Then he should still be authenticated and let in
```

```
Scenario: A company deactivates SSO
```

```
  Given an SSO-enabled company
  When their CISO decides to disable SSO
  Then the employees need to enter credentials in order to get in
```

The scenarios require the IT security team to point Activitee's software toward a working API endpoint that gives the user account information Activitee needs after identity confirmation. The security team also provides a client ID and a client secret, which the identity provider uses to select the correct company's user base. A callback URL is then required to redirect the user back to Activitee. The third new scenario deals with a company that decides to stop using a given SSO provider; in this case, Activitee must force employees to generate new passwords, because the Activitee platform didn't store them (the SSO provider did).

The overarching lesson here is that the Activitee team could have reacted more quickly to the fact that a new business need emerged and became increasingly demanding. Had they done so, they would have understood much earlier that there was a stakeholder they hadn't identified who was working behind the scenes, influencing their results. If they had talked to that stakeholder directly in the first place, they would have been able to present a scope that was smaller and tailored to the CISO's needs from the outset. Instead, they ended up committing to scenarios they thought were only proposals—and also had to implement three new SSO-related scenarios. In the end, it was all an issue of stakeholder management.

9.3.3 *Refactoring functional scenarios in business needs into individual abilities*

So far, all the security-related scenarios are in a single business need. Figure 9.3 shows the specification suite.

Although Activitee's business need started as a simple feature file with a single scenario, it's now vastly different. After all the iterations, there are eight different scenarios related to various areas of the product, such as passwords, two-factor authentication, and SSO integration. Now that we know CISOs are important stakeholders with their own requests, we suspect that the number of scenarios will keep growing—which means it's time to break the business need into several smaller abilities that will grow independently in the future.

Let's start with the SSO scenarios, because they're distinct from the scenarios prepared by the application security team and will be the easiest to extract. Extracting

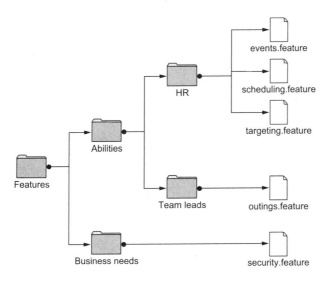

Figure 9.3 **A specification suite with both abilities and business needs becomes a map of functional requirements and stakeholders who find them important, as well as functional aspects of nonfunctional requirements important to the entire system.**

these SSO scenarios lets us add a specification brief with a lexical definition—just like you practiced doing in chapter 7.

Listing 9.12 SSO ability broken up from the previous business need

```
Ability: CISOs can manage employees easily by integrating with an SSO provider

    SINGLE SIGN-ON (SSO) is a session and user authentication service
    that permits a user to use one set of login credentials
    (e.g., name and password) to access multiple applications.

    Big companies with hundreds of employees find it hard to manage
    employees' data across many different internal services while adhering
    to internal security or privacy policies (e.g. some organizations
    change employees' passwords once a month because of security issues).
    Some might want to implement a custom registration process due
    to legal reasons. All of them will eventually part ways with some of
    their employees and will have to make sure that these ex-employees'
    private data is deleted across all of the internal services.

Scenario: CISOs should be able to have the IT Security team set SSO up

    Given a valid SSO API endpoint provided by an IT Security team
      And a client ID
      And a client secret
      And a callback URL
    When IT Security team activates SSO
    Then the company's Activitee should start pointing to the Identity Provider

Scenario: SSO-enabled users should be authenticated and let in

    Given an SSO-enabled company
      And James, an employee who's logged in to the Identity Provider's system
    When he doesn't re-enter his credentials on Activitee when he logs in
    Then he should still be authenticated and let in
```

```
Scenario: A company deactivates SSO

  Given an SSO-enabled company
  When their CISO decides to disable SSO
  Then the employees need to enter credentials in order to get in
```

The application security team also decides to extract the password-strength scenarios into their own ability.

```
Ability: Employees can secure their passwords

  Scenario Outline: Passwords should be secure

    Given Simona has to set a password
    When she tries to set the password to <password>
    Then the password should be considered <secure>

    Examples: Too short
      | password | secure   |
      | shorty   | insecure |

    Examples: No repetitive or sequential characters
      | password | secure   |
      | aaaaaaaa | insecure |

    Examples: No usernames, first names, or surnames
      | password     | secure   |
      | simonajenkins | insecure |

    Examples: Good password
      | password          | secure |
      | nevergonnagiveyouup | secure |

  Scenario Outline: Users should be able to see a password strength meter

    Given Simona has to set a password
    When she tries to set the password to <password>
    Then Simona should see that her password is <strength>

    Examples: Short passwords
      | password | strength |
      | shorty   | weak     |

    Examples: Longer passwords that are common dictionary words
      | password    | strength |
      | imagination | medium   |
      | imagination | medium   |
      | imagination | medium   |

    Examples: Long, non-obvious passwords
      | password          | strength |
      | nevergonnagiveyouup | strong   |
```

The only scenarios that remain in the security business need deal with employees authenticating themselves and managing their identity.

```
Listing 9.14   Ability for employee authentication and identity management
```

```
Ability: Employees can authenticate and manage their identity

  Scenario Outline: Users should be able to use two-factor authentication

    Given <authentication> for Simona
      And Simona's desire to log in
    When she provides her username
      And she provides her password
      And she enters <code>
    Then she should be <authenticated>

    Examples: Two-factor authentication
      | authentication | code             | authenticated  |
      | two-factor auth | the correct code | logged in     |
      | two-factor auth | a wrong code    | not logged in  |

    Examples: Make sure single-factor authentication still works
      | authentication | code    | authenticated |
      | traditional auth | no code | logged in    |

  Scenario Outline: Users should be able to review their login history

    Given Simona's previous logins were from <country>
    When somebody logs in to her account from <login>
    Then her account should be considered <compromised>
      And Simona should be notified about the security breach

    Examples:
      | country | login   | compromised |
      | the USA | the USA | secure      |
      | the USA | the UK  | compromised |
      | the UK  | the UK  | secure      |
      | the UK  | the USA | compromised |

  Scenario: Users should be able to log out remotely

    Given Simona was notified about the security breach
    When she confirms her identity via two-factor authentication
    Then she should be able to log herself out from all devices remotely
```

We have three more feature files than we started with, but the upside is that the application security team will be able to grow each area of implementation independently in the future. You can also see that each of the specifications we ended up with has two or three tightly connected scenarios instead of eight scenarios that try to specify the security aspect holistically within a single business need.

It's not that the previous business need was bad; it just outgrew its purpose. Business needs are used to identify areas where new stakeholders may potentially emerge. As soon as that happens, you can begin working with the stakeholders to develop their areas of interest—and abilities are much better for doing that (see figure 9.4).

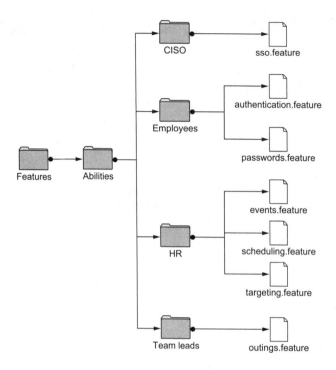

Figure 9.4   The specification suite with new security stakeholders, such as CISOs, and new security abilities, such as authentication, which were broken out from a prior business need when it had too many functional aspects to keep in a single feature file

9.4   Summary

- You can convey your requirements as abilities or business needs when deriving them from user stories.
- Adding too many new scenarios to existing executable specifications makes them cover too many topics at once.
- To avoid covering too many topics, refactor large specifications into smaller ones.
- Even though many teams use the `Feature` keyword at the beginning of their Gherkin journey, they should consider switching to abilities and business needs later on.
- You can refactor existing features into smaller abilities by splitting the scenarios just like the user stories from which they were derived.
- Specify functional aspects of nonfunctional requirements like security using business needs.
- New business needs usually imply that there's a stakeholder whom the team hasn't yet explicitly identified.
- When a business need grows into having too many functional scenarios, you can move each function to its own ability.

Building a domain-driven
specification suite

10

This chapter covers

- Recognizing good domain models
- Analyzing a ubiquitous language
- Distilling business domains from scenarios
- Recognizing different kinds of business domains
- Organizing a specification suite according to available domains

This is the third chapter in a four-chapter series about managing large specification suites. Chapters 8 and 9 discussed actors and using their abilities and business needs as replacements for the Feature keyword. In this chapter, we'll analyze what happens when actors have too many scenarios and another level of hierarchy is needed—which usually happens in medium-sized projects.

Figure 10.1 shows a specification suite for the fictional company Activitee of chapters 8–11. We built most of this suite in chapters 8 and 9; the figure presents a slightly expanded version, after the product has grown into a medium-sized project. We'll talk about the new specifications in section 10.3.

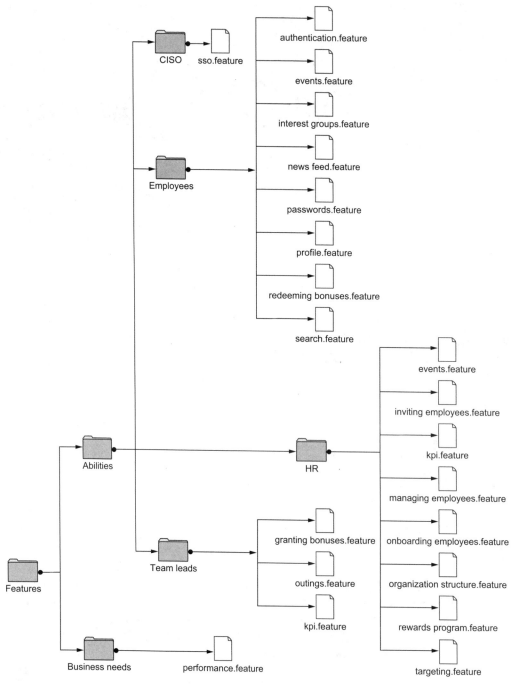

Figure 10.1   Actors in medium-sized projects can have too many abilities, which makes the specification suite more difficult to understand.

Before writing this chapter, I looked at some of the real projects I've worked on over the last few years. In one of these projects, a specification suite with about 60 scenarios had 380 steps spread between two actors. If you had such a project, then assuming every feature file had about three scenarios, as I advised in chapter 8, you'd end up with about 20 feature files in the suite—10 per actor. A slightly bigger project of mine had 170 scenarios written for 4 actors, 1,120 steps, and about 60 feature files—15 per actor. In such cases, a simple split between actors' abilities and the system's business needs, introduced in chapter 8, may not be enough. We're approaching a similar threshold with the Activitee specification suite.

The concepts we'll be using to manipulate and comprehend these large domains come from the field of domain-driven design (DDD). This chapter and the next one will rely heavily on ideas borrowed from DDD. You may be familiar with DDD; I first mentioned it in chapter 1 when I talked about ubiquitous languages in specifications. In this chapter, we'll discuss domains—subdomains, core domains, secondary domains, and generic domains—as well as domain models, a ubiquitous language, glossaries, bounded contexts, and context maps. This chapter is be a high-level summary of the most important concepts of *strategic domain-driven design* and shows how you can use these techniques in designing your specification suites.

You'll begin by distilling business domains from a ubiquitous language. Then, you'll use the distilled domain to build a domain model. Finally, you'll reorganize a large specification suite according to that model, grouping similar feature files together. Some of these methods were discussed earlier in the book; for example, I talked about a ubiquitous language in various parts of chapters 1, 2, 5, and 7. Chapter 7, which discussed living documentation, also talked about creating glossaries. We'll now revisit these concepts in the context of DDD and also introduce new ideas. Keep in mind that this chapter is by no means a full introduction to DDD. If interested, you can read more in Eric Evans' canonical work on the topic: *Domain-Driven Design* (Addison-Wesley, 2003). In this case, just as in Evans' book, everything starts with a ubiquitous language.

10.1 Distilling business domains from a ubiquitous language

A *ubiquitous language*, first mentioned in section 1.2.2, is a language cultivated in the intersection of technical and business jargons, derived from multiple sources (see figure 10.2). Each project has its own ubiquitous language. It's *not* the language of the business, nor is it the language of technology. It's a mix of both.

Domain experts—people with authority in a particular area or topic—have different design jargons. Technology experts—such as designers, testers, analysts, and engineers—also have their own jargons. Design jargon is just as bad as technical jargon. When bankers talk too much about their work, they can be as annoying at the dinner tables as programmers, designers, or testers—and they can be just as difficult to understand for a layperson inexperienced in their domain. The narrower the business

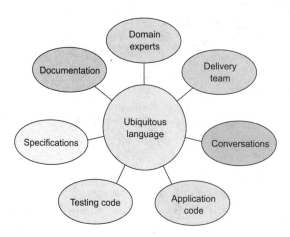

Figure 10.2 **The sources of a ubiquitous language—a language that's created by mixing the jargons of technology and business in order to build a unified lingual model that can be used by both the domain experts and the technology experts**

domain of a project, the more difficult the language seems to outsiders. But most people can understand the consumer-facing aspects of businesses. Pop culture can help, too: for example, movies about Wall Street have helped people understand basic finance keywords such as *shorting*, popularized by the 2015 movie *The Big Short*; and *initial public offering (IPO)*, depicted in the critically acclaimed *The Wolf of Wall Street* in 2013.

Businesses like Activitee aren't likely to receive that type of publicity. So, a ubiquitous language must grow out of blending technological expertise with business expertise in reasonable proportions. This section explores how you can analyze a ubiquitous language to derive a model of the business domains used in a specification suite. Deriving the model is the first step in getting to the end goal: creating a proper system for organizing large specification suites according to the business domain.

Before we continue our work on Activitee's specification suite, let's analyze a simpler example.

10.1.1 Spotting different domains in your scenarios

Ubiquitous language lies at the heart of DDD. Gherkin scenarios can be a great source of a ubiquitous language, because each scenario is a recording of a conversation that business experts had with technology experts about requirements. If the recording is truthful, the scenario should easily capture a ubiquitous language that the experts created during their conversations, both face-to-face and in writing.

Naturally, a raw record won't be perfect. Let's say you're sitting in a specification workshop for a simple cloud storage service similar to Dropbox, Google Drive, Apple iCloud, or Microsoft OneDrive. A domain expert is explaining a behavior, and you're writing it down as a Gherkin draft. The following record ends up on the whiteboard.

Listing 10.1 Conversation recorded as a Gherkin scenario

```
Given a 2 GB limit on free cloud drive accounts
  And 2 GB of files on Simona's free cloud drive account
When she upgrades to the premium plan
```

```
Then her credit card should be charged $5
And her storage should be upgraded to a 40 GB limit
```

It's a good enough draft—at least for the brainstorming stage. But if you look at the scenario more closely, you'll see that it introduces terms from several domains into a ubiquitous language for the team:

- Terms like *cloud drive* are from the cloud domain.
- *Gigabytes*, *files*, and *storage* are from the more general storage domain, which, nonetheless, must stay connected to the cloud domain.
- Terms like *premium plan*, *free*, and *credit card* are from the payments domain, also called the commercial offering domain, which all nonfree products share.

TIP   Chapter 7 discussed which elements of Gherkin scenarios are important parts of a ubiquitous language. They're elements such as actors, states, outcomes, domain concepts, and actions.

We can easily illustrate how different domains map onto the scenario, as shown in figure 10.3. Notice that some of the domains don't have to be tightly coupled. For example, the payments domain doesn't have to be connected so closely to the storage domain. Upgrading an account to the premium plan will also make available other, nonstorage features, such as team collaboration—so maybe you should look for a more general way to specify the details of the business model. But that doesn't mean you can uncouple *all* domains. The storage domain, for example, often remains connected to the cloud domain, because there can be no cloud storage without having storage in the first place.

```
Given a 2 GB limit on free cloud drive accounts
And 2 GB of files on Simona's free cloud drive account
When she upgrades to the premium plan
Then her credit card should be charged $5
And her storage should be upgraded to a 40 GB limit
```

▬▬▬ Cloud domain
▨▨▨ Storage domain
▨▨▨ Payments domain

Figure 10.3   **Different domains can appear in a single scenario, depending on how you formulate the behavior using a ubiquitous language.**

Exercise 1

Choose one state, one action, and one outcome from listing 10.1, and assign a domain to each one. If you notice multiple domains in any of the steps, decide which domain should be the most important in this step.

What should you do about all the different domains in a scenario?

Listing 10.1 presents a scenario that contains multiple subdomains. Should you leave it that way or refine it?

You faced a similar dilemma in section 3.3.4, which talked about a technique called *outcome questioning*. This technique requires you to ask, "Is there another outcome that also matters but isn't included in the scenario?" When you asked that question in chapter 3, you found another outcome—but it belonged to a completely different business domain!

You're facing a similar problem here. In fact, I based this example on the example from section 3.3.4, with some modifications. You can see the similarities if you compare listing 10.1 with the scenario from chapter 3, repeated here:

```
Scenario: Upgrading cloud plans

  Given a 50 MB limit on Vladimir's cloud drive
    And 50 MB of text documents on Vladimir's cloud drive
  When Vladimir tries to save a new revision in the cloud
  Then he should be upgraded to a plan with more space
    And his credit card should be charged $5
```

In the suggested answer to the exercise, which asked you to consider whether the outcomes from different domains that appeared back in chapter 3 should be separated, I wrote that, in my opinion, you should specify cloud functionality and paid plan limits separately. I stand by this opinion.

The cloud and storage domains can stay together because they're closely related, but the payments domain should be specified elsewhere in the specification suite. You could, for example, reword the scenario in terms of dealing only with remaining free space on a user's cloud drive and block the user's ability to upload new files. Then, in a separate specification, you could have all the scenarios that deal with premium accounts and payments. Among them, you'd be able to include a scenario to specify how much disk space free and premium accounts have.

10.1.2 *Distilling the core domain from scenarios*

Domain design, like any other design, is an art of trade-offs. We can clearly see that the domains in listing 10.1 aren't equal. Delivering products and services is a complex endeavor that requires many different activities coordinated among many diverse departments. Some domains are inherently more important than others, and some are more generic than others. This is natural. Your task is to untangle and prioritize domains so that you can decide which ones to focus on. DDD calls such a prioritization process *distillation*.

> **DEFINITION** *Distillation*—A procedure whereby the components of a mixture are separated in order to extract the various ingredients, particularly the most valuable one: the *heart* of the distillate

In the case of the storage service, if you were to distill the business into the several domains mentioned in section 10.1.1, the cloud domain would clearly be the heart of the distillate. In other words, the cloud domain is the *core domain*.

> **DEFINITION** *Core domain*—A domain most closely associated with the strategy and market positioning of a company. It's a domain of the utmost value.

A competitive company must excel at its core domain. The cloud storage company in the example must excel at the cloud domain if it wants to deliver enough value to its customers in this crowded market. By distilling the core domain, you can understand which scenarios and domain concepts are the heart of your software system and therefore should be more important than others.

10.1.3 *Distilling subdomains accompanying the core domain*

In addition to the core cloud domain, the example company distills into two other domains: storage and payments. If the core domain is *the* most important domain, then, by definition, you can have only one core domain. What are the other domains? They're *subdomains*: domains other than the core domain, which aren't at the heart of the company but are nonetheless necessary to sustain its strategic mission.

To understand the concept of subdomains more easily, look at your own life. We all have something important at the center of our lives. For some people, it's family. For other people, it's a passionate interest. This is a core domain. Although you know that it matters to you above all else, you know that a full human life has other, less important aspects, too, which support your well-being. Work is a good example. Other aspects are more mundane—like going shopping and paying taxes. They're the remaining subdomains of your life.

SUPPORTING SUBDOMAINS

Let's get back to the storage service. If you were to point out the domain that's next-most-important after the core domain, you'd probably choose the storage subdomain. Cloud storage obviously differs from physical storage, but the company needs some classic storage expertise, too, to become a viable player in the cloud industry. This is why domains like the storage domain from the example are called *supporting subdomains*.

> **DEFINITION** *Supporting subdomain*—A domain that indirectly supports the core domain without belonging to it. Even though only one domain can lie at the heart of a company, each core domain needs subdomains to support its strategic mission.

A company doesn't have to excel at its supporting subdomains. The value of supporting domains, in isolation, is weak. You just have be good enough not to fall too far behind the competition. In the example, storage is a well-penetrated area with multiple industry standards and established solutions that we don't have to develop on our own. The company doesn't have to drive innovation in this subdomain. You only need to make sure it works at a standard level that customers have learned to generally accept.

By distilling supporting subdomains, you learn which domain concepts should be taken care of after you deal with your core domain. Learning that is important because it lets you allocate appropriate resources to the supporting subdomains and, therefore, avoid over- and underinvestments.

> ### Exercise 2
> Think of one more supporting subdomain that could be relevant to the cloud storage service.

GENERIC SUBDOMAINS

The payments domain is also a subdomain—but it's different than storage. Storage is at least thematically related to the core domain. The payments domain is, in this case, a generic domain, like authentication or account management. It's like paying taxes in my earlier metaphor comparing subdomains to areas of life.

Such domains are required for the software to function, but they don't come from or influence the core domain. This is why we call such domains *generic subdomains*.

> **DEFINITION** *Generic subdomain*—A universal subdomain that can appear in any kind of software and includes standardized solutions such as account management and support functionalities. Whereas supporting subdomains support the core domain without belonging to it, generic subdomains don't have to be related to the core domain; they're meant to increase utility and make basic services work.

Some other classic examples are accounting, human resources, and project management. Some technical solutions, such as search, can also be generic subdomains. Generic subdomains are usually the least important subdomains in terms of market competition—I've never heard of anyone choosing a product or a service because of its great payments system. Still, generic subdomains *are* essential and can't be ignored. For example, you instinctively know that you can't ignore the payments subdomain—but at the same time, you could delegate it or even outsource it to a third-party service.

> ### Exercise 3
> Can you think of another generic subdomain?

10.2   Creating a domain model from distilled domains

Together, the core domain and the subdomains, distilled from a ubiquitous language, create a *domain model.* Chapter 1 said that a domain model is a simplification of the real-world business domain—an interpretation of reality that abstracts only the aspects relevant to solving the problem at hand.

Better models help you solve problems more reliably and easily. If you can not only organize scenarios by requirements, as you did in chapter 8, but also *organize requirements by their corresponding domains*, then you can build better domain models—which, in turn, will help you maintain and organize large enterprise systems and start harnessing DDD's benefits. In this section, you'll prepare to create a domain model from the subdomains distilled from the ubiquitous language. We'll look at why good models are important and what makes a good model.

10.2.1   The domain model and the specification suite

Here's a quick example of how you can organize the requirements in a specification suite by their corresponding domains, thus creating a visual representation of the domain model included in that specification suite. This example is also based on the cloud storage service, to maintain continuity.

Let's assume that the distillation process is finished, and you've extracted all the relevant subdomains. You end up with a complete list of actors and their abilities, prepared based on the practices covered in chapter 8, as well as several business needs that specify a few functional aspects of your nonfunctional requirements (see figure 10.4).

As you can see, the abilities—or functional requirements—in the system are organized by their corresponding subdomains. (I added a new generic subdomain for access control to make the specification suite a little more complex.) Now, even if a single actor has multiple capabilities, you can split all of them among various subdomains. You can also see which actors are present in which subdomains, which will help you understand which subdomains are important to which stakeholders. In addition, you can make an inverse deduction: you're able to see which stakeholders can be instrumental in developing the subdomains. Also notice that you haven't done anything with business needs; they're nonfunctional requirements, and nonfunctionals are general qualities like speed or usability—they belong to the entire system instead of specific subdomains.

Such a specification suite can become a visual representation of the domain model specified by this suite. You can see a clear hierarchy of subdomains, actors, and requirements. Moreover, a representation like this can evolve naturally over time, because the requirements are tied to the domain logic code by the automated tests. If you change the requirements or change the domain logic, you'll probably need to add, delete, or move the feature files related to the changed requirements—and your visualization of the model will change alongside the model.

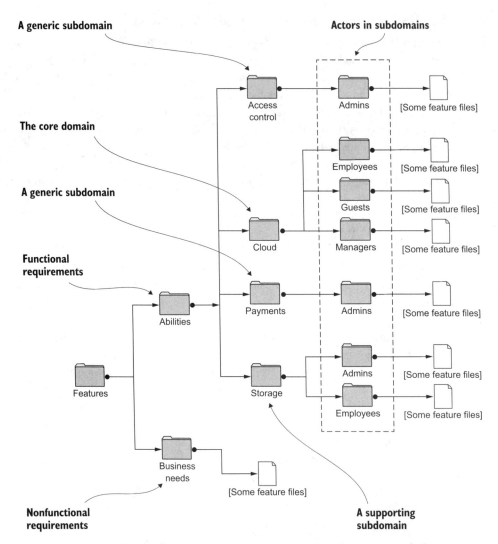

A generic subdomain

Actors in subdomains

Access control

Admins   [Some feature files]

The core domain

Employees   [Some feature files]

Guests   [Some feature files]

A generic subdomain

Cloud

Managers   [Some feature files]

Functional requirements

Abilities

Payments

Admins   [Some feature files]

Features

Storage

Admins   [Some feature files]

Employees   [Some feature files]

Business needs

[Some feature files]

Nonfunctional requirements

A supporting subdomain

Figure 10.4   A specification suite organized by the subdomains present in the suite. Each subdomain features a list of actors relevant to this subdomain. Every actor can have various capabilities in each of the subdomains.

10.2.2 Why are good domain models important?

Now that you know how to create a simple domain model based on a ubiquitous language, we can discuss why good models are important. In chapter 1, you learned that 80% of all product defects are inserted when delivery teams define their requirements. If you look at each requirement as a problem to solve on behalf of your customers, you can assume that building better domain models will result in fewer misunderstood requirements. To build a realistic model of your business domain, you

Why organize specification suites by subdomains?

An early reviewer of this book asked the following question:

> *The book talks about the idea of organizing specifications by domains. Fine, but why not organize them by actors instead?*

It's an interesting question. Chapter 8 left you with a simpler organization system that had actors at the top. Why should you now adopt a different system, with business domains at a higher level of the hierarchy?

The reason is that actors and stakeholders don't always define business domains, but business domains always define the stakeholders and actors. Business value is always dictated by the core domain. For example, a banking company will only hire banking personnel—the actors are derived from the business domain. The ubiquitous language, too, is created out of particular domains: you aren't interested in the way domain experts talk, but rather in their subject-matter expertise.

must not only understand particular requirements, but also understand how they relate to each other.

Maps can help. Maps often show how we think about the world around us. When the model depicted in a map is wrong, the decisions made based on the incorrect map are more likely to be wrong, too. By *more likely*, I mean that you won't necessarily be wrong every time you use a wrong model—but you'll *increase the long-term risk factor* of being wrong. Let me explain what I mean.

The geocentric map of the solar system, also called the Ptolemaic model, depicted a universe where the sun, moon, stars, and planets all circled Earth. The geocentric model was eventually replaced by the heliocentric model, including Copernican heliocentrism. But the Ptolemaic model was good enough for scientists to successfully perform many calculations. Both the Copernican and Ptolemaic models provided identical results for identical inputs. Only after Kepler demonstrated that the sun is directly involved in determining a planet's orbit was a new model required. If you abstain from talking about the real world for a moment, the geocentric model is only wrong when you go deep into the details.

At times, something similar happens with software. I've seen projects that didn't care much about mapping the business domain but that still delivered working software, even though it was based on imperfect models. Some of these projects worked well enough for a long time because they were all the business owners needed. Good for them. But other projects turned out to be unmaintainable in the long term and failed spectacularly when the teams tried to modify the scope by adding new requirements or expanding existing capabilities. Every time, it was a truly Copernican moment, in the sense that finding out a Ptolemaic model is wrong is usually very painful—and very expensive.

10.2.3 *What makes a good domain model in software?*

Bad models lead you to make wrong decisions. Good models, on the other hand, have these characteristics:

- Accurate enough to find a good solution to a problem
- Unified, as in "the model is internally consistent"
- Stable in finding good solutions over time
- Realistic and empirically based on the real world

Attributes such as accuracy are easy to accept. But some attributes are more controversial.

If a good model has to be stable, should you advocate iterative software development? Throughout the book, I've talked about the process of discovering requirements and refining models over time. Discovering requirements sounds fine, but what if your discoveries lead you to a painful Copernican moment, as described in the previous section?

Just as software development can be iterative, so can science. New theories replace old theories and tend to be better. The same is true with software development. New domain models tend to be better than old models. The challenging issue is how to manage the transition risk between the old and new models. The risk is lowered if the transition is small and the model improves iteratively over small batches of changes. The risk is also reduced if the model is strengthened by automated tests. In general, tests make a model stronger because automation ensures that you're tying the model directly to code, which creates powerful feedback loops between changes in the model and changes in the code. (Feedback loops were discussed in chapter 6.) SBE and Gherkin, as explained in this book, employ both of these practices.

Feedback loops help with unification of the model, too. When a model is frequently validated by automated tests, you can be sure that it's internally consistent to the level covered by the tests.

10.3 *Building a domain-driven specification suite in practice*

We can now get back to the Activitee example. In this section, we'll derive domains from a few of the specifications created for Activitee in the previous chapters. We'll do the same for a few new specifications shown in figure 10.1, when we were imagining what a medium-sized suite could look like in Activitee's case. Thanks to the distillation process, you'll be able to add another layer to your suite-building skills as we organize Activitee's specifications and actors by their subdomains. The new layer should result in something we'll call a *domain-driven specification suite.*

> **DEFINITION** *Domain-driven specification suite*—A specification suite organized according to its various domains. Domain-driven suites are easier to manage when you have too many actors or when actors have too many abilities.

10.3.1 *Distilling subdomains from unequivocal scenarios*

Let's begin with an easy, unequivocal example. Back in chapter 9, we wrote the following ability, which specifies how employees can authenticate and manage their identity on the Activitee platform.

> **Listing 10.2 features/abilities/security/employees/authentication.feature**

```
Ability: Employees can authenticate and manage their identity

  Scenario Outline: Users should be able to use two-factor authentication

    Given <authentication> for Simona
      And Simona's desire to log in
    When she provides her username
      And she provides her password
      And she enters <code>
    Then she should be <authenticated>

    Examples: Two-factor authentication
      | authentication   | code             | authenticated  |
      | two-factor auth  | the correct code | logged in      |
      | two-factor auth  | a wrong code     | not logged in  |

    Examples: Make sure single-factor authentication still works
      | authentication   | code     | authenticated  |
      | traditional auth | no code  | logged in      |

  Scenario Outline: Users should be able to review their login history

    Given Simona's previous logins were from <country>
    When somebody logs in to her account from <login>
    Then her account should be considered <compromised>
      And Simona should be notified about the security breach

    Examples:
      | country | login   | compromised |
      | the USA | the USA | secure      |
      | the USA | the UK  | compromised |
      | the UK  | the UK  | secure      |
      | the UK  | the USA | compromised |

  Scenario: Users should be able to log out remotely

    Given Simona was notified about the security breach
    When she confirms her identity via two-factor authentication
    Then she should be able to log herself out from all devices remotely
```

The three scenarios are very focused. They talk about one thing, and one thing only: security (see table 10.1). Their business context explains that; they were created when Activitee signed a new client that had an active Chief Information Security Officer responsible for its IT and computer systems.

Table 10.1   Domain in listing 10.3

Domain	Ubiquitous language
Security	Authentication, two-factor authentication, password, compromised account, secure, security breach, identity, remote logout

Specifications like this are easy to analyze, because they're unequivocal. You can derive the domain easily, because the scenarios talk about a single topic. If all Gherkin specifications maintained this one-to-one relationship between scenarios and domains, our job in this section would almost be done. Unfortunately, as you saw in figure 10.3, and as you'll see in the sections to come, reality isn't always organized so neatly.

10.3.2 *Distilling subdomains from mixed scenarios*

Security wasn't the only topic covered in chapter 9. You also prepared specifications that allowed HR representatives to target programs to specific audiences.

> **Listing 10.3   features/abilities/events/HR/targeting.feature**

```
Ability: HR reps can target wellness programs by choosing specific audiences

  Scenario Outline: Managing invited participants

    Given James drafted a new event
     When he invites <invitee>
     Then only <invitee> should be notified about the invite
      But <uninvited> should not be notified

    Examples: Invites to one-on-one events such as annual reviews
      | invitee | uninvited |
      | Simona  | Jane      |

    Examples: Invites to local events in specific locations
      | invitee           | uninvited           |
      | Atlanta employees | New York employees  |

    Examples: Inviting one department, but not the other (all locations)
      | invitee   | uninvited   |
      | engineers | salespeople |

    Examples: Inviting a specific department from a specific location
      | invitee          | uninvited                      |
      | Atlanta engineers | New York engineers, salespeople |
```

The language in the four scenarios from listing 10.3 isn't as unequivocal as in the previous specification (see table 10.2). At least two domains can be derived from the new steps. Some domain concepts refer to the events domain, others to the domain of organization.

   If we only wanted to analyze the ubiquitous language of the specification suite, saying that there are two distinct domains at play would be fine. The problem is that we want to organize the suite by its domains. Because the file system is a hierarchical structure, we can only assign the feature file that includes the ability from listing 10.4

Table 10.2 Domains in listing 10.4

Domain	Ubiquitous language
Events	Event, draft, invite, participants, annual review
Organization	Employee, team, location, department

to a single domain (if we want various directories to represent various domains). That's why we have to choose between the two domains we just distilled.

We can make the choice based on multiple approaches:

- *Treat the core domain as more important than other subdomains.* In Activitee's case, the events domain clearly is the core domain. The downside of this approach is that the core domain will *always* take precedence in every scenario it appears in—which isn't something we want, because most scenarios have to deal with the core domain in one way or another.
- *Count the domain concepts (terms) in each domain, and assume that the more popular domain is also more important.* The first downside is that we have no guidelines for dealing with draws (ties). The second downside is that some domains will be more popular only because they're more generic than others or because they have more nonfunctional aspects, making it easier for them to spread horizontally across the suite.
- *Combine the two previous approaches in an attempt to calculate the relative weight of each domain.* This approach acknowledges that some domains (such as the core domain) are inherently more important than others. But it also acknowledges that domains with more domain concepts can, in some cases, be even more essential than the core domain.

Table 10.2 shows that the specification from listing 10.4 is close to a draw, with a 5-4 result. We can assume that the distilled domains are almost equally important to the distillate. Personally, I recommend choosing the events domain, because the scenarios only talk about managing participants, and the core domain can take precedence in this case.

Next, let's talk about an example where the opposite is true. In chapter 8, we prepared a specification similar to the one from listing 10.4. It said that employees should only see Activitee content that's relevant to them—and that relevancy should be calculated based on their branches and departments.

Listing 10.4 features/abilities/organization/employees/news feed.feature

```
Ability: Employees can see content they like in the news feeds for their branches

  Scenario Outline: Employees should only see content relevant to them

    Given <person> from <branch> who works in <department>
    When <person> looks at the company dashboard on Activitee
    Then <person> should see <type> <content>
```

```
Examples: Employees should see after-work content only from their location
  | person | branch   | department  | type                 | content |
  | Jane   | New York | Engineering | New York after-work  | events  |
  | Mike   | New York | HR          | New York after-work  | posts   |
  | Tom    | Atlanta  | Sales       | Atlanta after-work   | events  |
  | Ramona | Atlanta  | Engineering | Atlanta after-work   | posts   |

Examples: Employees should see work-related content from all locations
  | person | branch   | department  | type                 | content |
  | Mike   | New York | HR          | Atlanta HR           | events  |
  | Jane   | New York | Engineering | Atlanta engineering  | posts   |
  | Jane   | New York | Engineering | New York engineering | events  |
  | Tom    | Atlanta  | Sales       | Atlanta sales        | events  |
  | Ramona | Atlanta  | Engineering | Atlanta engineering  | posts   |
  | Ramona | Atlanta  | Engineering | New York engineering | events  |
```

NOTE   I counted *posts* as part of the organization subdomain because Activi-tee's news feed treats posts as pieces of content published in various interest groups. *Groups* belong to the organization domain.

If you look at table 10.3, you'll see that listing 10.5 is the opposite of listing 10.4. It's close to a draw again—but this time, it's a 3-5 result in favor of the organization subdo-main. This, together with the fact that the examples talk not only about events but also about posts in interest groups, impels me to recommend adding this specification to the organization subdomain.

Table 10.3   Domains in listing 10.5

Domain	Ubiquitous language
Events	Events, after-work, work-related
Organization	Employee, branch, department, location, posts

10.3.3 *Distilling subdomains from other scenarios*

We now have three domains with at least one scenario assigned: security, events, and organization. We can use the same decision-making framework for other specifica-tions in the suite, so we won't focus as much on the distillation process as in the previ-ous examples. Instead, we'll look at examples that introduce new subdomains, so that our analysis will be more diverse.

Let's analyze a specification that wasn't included in chapters 8 or 9. At the begin-ning of the chapter, I added it to figure 10.1: the kpi.feature file.

Key performance indicators (KPIs) are a common type of performance measure-ment. KPIs evaluate the success of an organization or a particular activity in which it engages. Activitee provides HR departments with analytical tools that help them track their KPIs. The rationale is that analytics give HR representatives a sense of current direction and let them plan their event strategy in the long term. One of the KPIs in Activitee is the adoption metric.

Listing 10.5 features/abilities/analytics/HR/kpi.feature

```
Ability: HR can analyze adoption metrics to keep track of their KPIs

  Scenario Outline: Calculating adoption goals

    Our assumption is that employee distribution
    between interests should be that every
    interest group should aim to have at least 5%
    of the overall employee base. This is meant to ensure
    that there are no "dead" interests nobody
    likes.

    THE FORMULA FOR THE ADOPTION GOAL
    the adoption goal = (`active_groups` * 100%) / all interest groups
    `active_groups` = groups with more users than `required_users_per_group`
    `required_users_per_group` = 5% of all employees

    Given HR set the adoption goal to 60%
      And the company has <users> employees registered
      And there are <groups> interest groups in the organization
      And only <active> interest groups have more members than <required>
    When the current adoption goal is calculated
    Then it should be at <goal>
      And Mike's company <should> be meeting their KPIs

    Examples: Must be enough active groups
      | users | groups | active | required | goal | should     |
      | 200   | 20     | 12     | 10       | 60%  | should     |
      | 200   | 20     | 11     | 10       | 55%  | should not |

    Examples: The size of the user base should affect the goal
      | users | groups | active | required | goal | should     |
      | 2000  | 20     | 12     | 100      | 60%  | should     |
      | 2000  | 20     | 11     | 100      | 55%  | should not |
```

This time, the choice is easy. The analytics subdomain is both the most frequently mentioned and, based on the examples, is the most important subdomain in listing 10.6 (see table 10.4).

Table 10.4 Domains in listing 10.6

Domain	Ubiquitous language
Events	Interests
Organization	Employee, employee base, interest groups
Analytics	KPI, adoption, goal, activity

The last specification we'll analyze is an ability for employees to redeem bonus points as engagement rewards (see listing 10.6). Team leaders who use Activitee can grant their subordinates bonus points for teamwork. The employees can later redeem the points to get rewards from a special rewards catalog prepared by the HR department.

```
Ability: Employees can redeem their bonuses to get engagement rewards

  Scenario Outline: Redeeming a bonus as an employee

    Given a Fortune 500 company like Coca-Cola
      And a bonus of 100 points granted to Simona by her team lead
      And a company rewards catalog:
        | reward                | points needed |
        | A Starbucks Gift Card | 100           |
        | A dinner with the CEO | 100000        |
    When Simona tries to redeem her bonus points to <reward>
    Then she should <outcome>

    Examples:
      | reward                | outcome                       |
      | A Starbucks Gift Card | get her reward                |
      | A dinner with the CEO | see she doesn't have enough points |
```

Table 10.5 shows that the bonuses subdomain is the clear winner in this case.

Table 10.5 Domains in listing 10.6

Domain	Ubiquitous language
Organization	Company, team lead
Bonuses	Bonus, points, reward, rewards catalog, redeeming

10.3.4 Creating a specification suite from distilled domains

We end up with five distinct domains (see table 10.6). We're also able to prioritize the domains. I've already said that the events domain is the core domain because it lies at the heart of Activitee's platform. Security, on the other hand, is a classic generic subdomain: the company is only required to adhere to industry standards that almost all enterprise applications have to deal with. We'll automatically treat all the other domains as supporting subdomains.

Table 10.6 Domains in Activitee's specification suite

Type	Domains
Core domain	Events
Supporting subdomains	Organization, bonuses, analytics
Generic subdomains	Security

NOTE An early reviewer of this book argued that the analytics domain should be a generic subdomain instead of a supporting subdomain. I would usually agree, but I think Activitee's case is different. Metrics are becoming more important in the HR world. Activitee's sales team uses their data-driven product and analytical tools as important parts of their sales pitch. That's why I decided to list the analytics domain as a supporting subdomain: it's important to the most important stakeholders—HR representatives.

Now that all the important subdomains have been distilled, we can reorganize Activitee's specification suite according to everything learned in this chapter (see figure 10.5). Here's what you can do with a domain-driven suite like this one:

- Close branches of the directory tree to reduce noise from the many subdomains in the specification suite.
- Grade subdomains on their importance by counting how many specifications are featured in each subdomain.
- Track subdomains' growth over time.
- See how many actors each subdomain has to deal with, and map the relevant stakeholders and their interests.
- Watch new stakeholders appear in selected subdomains.

If you're using a version control system to store your specification suite, you should be able to track all that at any point in time—the feature files and their file structure will be stored in the commits. For example, you should be able to rewind and statistically determine which areas of your product have grown the most in the last six months. And because domains are mostly derived from the business aspects of a project and are seldom dictated by technology, you can also determine where the most business value was added. If you do that, you will, for example, be able to say which aspects of your product you should continue investing in—and which maybe aren't worth the effort.

10.4   *Answers to exercises*

EXERCISE 1   Choose one state, one action, and one outcome from listing 10.1, and assign a domain to each one. If you notice multiple domains in any of the steps, decide which domain should be the most important in this step:

- A storage state: a 2 GB limit
- A commercial offering action: upgrade to the premium plan
- A payments outcome: her credit card should be charged

EXERCISE 2   Think of one more supporting subdomain that could be relevant to the cloud storage service:

A file access-control subdomain can be a good example. Some files should only be accessible to the people they were shared with.

EXERCISE 3   Can you think of another generic subdomain?

A user access-control subdomain would be generic in most systems. Although file access control would be connected to the core domain of the cloud storage system and thus be a supporting subdomain, a user ACL, regulating which user could access which teams, would be a generic subdomain. User access control, along with authentication, could even be in the same bounded context for account management.

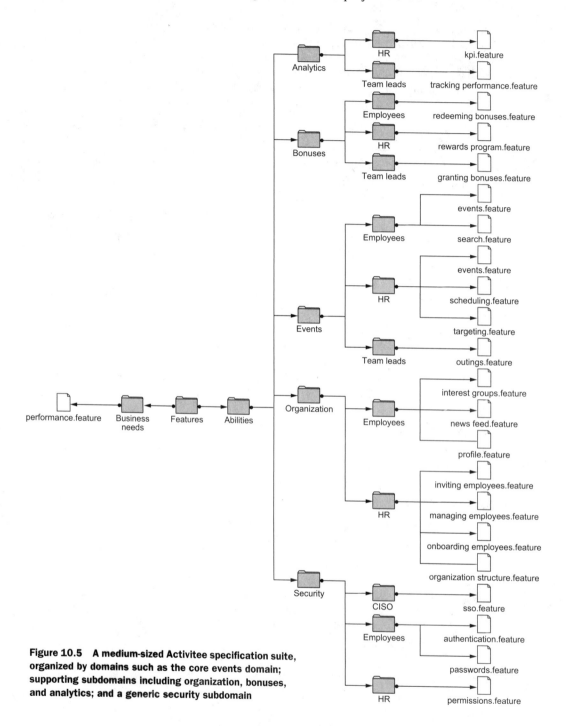

Figure 10.5   A medium-sized Activitee specification suite, organized by domains such as the core events domain; supporting subdomains including organization, bonuses, and analytics; and a generic security subdomain

10.5 *Summary*

- Gherkin helps you build better domain models by capturing a ubiquitous language, one of the main concepts from a software development methodology called domain-driven design (DDD).

- DDD is an approach to software development for complex needs that connects the implementation to an evolving model created with domain experts.

- Domain experts are the people who know the most about a high-priority area of the business. When domain experts and technical experts communicate, they use—and simultaneously create—a shared, ubiquitous language.

- Through a ubiquitous language, you can distill all the different subdomains and build a better map of your business domain by organizing the requirements in the specification suite according to their subdomains.

- The core domain is the domain where the most value should be added in your system.

- A supporting subdomain models some aspect of the business that is essential, but not core.

- A generic domain captures nothing special to the business, but it's required for the overall business solution.

Managing large projects
with bounded contexts

11

This chapter covers

- Refactoring large specification suites
- Recognizing false cognates and duplicate concepts
- Managing bounded contexts
- Drawing context maps
- Fitting domain-driven design into an SBE process

This is the final chapter in our four-chapter series about managing specification suites. Chapters 8, 9, and 10 talked about managing small- to medium-sized suites. In this chapter, we'll split a large specification suite into several smaller suites, each of which will be a unified model of a particular subarea of a complex business domain. In doing this, you'll see how the challenge of managing large specification suites can be viewed as a task of managing multiple medium-sized suites, which is something you already know how to do.

One of the biggest projects I've worked on while using SBE and Gherkin spread into multiple applications, each having its own specification suite. The applications dealt with the same business domain, but they were managed by separate teams, some of which were outsourced. As systems grow too complex to know completely at the level of individual capabilities, you need techniques for manipulating and comprehending large domains easily, as well as sharing consistent organization models among multiple technical teams.

This hasn't yet happened in the Activitee example. In the previous chapters, you saw Activitee evolve from having a small specification suite to a medium-sized one. In this chapter, we'll fast-forward its evolution to a later stage so that you can learn the techniques necessary to deal with really large suites. By *large*, I mean that it would be pointless to try to show you an illustration of this suite—it wouldn't fit on a single page, and we'd have to take too much time to analyze it.

Given the way I've been talking about the domain model, you might assume that the goal is to create a single, cohesive, all-inclusive model of the organization's entire business domain. That's not correct. Experience shows that no matter how hard you try, you'll never be able to create a unified model for an entire organization. The subject-matter experts will keep expanding their ubiquitous languages by adding, modifying, and removing domain concepts as they see fit—often without maintaining consistency within the larger organization. In this regard, ubiquitous languages are like dialects. Dialects are based on the same core language, just as ubiquitous languages are based on the same core domain in the corporate world. If you tried to force people to unify their dialects into a single official language, the task would take years—even if you assumed total cooperation. The process wouldn't be impossible, but the cost could end up outweighing the benefit. Now, imagine the same challenge in the corporate world. Yuck, right?

Integrating different ubiquitous languages isn't worth the effort required to create a unified model of the entire business domain. If making a unified model of a complex domain isn't an optimal choice, how can you organize large enterprise specification suites according to a domain model? Fortunately, domain-driven design (DDD) has an answer to this question. The answer, as often happens in DDD, begins with the concept of ubiquitous language and the process of translation.

11.1 *Analyzing domain concepts in context*

This section explores the process of translation among dialects that appear in a specification suite as it grows larger and includes more subdomains. Each subdomain comes with its own dialect; in different dialects, the same word can mean opposite things, or the same thing can have two names. Soon, you'll see how to spot such words in a specification suite and how to deal with them. If you understand the problem of dealing with coexisting dialects, you'll be able to solve it later in the chapter and learn how to manage large specification suites.

11.1.1 Spotting false cognates

Activitee is becoming larger. The product is growing, the specification suite is growing—and there have been growing pains. For example, a new team member will quickly notice that there's something called an *event* in multiple places in the growing specification suite. Sometimes events are put in an obvious context (see listing 11.1), but other times they're found in places where, at face value, they shouldn't be—like the application security subdomain (see listing 11.2).

Listing 11.1   Event concept in the core events domain

```
Scenario: Team leads and HR should be able to cancel events

  Given an event created by Mike for his team:
    | name    | date       | time  |
    | Bowling | 10-03-2017 | 10 AM |
    And Simona's confirmed attendance
  When Mike cancels the event
  Then Simona should receive a cancellation notification
```

Listing 11.2   Event concept in the application security subdomain

```
Scenario: Employees can review events in the security log

  Given Simona's previous logins were from the USA
    And her latest login was from the UK
    And somebody attempted to change her password
  When she reviews her activity log
  Then she should see the following events:
    | event                  | from | created at |
    | log in                 | USA  | yesterday  |
    | log in                 | USA  | yesterday  |
    | log in                 | UK   | today      |
    | change password attempt | UK  | today      |
```

It turns out that there are two different kinds of events in the specification suite (see also figure 11.1):

- *Core domain events*—Events that take place in the real world and at which employees have fun
- *Application security events*—Digital footprints on the Activitee platform that can be used to review suspicious activity

DDD calls such concepts *false cognates*.

> **DEFINITION** *False cognate*—A domain concept that shares its name with another domain concept. False cognates lead people to think they're talking about the same thing when they aren't.

In linguistics, false cognates are also called *polysemes*: words that can have multiple meanings depending on the context. Polysemy is distinct from homonymy, which is an

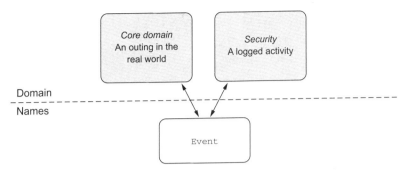

Figure 11.1 Two different domain concepts can sometimes share the same name in the ubiquitous language.

accidental similarity between two words; whereas homonymy is often a linguistic coincidence, polysemy isn't. The difference between polysemy and homonymy is that polysemy is more contextual. You've already seen that difference: context led us to determine that events in listing 11.1 aren't the same as events in listing 11.2 and that they belong to different domains. The context was provided by the examples in the tables and by the differences in ubiquitous languages used in the scenarios.

11.1.2 Dealing with false cognates

False cognates aren't necessarily *mistakes*. As I said before, different groups of people will use subtly different vocabularies in different parts of a large organization. You can't force security experts to abandon their vocabulary—in which the concept of *event* as a logged activity is used often—just because you have another domain that uses a similar name for a different concept.

But false cognates, like polysemes in natural languages, can introduce confusion. Trying to eradicate them isn't a domain-driven way of dealing with false cognates. Instead, you can try to explicitly define the relationships between different contexts in which the domain concepts in question appear. Gherkin and Cucumber let you do that with *glossaries*.

In chapter 7, we defined a glossary as a separate file in the specification suite that contains the definitions of all domain concepts required to understand a suite. This definition was fine for small specification suites of limited complexity. But now you know that in larger suites, some names can have multiple meanings in different contexts. And I've already said that trying to create a single, unified, all-encompassing glossary is often too difficult and yields little return on investment.

But what if you tried to create multiple contextual glossaries, like the ones shown in figure 11.2? A *contextual glossary* defines domain concepts from a shared context where no polysemes exist. A glossary for the core domain will define *event* as unequivocally a domain concept.

Listing 11.3   features/abilities/events/glossary.md

```
EVENT is a social outing in the real world.                        ⬅

COMPANY-WIDE EVENT is an event targeted at everyone within an entire
➥organization.

LOCAL EVENT is an event targeted for some specific location like New York,
➥Boston, Atlanta.
                                                    Ambiguous term in the context
    (...)                                              of the core events domain
```

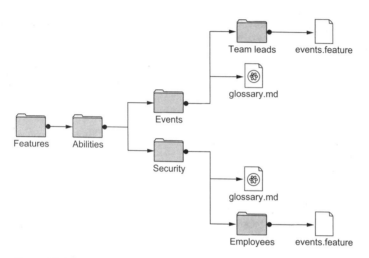

Figure 11.2   A specification suite can have multiple glossaries, each defining domain concepts in different contexts.

A glossary for the security context will define *event* as a domain concept from the security domain. In this context, events are also unequivocal—as long as you don't mix one context with the other.

Listing 11.4   features/abilities/security/glossary.md

```
EVENT is any logged activity.                          ⬅

SINGLE SIGN-ON (SSO) is a session and user authentication service that permits
    a user to use one set of login credentials (e.g., name and password) to
    access multiple applications.

TWO-FACTOR AUTHENTICATION (2FA) adds a second level of authentication to an
    account log-in. When you have to enter only your username and one
    password, that's considered a single-factor authentication. 2FA requires
    the user to have two out of three types of credentials before being able
    to access an account.

    (...)
                                        Ambiguous term in the context of the
                                            application security subdomain
```

Context rules everything. The more you think about it, the more often you'll notice that subdomains, actors, and domain concepts always appear in context. The larger the specification suite, the more you must be aware of the contexts that exist within it. You'll soon see how contexts will let you manage large specification suites, too. Unfortunately, you aren't ready to do that just yet, because specifying false cognates isn't the only issue you'll face when dealing with context in specification suites.

11.1.3 Spotting duplicate concepts

The ubiquitous languages of different contexts sometimes interact. That's why a single domain concept can appear in multiple contexts. It's an inversion of what we talked about in the previous section, where two domain concepts appeared to be the same but weren't.

For example, the Activitee platform uses the concept of *interest* in multiple contexts (see figure 11.3). In the employee context, interests mean hobbies and activities that users are interested in. In the core domain context, interests are used to target events at particular employees. In the organization context, each interest has its own *interest group*, which is a simple message board for like-minded people.

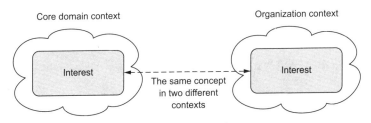

Figure 11.3 Dialects and contexts can share the same domain concepts under the same names. Each context usually requires a slightly different implementation, but the underlying concepts remain the same. Each context uses different aspects of the concept.

If interests from the three contexts I just mentioned were false cognates, they would all be different concepts—and different domain concepts deserve their own definitions. But in this situation, the domain concept is the same for all, so we only have to write a single definition for it and duplicate it in every context. Compare the glossaries in listings 11.5. and 11.6.

> **Listing 11.5 features/abilities/events/glossary.md**

```
EVENT is a social outing in the real world.

COMPANY-WIDE EVENT is an event targeted at everyone within an entire
organization.

LOCAL EVENT is an event targeted for some specific location like New York,
Boston, Atlanta.

INTEREST is a hobby or activity that our employees may want to participate in.
```
(...)

                                                        Interests in the core domain context

> **Listing 11.6   features/abilities/organization/glossary.md**

```
INTEREST is a hobby or activity that our employees may want to participate in.

INTEREST GROUP is a group of like-minded people who share the same interest
and can use an Activitee message board to discuss it.

(...)
```

**Interests in the
organization context**

DDD calls such concepts *duplicate concepts.*

> **DEFINITION**   *Duplicate concept*—One of at least two models of the same domain
> concept. Each model represents and implements the same domain concept
> in a different context.

In chapter 10, I said that a *model* is an interpretation of reality that abstracts only the
aspects relevant to solving the problem at hand. Because different contexts deal with
different problems, they can abstract different aspects of the same domain concept
(see figure 11.4).

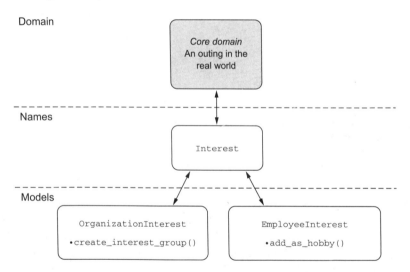

**Figure 11.4   The same domain concept can have two different models in two
different contexts, each model having its own implementation with unique functions.**

Each context will imply slightly different functions when implemented as code, even
though the underlying concept is the same. For example, an `Interest` model in the
organization context will implement a `create_interest_group()` function, which will
contain code used to create interest groups. An `Interest` model in the employee context will implement an `add_as_hobby()` function, which will assign interests to
employees who choose them.

Tracking duplicate concepts is just as important as tracking false cognates, because errors introduced into a duplicate in one context can influence another context—for example, through a shared database. Having multiple possible implementations can also introduce new political issues over ownership of a concept. If two teams work in two different contexts that share a single domain concept, how do these teams manage the differences between their visions of the concept? This is a common situation. I'll try to answer this question in the next section.

11.2 Modeling specification suites as bounded contexts

Duplicate concepts are common and to be expected. Large projects are often decentralized, and decentralization invites duplication. In the long run, it's not efficient to try to avoid this. False cognates are less common and more harmful: they can lead to delivery teams prying into each other's code, inconsistent databases, and confusion in communication. Uninvited as they are, multiple false cognates often happen in a typical large software development project.

DDD doesn't deal with duplicate concepts and false cognates by creating an all-encompassing domain model where inconsistencies don't appear. Rather, it recognizes the splinters and either removes (when they're design mistakes) or contains the inconsistencies within multiple smaller models that interact with each other. The interaction process is key. It's like translation. Every model must figure out a way to resolve the splinters in order to exchange information (send or retrieve data) required to complete the interaction. Such models are called *bounded contexts*. I used the word *context* a lot in previous sections—and that was a conscious decision. In this section, I'll explain what bounded contexts are and how they can help you manage large specification suites.

11.2.1 Understanding bounded contexts

A bounded context is a fragment of the domain that has a unified model. A model is meaningless unless it's logically consistent, so each bounded context must have a unified model that's internally valid.

> **DEFINITION** *Bounded context*—A fragment of the domain that has a unified model

The internal consistency of a model—meaning that each term is unambiguous and there are no contradicting rules—is called *unification*. You know that a model is unified when the following are true:

- It has an unambiguous glossary.
- It's validated by specification suite tests.
- It's continuously integrated.

Even though the context is internally consistent, it may not be consistent with other bounded contexts. Within the context, you should work to keep the model logically unified, but don't worry about applicability outside those bounds. The translation process will handle that job later. We'll talk more about how to resolve inconsistencies between contexts in section 11.2.4.

How do you define contextual bounds? You can use a rule of thumb and identify contexts by their glossaries. Whenever a fragment of the domain has an unambiguous glossary, it can be represented as a bounded context. An unambiguous glossary is a sign of unification. Other than that, contexts can be flexible.

Remember that a bounded context is always a model. Models are abstract interpretations of reality made to solve problems at hand. As long as your interpretation makes sense and you can keep the ubiquitous language consistent, you may choose from many potential splits between contexts. Any split can be more or less optimal, depending on the problem at hand. You can assume that the more you get to know about the domain and your stakeholders, the more optimal the contexts you create will become.

11.2.2 Splitting a large specification suite into multiple bounded contexts

Defining bounded contexts catalyzes the split of a single large specification suite into several smaller specification suites. Each context is a fragment of the domain. Each fragment becomes a potential split line. In this section, we'll define a few contexts for Activitee, based on the contextual glossaries discussed earlier. We'll then do a few splits based on those contexts. We should end up with a clearly organized project with a lot of room to grow for new abilities and business needs.

At the end of the previous chapter, five subdomains were in play (see figure 11.5):

- Analytics
- Bonuses
- Events
- Organization
- Application security

In figure 11.2, we use bounded contexts that include only a single subdomain. There's a separate context for the events subdomain, which has its own glossary—and there's a second context for the application security subdomain with another glossary. That can happen, but it doesn't have to be the case every time. A bounded context can easily deal with multiple subdomains, as long as they can share a single glossary (see figure 11.6). For example, we can define a bounded context for the core Activitee experience, which deals with subdomains such as events, bonuses, and organization. The ubiquitous languages in these subdomains are generally consistent and fit together easily.

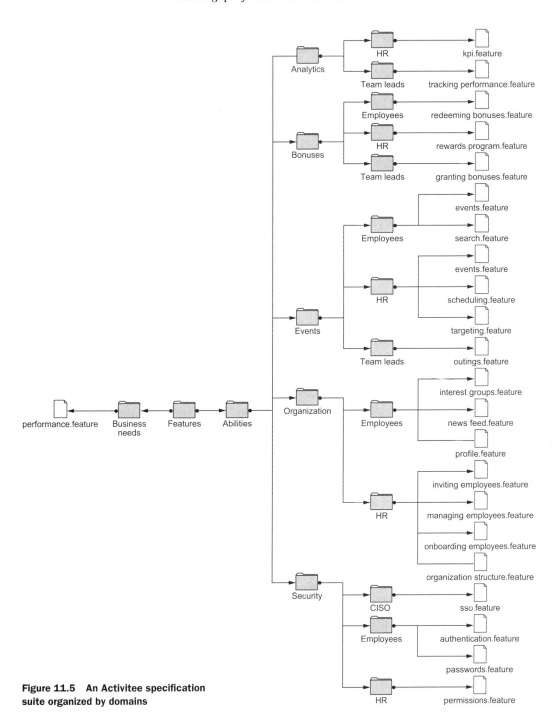

**Figure 11.5   An Activitee specification
suite organized by domains**

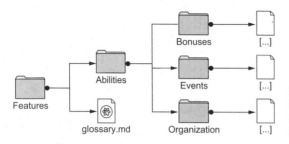

Figure 11.6   A bounded context for the core Activitee experience, with a single unified glossary for three subdomains

Figure 11.6 shows a specification suite with three subdomains and a single unified glossary. From the modeling perspective, the unification aspect is the most important. From the technical perspective, having a separate specification suite for several subdomains often means you've decided to split a so-far-unified product into multiple applications called *services,* each of which is responsible for certain aspects of the business domain. That's because Cucumber can read only one features directory per project. (If you wanted to keep your bounded contexts in a single application, you'd need to create a separate folder for each context in the features directory—a less elegant solution.)

After extracting three subdomains from figure 11.6, we still have two other subdomains to deal with: analytics and application security. I talked a bit about the security subdomain when we analyzed false cognates. You may remember from chapters 9 and 10 that this subdomain cares mainly about identity issues, such as authentication, authorization, and SSO. That's why we can extract it into a separate bounded context called the *identity context* (see figure 11.7).

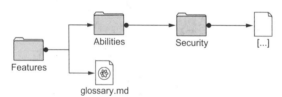

Figure 11.7   Activitee's identity context and its glossary only specify scenarios that deal with the application security subdomain—for example, authentication and authorization.

We can do the same with the analytics subdomain (see figure 11.8). Although key performance indicators (KPIs) are an important part of Activitee, they've always been separated from the rest of the platform. There are a couple of reasons to keep this subdomain in a separate bounded context. First, the analytics product doesn't introduce any new functionalities on its own; it feeds on data from other features. This data feed product has to interact with other ubiquitous languages on a daily basis. A separate glossary would be a great tool to define the interactions between different dialects and resolve possible conflicts. For example, the analytics product could be able to analyze the frequency of both HR events and security events, with a glossary specifying which is which. You can also look at similar products from other companies. For instance, at the time of writing, Twitter Analytics is a separate application, complete with its own design and a URL different than the core Twitter experience.

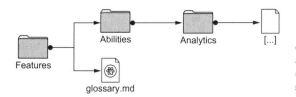

Figure 11.8 Activitee's analytics context focuses only on analytical abilities, with a glossary that can unify the ubiquitous language in the specification suite presented in the diagram.

The real relationships between bounded contexts and subdomains is usually more complex than in these simple examples. For instance, we've assumed that the contexts contain entire subdomains, which can happen—but the opposite is just as likely. A subdomain can be split into parts, each part implemented in a different bounded context; there's nothing wrong with that.

11.2.3 Managing bounded contexts with context maps

Creating bounded contexts is a good first step toward manipulating and comprehending large domains easily. It reduces the problem of managing large specification suites into managing multiple medium-sized specification suites. But how can you work with, organize, and comprehend multiple bounded contexts? The solution is to create a *context map*: a map that describes the points of contact between different bounded contexts. I'll show you an example in a moment.

> **DEFINITION**   *Context map*—A map that describes the points of contact between different bounded contexts (different specification suites), outlining explicit translations for any communication and highlighting any sharing

I've talked about maps already:

- In section 8.2.3, when discussing the concept of a specification suite as a map of requirements
- In section 10.2.2, when likening the domain model to a map of the domain that helps you make good decisions on your journey to deliver software that will be valuable in that domain

A context map is an entirely new kind of map. If a specification suite is a map of requirements organized according to DDD principles, then a context map is a map of specification suites and the relationships between suites.

Why are context maps important? Splitting the domain model into multiple contexts won't automatically make the domain model smaller, easier to comprehend, or less complex. It will decentralize complexity.

Decentralization is a huge topic in DDD. For example, each time you find out that two decentralized contexts aren't synchronized (for example, if you find a false cognate and haven't decided what to do with it), you can make one of two decisions:

- Pull the model back together, and refine it to prevent fragmentation.
- Accept the fragmentation as a result of diverse groups who want to push the model in different directions for good reasons, and let them develop their contexts independently.

If you make the second decision, you'll need a way to track fragmentation and see where different bounded contexts converge and diverge. A good first step is creating and maintaining separate glossaries for each bounded context—something you've already done. A good second step is to mark relationships such as false cognates and duplicate concepts in different contexts. Here's where context maps come in handy.

11.2.4 Drawing context maps

Figure 11.9 shows what a context map looks like in theory. It shows two models, each in its own bounded context. Each model is a visual representation of the domain concepts present in each context as well as the relationships between the concepts. (In practice, such diagrams are most often drawn in UML, a popular modeling language that provides a standard way to visualize the design of a system.) You can also see the translation map, which is a space where you can define the points of contact between different bounded contexts. Each point of contact can specify interactions such as false cognates, duplicate concepts, and any other relation that you deem important.

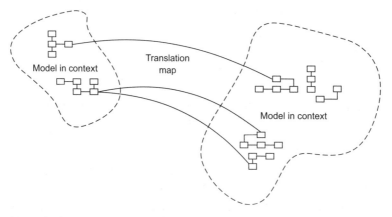

Figure 11.9   A simple context map that lists translations such as false cognates and duplicate concepts between two theoretical models in their bounded contexts

Figure 11.10 shows a more practical example based on the Activitee platform and the false cognates and duplicate concepts we dealt with in section 11.1. Software development teams often draw maps like this one to outline explicit translations for any communication and highlight any sharing between contexts. The map defines the territory of each context and the borders between contexts. Without a context map, people on other teams may not be aware of contextual bounds and may unknowingly make changes that blur the edges or complicate the interconnections.

A context map is different than the map I talked about when comparing a specification suite to a map. Due to automation and its link to real working code, a specification suite can only be a model of the bounded contexts in a single codebase. So if you have to split your bounded contexts into separate codebases due to the complexity of

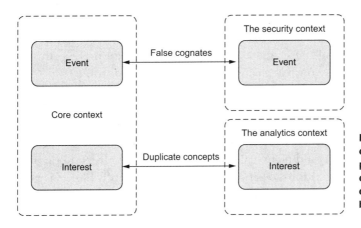

Figure 11.10 A simple context map that lists previously defined false cognates and duplicate concepts between Activitee's bounded contexts

the system or your system architecture, each specification suite will be able to map only what it can automate; therefore, it will always be limited to the reach of its testing code. A simple, practical example is that two different subsystems can be written in two different programming languages, which makes unified testing more difficult. You have to resort to non-automated methods, such as context maps. It *really* is just a simple drawing. Still, each specification suite with a glossary will help you create better context maps because it's an automated, frequently validated, always up-to-date map of each bounded context. But the context map itself must be maintained manually.

In DDD, contexts map are an important element of *strategic design*. Strategic design is not only a way to map a business domain, as in the example, but also a way to show which parts of the system matter most to the business and where to focus design efforts in order to be effective. Eric Evans defined several design patterns.[1] The conformist pattern is a good example. A conformist context adheres to other models in order to simplify integration by adopting to a provided language and data without questioning it. Therefore, conformity eliminates the complexity of translation.

Another example is the anticorruption layer pattern, which creates an isolating layer to provide clients with functionality in terms of their own domain model. Thanks to DDD's strategic patterns, you can not only define the points of contact shared by the ubiquitous languages of different bounded contexts, but also define how, in the long term, each team should manage their context's interactions with other contexts and, therefore, other teams.

Unfortunately, it's beyond the scope of this book to discuss techniques from the field of DDD. If you're interested in the topic, you can read Evans' book, which is a great introduction to the topic and will give you a fuller overview of what DDD is all about.

---

[1] Eric Evans, *Domain-Driven Design*, chapters 14–17 (Addison-Wesley, 2003).

11.3 *Fitting DDD into an SBE process*

Paired with SBE and Gherkin, DDD can be a powerful tool. To solidify your understanding before we end the chapter, let's review the general process, this time from start to finish. This section features some new material that will let you see the processes of modeling and specifying from the perspective of different team members; programmers, designers, analysts, and testers will be able to understand how the domain-modeling process will affect their jobs.

Everything starts with the ubiquitous language, created thanks to the cooperation of both domain experts and technical experts. When they converse about the requirements and their organization's business domain, they naturally flesh out domain concepts and mix their jargons to create the ubiquitous language—the language of the domain in a given technological context, also called a bounded context.

That's when Gherkin steps in. Gherkin allows for the recording and long-term storage of short-term conversations. When the experts write down their conversations in Gherkin, they can refine their domain models more easily. As section 10.2.2 explained, you can analyze Gherkin scenarios to distill different domains from each conversation and decide which is the core domain and which are secondary or generic domains (and thus less important). And section 10.2.3 showed that analyzing false cognates and duplicate concepts between different scenarios can lead to creating different bounded contexts, which fragment the domain into several smaller context-dependent models.

Thanks to Gherkin's connection to the realm of automated testing, each bounded context binds the testing code of its specification suite and the real code meant to implement the actual requirements. Thanks to automated tests, which frequently verify the suite's consistency, as well as Gherkin's focus on the ubiquitous language, you can be sure that each specification suite based on a bounded context presents a unified, consistent model of the subdomain the current code is dealing with.

The requirements are organized according to their corresponding subdomains. You can quickly inspect the subdomains used in each context by analyzing the structure of directories within the specification suite, as well as create and maintain a unified glossary of domain concepts for each bounded context. The structure of your specification suites becomes a visual and hierarchical domain model—a map of the fragments of your business domain that you've already specified—in which requirements and glossaries are connected to their corresponding domains.

Thanks to bounded contexts, the problem of managing large specification suites is reduced to a problem of managing multiple medium-sized specification suites—a topic we discussed in chapters 8–10 and that you should be ready to deal with. The only remaining issue is figuring out how to deal with interactions among multiple suites. The relationships among different specification suites can be clarified by using context maps. By describing the points of contact between different bounded contexts, context maps can give you a fuller overview of your business domain and provide a translation framework between the bounded contexts. The translation framework can help you deal with false cognates and duplicate concepts more easily.

Refining the domain model as well as defining and analyzing bounded contexts can yield multiple positive outcomes to each delivery team. DDD emphasizes that different parts of your system matter differently to your business and provides a methodology to focus your team's design efforts most effectively. Designers and analysts can benefit from DDD by understanding where business value comes from, thanks to seeing which domains and contexts grow the fastest.

Better domain models yield better code designs, without unnecessary coupling of concepts that should stay separate; this makes code more stable for developers and automated testing easier for testers. For free, developers also get a methodology for naming their domain objects in code according to the ubiquitous language—which reduces the cost of mental translations.

On a personal note, I wish I'd known all this years ago when my team and I were working on a particular enterprise project. It would have saved us considerable time and stress. The complexity was eating us up on a daily basis. We were on the right track to curb it, but the project lacked the finishing touches. We knew how to use Gherkin and Cucumber, but we had no idea how to organize large specification suites. We understood the concept of a ubiquitous language, but we didn't yet grasp all of its implications for software design. The only element almost completely missing was DDD. (We learned about the ubiquitous language through Gherkin.) As I reminisce, I see how we could have used glossaries, bounded contexts, context maps, and DDD design patterns to improve our processes. I can only hope that this chapter—a culmination of the previous lessons—will aid you in writing great specifications so that you can harness the true power of executable Gherkin much more quickly and easily than I did.

11.4 Summary

- A false cognate is a domain concept that shares its name with another domain concept.
- False cognates lead people to think they're talking about the same thing when they aren't.
- Duplication of concepts leads to two different implementations of the same domain concept in two different contexts.
- False cognates and duplicate concepts are examples of why it's difficult to create a unified, all-encompassing domain model—repetitions, inconsistencies, and equivocation creep in.
- Even though domain models lie at the center of domain-driven design, DDD's goal isn't to build a single model of an organization's entire business domain. Instead, DDD practitioners use bounded contexts.

- A bounded context is only a *fragment* of the domain with a unified model. A fragment can be small and consistent enough to avoid equivocation within its model.

- A specification suite of a bounded context specifies the ubiquitous language of its model.

- Thanks to bounded contexts, the problem of managing large specification suites is reduced to a problem of managing multiple medium-sized specification suites.

- Each bounded context needs to figure out how to communicate with other bounded contexts, just as different departments learn to share information within a company.

- Bounded contexts share information through context maps. A context map describes the points of contact between different bounded contexts, outlining explicit translations for any communication and highlighting any sharing.

appendix
Executing specifications
with Cucumber

This appendix is a quick tutorial on how to write and run simple automated tests for feature files with Cucumber and Gherkin. I *do* realize that some readers will expect an explanation of the *executable* part of executable specifications. Execution is Cucumber's role. To execute a specification, you write tests based on a prepared scenario, which you later evolve into a scenario outline—and then you automate that, too. I'm assuming you've read at least chapters 2 and 5, which talk about scenarios and scenario outlines. You can, however, proceed up to section A.8 without having read chapter 5, and then come back later.

This tutorial will teach you the basic workings of the automation layer based on an example of a simple banking application that lets clients deposit and withdraw money. I'll try to keep the example simple and explain everything along the way, for readers who are nontechnical but want to learn more about the automation layer.

You can use the command-line interpreter of your choice. I'll assume you understand basic regular expressions and Ruby, which I'm using to write the code, as well as how to configure and use RubyGems to install Cucumber. I realize that not everybody needs to know Ruby, so I'm writing the simplest implementation code possible and testing it with the simplest testing code I can think of. This choice means the results won't be perfect according to Ruby's coding standards, but you should be able to understand my code regardless of your language of choice.

A.1   *Introducing test-driven development*

This appendix is more of a high-level overview of fundamental testing techniques rather than a complete explanation. It focuses on the two most important topics:

- Understanding test-driven development (TDD)
- Writing unit tests

TDD is one of the best-known practices inside and outside agile software development communities.

DEFINITION   *Test-driven development*—A software development methodology that requires developers to write failing tests first and then gradually create the implementation code to make the tests pass

This appendix relies on TDD heavily, so it's important that you understand what that means. Kent Beck, who popularized TDD, explained it as a practice that requires you to "test a little, code a little."[1] Each time you have a new feature to implement, Beck said, you should do the following:

1   Add a failing test first.
2   Run all of your tests, and confirm that the new test fails.
3   Write the minimum implementation code that causes the new test to pass.
4   Run the tests again to see them pass, thanks to the new code.
5   The minimum implementation code will usually be ugly even though it passes the test. Refactor and polish the code. Use the test repeatedly to check whether the code works as intended even with changes.
6   Repeat the entire process every time you want to add a new functionality.

This process is sometimes simplified into a three-step loop: *red-green-refactor*. Most test runners mark failing tests in red and passing tests in green. You start with a red test and gradually work to make it a green one. As soon as you get a green test, you refactor the code to polish it, and then you use the tests to be sure you didn't break anything while making your implementation more beautiful.

If you feel that writing failing tests before writing actual implementation code is weird, don't worry—I remember feeling that way. It becomes more natural as you get the hang of it. The benefit of TDD is that when you focus on writing only the code necessary to pass tests, your designs will often be cleaner and clearer than you can achieve with other methods.

A.2   *Introducing unit tests*

The tests you'll write in this appendix are called *unit tests*.

DEFINITION   *Unit test*—A low-level test that focuses on a small part of the software system called a *unit of work*

People often consider different things to be single units of work. In object-oriented design, a unit can be an entire interface, such as a class; but in functional design, it may be a single function. In the context of this appendix, it doesn't matter. I chose to use unit tests because they're short, simple, and quick, and they don't require you to

---

[1]   Kent Beck and Erich Gamma, "Test Infected: Programmers Love Writing Tests," Java Report, 3(7), July 1998, http://junit.sourceforge.net/doc/testinfected/testing.htm.

create an advanced implementation such as a database connection or a user interface. You can copy the code as is and make it run effortlessly on your machine.

Unit tests aren't the only type of tests. Most teams use Cucumber and Gherkin to run end-to-end tests with a runner like Selenium for web browser automation. Selenium-driven specifications simulate a user working with a real instance of the system. When I say *real*, I mean as real as possible. You can even configure Selenium to run Firefox or Chrome on your machine in order to watch Cucumber click over the simulated user interface as it tests the system. Personally, I like to use an approach based on domain-driven design (discussed in chapter 10) and write Cucumber tests that validate the domain layer without end-to-end testing, which tends to be slow and performance heavy. Unfortunately, a discussion of choosing domain logic tests over end-to-end tests is too complex for me to do it justice in an appendix. I wanted to mention it, though, in order to show you some possible future learning paths.

If you want to learn more about the automation aspects of Cucumber and Gherkin, read *The Cucumber Book* by Matt Wynne and Aslak Hellesøy (Pragmatic Programmers, 2012). If you're a Java person, you may want to look at *BDD in Action* by John Ferguson Smart (Manning, 2014), which features many code examples written in Java. You should have zero problems finding books that talk about any of the topics I've just mentioned, including TDD, unit tests, and end-to-end testing; they're all established software development practices.

A.3   *Configuring the environment*

To execute any tests, you first need to make sure you have a test runner on board and that your programming environment is configured to make the tests pass. A *test runner*—in this case, Cucumber—is a type of software written to automatically test other software. In this section, you'll install Cucumber and do the basic configuration required to execute any specifications.

You can install Cucumber by running the gem install cucumber command on your terminal:

```
$ gem install cucumber
Fetching: cucumber-2.4.0.gem (100%)
Successfully installed cucumber-2.4.0
Parsing documentation for cucumber-2.4.0
Installing ri documentation for cucumber-2.4.0
Done installing documentation for cucumber after 3 seconds
1 gem installed
```

> **NOTE**   The gem install cucumber command's output may be much longer in a clean Ruby environment, because all kinds of dependencies will have to be installed. I simplified the output for the sake of space.

Also, create a directory where you'll store your tests and scenarios:

```
$ mkdir bank
$ cd bank
```

Once you're in the new directory, you can run Cucumber to see what happens:

```
$ cucumber
No such file or directory - features. You can use `cucumber --init` to get
➥started.
```

> **TIP**   You can only use the cucumber command in a directory that contains a directory called features.

You haven't done any configuration yet, so Cucumber asks you to prepare the environment for future testing. Executing cucumber --init will create the file structure required to put your scenarios in the specification suite and write the tests:

```
$ cucumber --init
   create    features
   create    features/step_definitions
   create    features/support
   create    features/support/env.rb
```

The file structure is simple enough:

- You put your .feature files in the features directory.
- Step definitions (the testing code) go in features/step_definitions.
- The files in the features/support directory can be used to configure the specification suite. Don't worry about it for now; the default configuration will be all you need.

Thanks to the cucumber --init command, you have a good baseline. You've installed Cucumber and gotten it to work, and you know where to store scenarios and tests. Now you need to take care of those, if you want to execute any specifications.

A.4   *Preparing scenarios for automation*

TDD is a test-first approach, so you first need to write a test. Listing A.1 presents a very simple scenario for depositing money in a bank account. The scenario includes two Givens, in which you meet a user—Simona Jenkins—with an empty bank account; a When where she deposits the money; and a Then that checks whether her account balance was updated. In this section, you'll automate each of the Given-When-Thens.

Listing A.1   Scenario for depositing money

```
Feature: Bank account

  Scenario: Adding money to your account

    Given a bank account in Simona's name
      And that her current account balance is $0
    When she deposits $500
    Then the account balance should be $500
```

> **TIP**   You can choose any names for your feature files. Cucumber will read everything from the features directory.

Put the scenario in a feature file called account.feature in the features directory, and execute the cucumber command again. Even though this code looks like a big jump in complexity, the command just reprints the scenario, returns tests results, and generates missing code snippets:

```
$ cucumber
Feature: Bank account                    ◄——— Printed-out scenario

  Scenario: Adding money to your account       # features/account.feature:3
    Given a bank account in Simona's name      # features/account.feature:5
    And that her current account balance is $0 # features/account.feature:6
    When she deposits $500                     # features/account.feature:7
    Then the account balance should be $500    # features/account.feature:8

1 scenario (1 undefined)
4 steps (4 undefined)         Test results                Code snippets
0m0.003s

You can implement step definitions for undefined steps with these snippets:  ◄——┘

Given(/^a bank account in Simona's name$/) do
  pending # Write code here that turns the phrase above into concrete actions
end

Given(/^that her current account balance is \$(\d+)$/) do |arg1|
  pending # Write code here that turns the phrase above into concrete actions
end

When(/^she deposits \$(\d+)$/) do |arg1|
  pending # Write code here that turns the phrase above into concrete actions
end

Then(/^the account balance should be \$(\d+)$/) do |arg1|
  pending # Write code here that turns the phrase above into concrete actions
end
```

The test results are classified as undefined because you haven't written any testing code. That's why Cucumber generates a code snippet for every Given, When, and Then. The step definitions are marked as pending; Cucumber will ignore them unless you put some code in them. At this moment, the step definitions are more placeholders for future tests than real tests. You'll change that soon. As you write more code, the pending steps will be classified as either passed or failed.

Notice that steps and step definitions are matched through regular expressions. Cucumber lets you use regular expressions to extract attributes from the steps, and to make automation easier and reduce redundancy. For example, if you changed the she deposits $500 step to she deposits $1000, Cucumber wouldn't need a second step definition, because it treats \$(\d+) as a placeholder that can catch all numbers in any step that matches the rest of the regular expression—the she deposits part.

> **TIP** Be careful! Sometimes regular expressions in Cucumber can cause headaches. Cucumber reuses steps based on the expressions you write. If you write a regex that's too loose, you may end up with a step definition that's matched with a different step than you had in mind.

With a specification in place, you can proceed to writing your first testing code.

A.5   *Writing tests in a test-driven manner*

Here's where the challenge gets interesting. To make the development process really test-driven, you should write the tests before the implementation. Let's begin by copying the snippets generated by Cucumber and putting them in a file called account.rb in the features/step_definitions directory.

Listing A.2   features/step_definitions/account.rb

```
Given(/^a bank account in Simona's name$/) do
  pending # Write code here that turns the phrase above into concrete actions
end

Given(/^that her current account balance is \$(\d+)$/) do |arg1|
  pending # Write code here that turns the phrase above into concrete actions
end

When(/^she deposits \$(\d+)$/) do |arg1|
  pending # Write code here that turns the phrase above into concrete actions
end

Then(/^the account balance should be \$(\d+)$/) do |arg1|
  pending # Write code here that turns the phrase above into concrete actions
end
```

A.5.1   *Defining prerequisites with Givens*

In the case of the first `Given` in listing A.2, you'll have to create a bank account in the name of a client named Simona. The code should create Simona's client account with a hypothetical `Client` object and then create a bank account—for example, with an `Account` object—and assign it to Simona (see the following listing). Keep in mind that you haven't created any real objects yet. Instead, you're planning which objects and methods you'll need during implementation.

Listing A.3   Testing code for the first `Given` step

```
Given(/^a bank account in Simona's name$/) do
  @simona = Client.new(name: "Simona")
  @simona.account = Account.new
end
```

You'll probably reuse Simona's `Client` account in many other scenarios—even those that don't deal with deposits and don't interact with the `Account` object. It would be a good idea to extract creating the `Client` profile into a separate step, to simplify reusing that step in other scenarios. Cucumber lets you do that with its `step` method.

Listing A.4   Invoking steps from other step definitions

```
Given(/^a client called Simona$/) do
  @simona = Client.new(name: "Simona")
end

Given(/^a bank account in Simona's name$/) do
```

```
step "a client called Simona"
@simona.account = Account.new
end
```

Reusing a Given thanks to Cucumber's step method

The `step` method takes a `String` with the name of another step, runs it through Cucumber's regex engine, and executes the called step inside another step. You're probably being too careful, using the `step` function so soon in this case, because there's no explicit need for reusability; but the method is so useful that you couldn't leave it aside.

Having taken care of the first `Given`, let's proceed to the second one. This step should make sure the initial balance in Simona's account is the same in every test run so you won't end up with a different amount of money than defined in the scenario.

Listing A.5 `Given` step for setting the account balance

```
Given(/^that her current account balance is \$(\d+)$/) do |arg1|
  @simona.account.balance = arg1.to_i
end
```

This step definition uses a regular expression to extract the current account balance from the scenario. That's why you can use the `arg1` argument in the testing code to define Simona's account balance. Using a regular expression means that whatever number you write in the scenario will be extracted by Cucumber for use as the value of the `arg1` argument.

NOTE You have to recast `arg1` as an `Integer` because Cucumber treats every argument extracted from regular expressions as a `String`.

Even though you don't yet have any real code for the `Account` object, you know that it should have a method for setting the initial account balance. If it didn't, you wouldn't be able to execute your tests. In Ruby, this means instances of the `Account` object must implement a method like `balance=` with a numeric argument. That's how tests written in the TDD manner can influence the implementation code's design.

TIP If you want to, you can rename `arg1` to something more human friendly, like `current_balance`.

A.5.2 *Taking actions with Whens*

Two steps down, two steps to go. The `When` should allow the client to deposit the amount of money specified in the scenario, which is the primary action of the scenario.

Listing A.6 Defining the scenario's primary action in a `When`

```
When(/^she deposits \$(\d+)$/) do |arg1|
  @simona.account.deposit(arg1.to_i)
end
```

Again, you use an argument from the step definition; and again, you recast `arg1` as an `Integer`. You also know that every instance of the `Account` object will have to implement a deposit method, which will increase the account balance set by the `balance=` method you used in the previous step definition. In this scenario, you know that the deposit method should increase the balance by $500.

A.5.3   *Testing consequences with Thens*

This is the last step. It's a `Then`, so you programmatically define the consequences you expect from this scenario and test whether the actions you took in the previous steps had the desired effect.

Listing A.7   Pending Then step

```
Then(/^the account balance should be \$(\d+)$/) do |arg1|
  pending # Write code here that turns the phrase above into concrete actions
end
```

Programmers and testers test consequences with *assertions*.

> **DEFINITION**   *Assertion*—A statement that's expected to always be true when executed. If an assertion evaluates to false at runtime, an assertion failure results, which typically causes the program to crash or to throw an assertion exception.

I'm using RSpec to write my test assertions. RSpec is a behavior-driven development (BDD) testing framework for Ruby. You can easily combine RSpec with Cucumber, thanks to the `rspec-expectations` library; Cucumber will automatically load RSpec's matchers and expectation methods. The assertions check whether the output expected in the feature file matches the output from the executed tests. If it doesn't, RSpec will raise an error and stop executing the tests.

To use RSpec's assertions with Cucumber, you need to install the library using RubyGems:

```
$ gem install rspec-expectations
Fetching: rspec-support-3.5.0.gem (100%)
Fetching: diff-lcs-1.2.5.gem (100%)
Fetching: rspec-expectations-3.5.0.gem (100%)
Successfully installed rspec-support-3.5.0
Successfully installed diff-lcs-1.2.5
Successfully installed rspec-expectations-3.5.0
3 gems installed
```

As you can see, `rspec expectations` loads a few supporting libraries—that's fine. You'll need them all to use assertions.

> **TIP**   If you're using Bundler, you can add `gem 'rspec-expectations'` to your Gemfile, instead. Bundler provides a consistent environment for Ruby projects by tracking and installing the exact gems and versions that are needed.

Therefore, you can list the gems your project requires in a Gemfile and install them all at once, instead of going through the list one by one.

The last step required to use `rspec-expectations` in your testing code is to add a `require` line at the top of the account.rb file in features/step_definitions, as shown next.

Listing A.8   Including the `rspec-expectations` gem

```
require "rspec/expectations"

Given(/^a client called Simona$/) do
  @simona = Client.new(name: "Simona")
end

(...)
```

Now you can use RSpec's expect syntax to create a simple assertion that will check whether Simona's account balance equals `final_balance`—the number extracted from the scenario by Cucumber.

Listing A.9   Using an Rspec assertion to check the final account balance

```
Then(/^the account balance should be \$(\d+)$/) do |final_balance|
  expect(@simona.account.balance).to eq final_balance.to_i
end
```

In this case, you know that Simona's account balance should be $500, because you used the `deposit` method to increase it when you wrote the testing code for the `When`.

And that's all! (For now.) You've completed the testing code required to execute the specification. That doesn't mean, of course, that it will be executed *successfully*. As you'll soon see, you still have to write the implementation code.

A.6   *Writing implementation code based on tests*

Do you remember the red-green-refactor loop I talked about at the beginning of this appendix? You should periodically run Cucumber to check whether the code you've written so far is enough to make the tests pass. In this section, you'll see how failing tests can guide you in writing the implementation code that will later run in production. After a few iterations, you should end up with working code that makes the tests pass.

Let's not get ahead of ourselves, though. First, run Cucumber to see whether anything has changed since you used it to generate snippets for the step definitions:

```
$ cucumber
Feature: Bank account

  Scenario: Adding money to your account          # features/account.feature:3
    Given a bank account in Simona's name
      # features/step_definitions/tests.rb:3
      uninitialized constant Client (NameError)
      ./features/step_definitions/tests.rb:4:in
        `/^a bank account in Simona's name$/'
      features/account.feature:5:in `Given a bank account in Simona's name'
```

NameError exception
thrown during test execution

```
      And that her current account balance is $0
      ➥# features/step_definitions/tests.rb:8
      When she deposits $500
      ➥# features/step_definitions/tests.rb:12
      Then the account balance should be $500
      ➥# features/step_definitions/tests.rb:16
```

```
Failing Scenarios:
cucumber features/account.feature:3 # Scenario: Adding money to your account

1 scenario (1 failed)
4 steps (1 failed, 3 skipped)
0m0.005s
```

Ouch! The scenario failed in its first step because Cucumber threw an exception. Let's look at the step definition to see what's wrong:

```
Given(/^a client called Simona$/) do
  @simona = Client.new(name: "Simona")
end
```

Oh, that's it: there's a NameError because the step definition tried to use the Client object even though you haven't defined it. Let's write some implementation code to make the Client object more real—and make the test pass.

First, create a directory called features/implementation where you'll store implementation code for Cucumber to see:

```
mkdir features/implementation
```

> **TIP**   In real-world projects, you'll store your implementation code outside of the features directory. But for now, I want to keep things easy; so, you're putting the code where Cucumber can see it without your having to reconfigure Cucumber to see code in other directories.

You can now write the following simple implementation of the Client object that should make the step definition from listing A.10 pass.

Listing A.10   features/implementation/client.rb

```
class Client
  def initialize(name:)
    @name = name
  end

  def name
    @name
  end
end
```

The object has two simple methods for setting and reading a client's name. It's not much, but remember that TDD requires you to write only the code necessary to pass tests. Because setting the name is where you saw the tests fail, that's what you should fix.

To see what you should do next, though, you have to rerun Cucumber:

```
$ cucumber
Feature: Bank account

  Scenario: Adding money to your account          # features/account.feature:3
    Given a bank account in Simona's name
    ➥# features/step_definitions/account.rb:7
      uninitialized constant Account (NameError)              | Another NameError
      ./features/step_definitions/account.rb:9:in       ⊲──┘ exception
      ➥`/^a bank account in Simona's name$/'
      features/account.feature:5:in `Given a bank account in Simona's name'
    And that her current account balance is $0
    ➥# features/step_definitions/account.rb:12
    When she deposits $500
    ➥# features/step_definitions/account.rb:16
    Then the account balance should be $500

# features/step_definitions/account.rb:20

Failing Scenarios:
cucumber features/account.feature:3 # Scenario: Adding money to your account

1 scenario (1 failed)
4 steps (1 failed, 3 skipped)
0m0.008s
```

The tests are still failing, but at least you got a different error. This time, Cucumber tracked the source of the exception back to the ninth line of the features/step_definitions/account.rb file:

```
Given(/^a bank account in Simona's name$/) do
  step "a client called Simona"
  @simona.account = Account.new          ⊲─── Line 9
end
```

The step definition is trying to use the `Account` object even though it doesn't exist. Let's create the simplest possible implementation of the `Account` object that should make the tests pass—or at least let you progress to a different error.

Listing A.11 features/implementation/account.rb

```
class Account
end
```

Rerun Cucumber:

```
$ cucumber

(...)

undefined method `account=' for #<Client:0x007f87021cf788 @name="Simona">
➥(NoMethodError)
./features/step_definitions/account.rb:9:in
➥`/^a bank account in Simona's name$/'
```

Another exception. The implementation of the `Client` object still doesn't have a method for connecting bank accounts with their owners—but you use the method in listing A.12 when you invoke the `account=` method on the `@simona` instance of the `Client` object. Let's fix that.

Listing A.12   Expended `Client` object with an `account=` method

```
class Client
  def initialize(name:)
    @name = name
  end

  def name
    @name
  end

  def account=(account)
    @account = account
  end
end
```

The `account=` method sets the client's bank account to the account you put in the argument—just as the test expects.

Again, run Cucumber:

```
$ cucumber

(...)

undefined method `account' for #<Client:0x007fc42d34d9a8>
Did you mean?  account= (NoMethodError)
./features/step_definitions/account.rb:13:in
➥ `/^that her current account balance is \$(\d+)$/'
```

Again, the run fails—and again, with a different error. By this time, you should understand how TDD works. Writing the tests first lets you progress in small, incremental loops driven by tests. You test a little and then code a little.

This example was a bit far-fetched. In the real world, you wouldn't wait for Cucumber to notify you if you knew an implementation of an object was missing. Experienced programmers can sense how much code is needed from the outset and write the final methods on their first try. Now that you know how TDD works, you can skip the incremental changes and go straight to working implementation code.

Following is the working implementation of the `Client` object.

Listing A.13   features/implementation/client.rb

```
class Client
  def initialize(name:)
    @name = name
  end

  def name
    @name
  end

  def account=(account)
```

```
    @account = account
  end

  def account
    @account
  end
end
```

And here's the working implementation for the `Account` object.

Listing A.14   features/implementation/account.rb

```
class Account
  def initialize
    @balance = 0
  end

  def balance
    @balance
  end

  def balance=(balance)
    @balance = balance
  end

  def deposit(transfer)
    @balance += transfer
  end
end
```

With these two objects, you can expect your next Cucumber run to work without any problem. You'll soon see if that's true.

A.7   Executing the working specification

If you execute `cucumber` again, you'll see that the testing code works well and your scenarios pass (I cut out the content of the scenarios to make the listing shorter):

```
$ cucumber

(...)

1 scenario (1 passed)
4 steps (4 passed)
0m0.057s
```

Hooray! Now that the objects and tests work, you can rerun Cucumber every time you want to check whether the underlying implementation code still behaves as the testing code expects it to. Every time you make a change to the codebase—for example, when you introduce a new feature or fix an error in an existing feature—you can execute the `cucumber` command and see if the `Client` and `Account` objects work as they should.

A.8   *Executing scenario outlines*

In chapter 4, you learned that a scenario outline is a template that similar scenarios can share so you don't have to repeat the same Given-When-Thens throughout your feature file. Scenario outlines use more-technical elements of Gherkin's syntax, such as dynamic parameters and tables with examples. In this section, we'll explore whether and how such elements change the automation process for scenario outlines.

Let's begin by adding a second scenario with a contrasting outcome that you can rewrite as an outline later. You have a scenario for deposits; the following is a scenario for withdrawals.

Listing A.15   Adding a withdrawal scenario to the executable specification

```
Feature: Bank account

  Scenario: Adding money to your account

    Given a bank account in Simona's name
      And that her current account balance is $0
    When she deposits $500
    Then the account balance should be $500

  Scenario: Withdrawing money from your account

    Given a bank account in Simona's name
      And that her current account balance is $500
    When she withdraws $500
    Then the account balance should be $0
```

Now that you have two similar scenarios, you can rewrite the specification as a single scenario outline.

Listing A.16   Two similar scenarios reframed as a single scenario outline

```
Feature: Bank account

  Scenario Outline: Managing money in your account

    Given a bank account in Simona's name
      And that her current account balance is <balance>
    When she <action>
    Then the account balance should be <result>

    Examples:
      | balance | action         | result |
      | $0      | deposits $500  | $500   |
      | $500    | withdraws $500 | $0     |
```

Having done that, run Cucumber to check whether the tests pass or break:

```
$ cucumber

(...)

2 scenarios (1 undefined, 1 passed)
8 steps (1 skipped, 1 undefined, 6 passed)
```

```
0m0.009s
```

You can implement step definitions for undefined steps with these snippets:

```
When(/^she withdraws \$(\d+)$/) do |arg1|
  pending # Write code here that turns the phrase above into concrete actions
end
```

Cucumber generated a snipper for a pending step definition. That's because the new withdrawal scenario only changed the main action of the scenario from a deposit to a withdrawal.

Let's add the snippet to features/step_definitions/account.rb and write the testing code that will be run upon execution.

Listing A.17 Testing code for the step definition added in the outline

```
When(/^she withdraws \$(\d+)$/) do |arg1|
  @simona.account.withdraw(arg1.to_i)
end
```

This code is similar to the code you wrote for the deposit step back in section A.4.3. You just changed the deposit method in the Account object to a new withdraw method that will handle withdrawals.

You know what will happen if you run Cucumber: you'll see a NoMethodError exception, because the Account object doesn't yet know how to handle withdrawals. Let's take care of this now.

Listing A.18 Adding the `withdraw` method to the `Account` object

```
class Account
  def initialize
    @balance = 0
  end

  def balance
    @balance
  end

  def balance=(balance)
    @balance = balance
  end

  def deposit(transfer)
    @balance += transfer
  end

  def withdraw(transfer)
    @balance -= transfer
  end
end
```

The implementation of the withdraw method is the opposite of the deposit method. It should make the tests run successfully, though. Let's see if that's true:

```
$ cucumber
Feature: Bank account

   Scenario Outline: Managing money in your account
   ➥# features/outline.feature:3
     Given a bank account in Simona's name
     ➥# features/outline.feature:5
     And that her current account balance is <balance>
     ➥# features/outline.feature:6
     When she <action>
     ➥# features/outline.feature:7
     Then the account balance should be <result>
     ➥# features/outline.feature:8

     Examples:
       | balance | action          | result |
       | $0      | deposits $500   | $500   |
       | $500    | withdraws $500  | $0     |

2 scenarios (2 passed)
8 steps (8 passed)
0m0.011s
```

That's it. The examples passed! Even though you may have suspected that the programmatic elements of scenario outlines, such as dynamic parameters and tables, would complicate your code in the automation layer, the testing process looked the same. Cucumber goes through the parameters before execution and generates new scenarios out of the scenario outlines—and only then are the scenarios executed. That's why you didn't have to change anything in the step definitions from previous sections.

A.9   *Testing systems end to end with Capybara*

In this appendix, you've used Cucumber to write unit tests because they're short and easy to learn. But in the testing community, Cucumber is typically associated with using Capybara for an end-to-end system testing.

> **DEFINITION**   *Capybara*—An integration testing tool for web applications. Capybara helps you test web applications by simulating how a real user would interact with your app.

You can even configure Capybara to run Firefox or Chrome on your machine as a test driver in order to watch Cucumber click over the simulated user interface when it tests the system. The main benefit is that such tests check the system end to end, forcing it to integrate different elements such as the domain layer, API calls, and the user interface. The main drawback is that end-to-end testing is slow and performance heavy. In the banking example, the unit tests took 0.011 seconds; a single end-to-end integration test can take up to 30 seconds, depending on how many screens you want to test in a single run.

We won't be analyzing a Capybara end-to-end example in this appendix. To do so, you'd need to create a fully working web application—a task that's definitely beyond the scope of this book. Besides, other resources such as *The Cucumber Book*, referenced earlier, can help you learn more about end-to-end testing. What you *can* do, though, is rewrite one step definition to see what a test using Capybara looks like.

Listing A.19 When step rewritten to use Capybara

```
When(/^she deposits \$(\d+)$/) do |arg1|
  click_link "Deposit"
  find("input#deposit", match: :first).set arg1
  click_button "Deposit"
end
```

Capybara provides a new set of methods such as `click_link`, `find`, and `click_button` that you can use to interact with the user interface.

As of version 5.1, Ruby on Rails has Capybara working out of the box as the default solution for system tests. You get a Capybara wrapper that's preconfigured for Chrome and enhanced to provide failure screenshots as part of Action Dispatch. Different frameworks in other programming languages have their own equivalents of Capybara.

Even if your language doesn't provide something like Capybara, you can use the original Ruby version and write Cucumber tests in Ruby that will check your application written in any other language. This is possible because Capybara only interacts with the user interface, so you only have to run a web server behind the scenes that can serve a simulation of your web application. As long as you do that, you'll be fine.

index

MORE TITLES FROM MANNING

Specification by Example
How Successful Teams Deliver the Right Software
by Gojko Adzic

> ISBN: 9781617290084
> 296 pages
> $49.99
> June 2011

BDD in Action
Behavior-Driven Development for the whole software lifecycle
by John Ferguson Smart

> ISBN: 9781617291654
> 384 pages
> $49.99
> September 2014

Test Driven
Practical TDD and Acceptance TDD for Java Developers
by Lasse Koskela

> ISBN: 9781932394856
> 544 pages
> $44.99
> August 2007

For ordering information go to www.manning.com

Java Testing with Spock

by Konstantinos Kapelonis

   ISBN: 9781617292538
   304 pages
   $44.99
   March 2016

The Art of Unit Testing, Second Edition
with examples in C#

by Roy Osherove

   ISBN: 9781617290893
   296 pages
   $44.99
   November 2013

Effective Unit Testing
A guide for Java developers

by Lasse Koskela

   ISBN: 9781935182573
   258 pages
   $39.99
   February 2013

For ordering information go to www.manning.com

MORE TITLES FROM MANNING

Kanban in Action

by Marcus Hammarberg and Joakim Sundén

ISBN: 9781617291050
360 pages
$44.99
February 2014

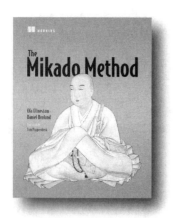

The Mikado Method

by Ola Ellnestam and Daniel Brolund

ISBN: 9781617291210
240 pages
$44.99
March 2014

Re-Engineering Legacy Software

by Chris Birchall

ISBN: 9781617292507
232 pages
$64.99
April 2016

For ordering information go to www.manning.com